Kant and the End of War

International Political Theory series

Series Editor: **Gary Browning**, Professor of Politics, Department of International Relations, Politics and Sociology, Oxford Brookes University, UK

The **Palgrave International Political Theory Series** provides students and scholars with cutting-edge scholarship that explores the ways in which we theorise the international.

Political theory has by tradition implicitly accepted the bounds of the state, and this series of intellectually rigorous and innovative monographs and edited volumes takes the discipline forward, reflecting both the burgeoning of IR as a discipline and the concurrent internationalization of traditional political theory issues and concepts. Offering a wide-ranging examination of how international politics is to be interpreted, the titles in the series thus bridge the IR–political theory divide.

The aim of the series is to explore international issues in analytic, historical and radical ways that complement and extend common forms of conceiving international relations such as realism, liberalism and constructivism.

Titles in the series include:

Keith Breen and Shane O'Neill (*editors*)
AFTER THE NATION
Critical Reflections on Nationalism and Postnationalism

Gary Browning
GLOBAL THEORY FROM KANT TO HARDT AND NEGRI

Mihaela Neacsu
HANS J. MORGENTHAU'S THEORY OF INTERNATIONAL RELATIONS
Disenchantment and Re-Enchantment

Raia Prokhovnik and Gabriella Slomp (*editors*)
INTERNATIONAL POLITICAL THEORY AFTER HOBBES
Analysis, Interpretation and Orientation

Howard Williams
KANT AND THE END OF WAR
A Critique of Just War Theory

Huw Lloyd Williams
ON RAWLS, DEVELOPMENT AND GLOBAL JUSTICE
The Freedom of Peoples

International Political Theory series
Series Standing Order ISBN 978-0-230-20538-3 hardcover
978-0-230-20539-0 paperback
(*outside North America only*)

You can receive future titles in this series as they are published by placing a standing order. Please contact your bookseller or, in case of difficulty, write to us at the address below with your name and address, the title of the series and the ISBNs quoted above.

Customer Services Department, Macmillan Distribution Ltd, Houndmills, Basingstoke, Hampshire RG21 6XS, England

Kant and the End of War

A Critique of Just War Theory

Howard Williams
*Professor in Political Theory, Department of International Politics,
University of Wales, Aberystwyth*

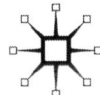

© Howard Williams 2012
Corrected Printing 2012

All rights reserved. No reproduction, copy or transmission of this publication may be made without written permission.

No portion of this publication may be reproduced, copied or transmitted save with written permission or in accordance with the provisions of the Copyright, Designs and Patents Act 1988, or under the terms of any licence permitting limited copying issued by the Copyright Licensing Agency, Saffron House, 6–10 Kirby Street, London EC1N 8TS.

Any person who does any unauthorized act in relation to this publication may be liable to criminal prosecution and civil claims for damages.

The author has asserted his right to be identified as the author of this work in accordance with the Copyright, Designs and Patents Act 1988.

First published 2012 by
PALGRAVE MACMILLAN

Palgrave Macmillan in the UK is an imprint of Macmillan Publishers Limited, registered in England, company number 785998, of Houndmills, Basingstoke, Hampshire RG21 6XS.

Palgrave Macmillan in the US is a division of St Martin's Press LLC, 175 Fifth Avenue, New York, NY 10010.

Palgrave Macmillan is the global academic imprint of the above companies and has companies and representatives throughout the world.

Palgrave® and Macmillan® are registered trademarks in the United States, the United Kingdom, Europe and other countries.

ISBN 978-1-349-31885-8   ISBN 978-0-230-36022-8 (eBook)
DOI 10.1057/9780230360228

A catalogue record for this book is available from the British Library.

A catalog record for this book is available from the Library of Congress.

10 9 8 7 6 5 4 3 2 1
21 20 19 18 17 16 15 14 13 12

Contents

Preface	vi
Acknowledgements	xviii
Introduction	1
1 The Motif of War in Kant's Critical Philosophy	10
2 Kant and Just War Theory: The Problem Outlined	40
3 *Perpetual Peace* and the Case against Just War Theory	56
4 The *Metaphysics of Morals* and the Case for Just War Theory	72
5 Bringing the Argument Together	91
6 Kantian Perspectives on Foreign Intervention	113
7 The Hegelian Premises of Contemporary Just War Theory and Their Kantian Critique	141
8 Conclusion: The Kantian Critique of Just War Theory	166
Notes	172
Bibliography	194
Index	199

Preface

This preface draws on an interview I gave to Richard Marshall in the online philosophy journal 3am which took place in 2013.[1] The interview was prompted by some of the reaction to *Kant and the End of War* (*KEW*) and especially a review of the book by Harry van der Linden that had appeared in the *Notre Dame Review of Philosophy*. Marshall Began by asking me what made me become a philosopher, was it always an interest I had had?

Having trained as a political theorist by completing a doctorate on Hegel and Marx in a Politics Department, I think of political theory as my initiation to philosophy. Studying political theory itself represented a migration from my undergraduate studies in economics and international relations. Whilst an undergraduate I became interested in Marx (in the late nineteen sixties) but I also increasingly discovered as I pursued my studies in economics and politics that at the root of many issues I was concerned with lay in philosophy. In this way I took a path diametrically opposed to Marx who had travelled in the other direction in the course of his intellectual development – from philosophy to political economy! I think what embedded in my mind the realisation that I was headed towards philosophy as my chosen field was when, in the final years of my doctoral research, I spent some time in Heidelberg University. There I discovered the problems I was interested in were, primarily, and best dealt with in the sphere of philosophy. I wanted to understand how Marx's revolutionary political outlook had grown out of his engagement with Hegel and Hegelian philosophy. The answers (or the best answers that were possible) lay in understanding philosophy and its history. Eventually my study of Marx and Hegel took me back to Kant. In the 1970s Kant's political philosophy was very little researched in the Anglo-American world. It was a topic where one had largely to start from scratch – although knowledge of Hegel and Marx represented a good starting point – since Hegel at least had a good understanding of Kant's philosophy of right. I found a response to my work in this field with my first major publication in the English language *Kant's Political Philosophy* (1983).

We then turned to this book which Marshall saw as a very timely work, given the current international situation. I argue that Kant shouldn't be placed in the 'just war' tradition, indeed that he is a critic of that tradition. Now the just war tradition can be traced back at least as far as the work of St. Augustine in the 3rd and 4th century where he argues that although Christians must be averse to war nevertheless there are certain circumstances where war must be engaged in by the followers of Christ. Although Christians should realize the imperfections of earthly power it is better to respect and uphold it rather than allow an even less satisfactory situation to emerge. Of course writers like Augustine did not think of themselves as beginning a just war tradition, but their ideas were seized upon by later thinkers in looking for classical authorities to support their theories. Just war theory reached the height of its influence in the seventeenth and eighteenth century when it was adopted by international law as one of its accepted doctrines. Hugo Grotius, the Dutch international lawyer, was one of the first to give it this status but his influential writings were followed by those of Samuel Pufendorf, Emmerich de Vattel and others to great effect.

An important mediator between the early Christian doctrine of just war and the international lawyers of the modern period was the medieval theologian philosopher Thomas Aquinas (c.1224–74). He developed with some thoroughness a doctrine of just war in relation to his theory of natural law. Some contemporary Catholic thinkers still draw upon his (Thomist) doctrines.

A major figure in contemporary just war theory is the American political philosopher Michael Walzer. He developed his ideas in response to the Vietnam conflict which greatly divided Western society. His object in reviving the just war tradition of thinking in the 1970s was to demonstrate that some wars (such as the Vietnam conflict) could not be justified. He contrasted the United States' intervention in Vietnam to protect its interests with the 'just' defence which the Israeli state had put up against the 'aggression' of its neighbouring states in the Six Day War in the 1960s. Walzer's book *Just and Unjust Wars* (1977) has been highly influential. A great deal of the debate that occurs on this issue centres on his writings. Walzer presents a very attractive theory which maintains wars are caused by aggression and aggression should be resisted. Indeed, this is what defines a just war for him: resistance to aggression.

Arguably the debate has moved on a little from Walzer's philosophy. There is a new generation of just war scholars such as David Rodin[2] who are prepared to question the just war paradigm. It is encouraging to see a greater heterogeneity emerging in relation to just war doctrine. One of my main objectives in writing *KEW* is to show that Kant's thinking cannot be integrated into the just war tradition and as a consequence cannot be tacked on to the debate arising from Walzer's work in an uncritical manner. There is ample evidence to show that Kant, insofar as he was familiar with the just war tradition – and it pretty much dominated natural law theory in its international dimension in his time – wants to avoid its vocabulary and arguments. Indeed the core of his argument is an attempt to establish an alternative paradigm to the just war view – one in which war is seen as an unacceptable manner of resolving disputes amongst societies.

One of the things Kant is saying is that just war theory is flawed because it is itself a part of an unjust international system. But this is not a simple critique of the rhetoric or ideology of the relations amongst states in his time; rather Kant's objection to just war theory arises from his understanding of the implications of human freedom, and the doctrine of right upon which it depends. Kant's understanding of international relations and his approach to war have to be seen in the context of his understanding of morality and human freedom in general. Kant does not isolate war as a question for states and international law solely; rather he sees war in the setting of the kinds of relations that are necessary to foster human flourishing. As the first chapter of the book seeks to show it is a pretty general conclusion of his whole philosophy that war stands in complete antithesis to the proper flourishing of human society. Even in his most theoretical work the *Critique of Pure Reason* Kant criticizes war as the most unsuitable model of human transaction – one from which philosophy must distance itself if philosophy is to remain true to its aims.

Marshall suggested Kant would not approve of big military interventions such as we've seen in Iraq and Afghanistan recently even with the purported aim of delivering humanitarian support and democracy and so forth. I replied that we have to be wary not to allow Kant to fight proxy battles on our behalf. *KEW* is an interpretation of Kant's philosophy. Here I am trying to outline what might be a consistent Kantian position on war. I do not claim the authority of Kant for my interpretation, rather I look for the critical approval of other philosophers and political scientists who have read the same texts and infer the same arguments from those texts as I do. I am pretty sure that those who deploy the same methods as Kant does in his moral and political philosophy would find it hard to approve of the interventions in Afghanistan and Iraq. So I am persuaded that those who have looked to Kant's writings to claim authority for intervention in these countries (by the US and its allies) are doing so on mistaken grounds. There are a whole host of good grounds that can be drawn from Kant's reasoning on war to show these interventions are wrong.

In the first place, Kant thinks sovereign states should be left to sort out their own problems. Of course many of today's independent states do not have ideal political constitutions and their people are often unfairly treated. But these are matters for the people of those states themselves to improve. In the second place, Kant is absolutely clear that one should only engage in war for defensive purposes. And this should be a war that is actively willed by the majority of the population. Kant is happy for representatives to take decisions on our behalf in most political situations (those representative should be periodically accountable through election). However, when it comes to war Kant looks for a more active consent on the part of citizens. He emphasizes in *Perpetual Peace* that citizens should be involved in their own defense and it is important for him that they concur as a body when a decision for war is made. Thirdly, if states are to get involved in the internal troubles of other states they have to show that this intervention is requested by the people they aim to help. Where Kant notes that involving yourself in the troubles of another states may be acceptable he primarily has in mind those states which border on the distressed region. The grounds on which he thinks involvement may be acceptable only begin to come into play once it is absolutely clear that central sovereign authority has broken down in the affected territory and rival factions are engaging in war with one another.

In such a situation a neighbouring state might understandably want to support one side or another to see some semblance of legal order restored. Kant seems not to indicate how one should choose which warring faction to support, but given his general political philosophy which strongly recommends republican rule (in modern parlance: representative democratic government) it seems most likely that a Kantian would seek to aid the faction which is most likely to set the troubled territory onto a republican path. This is of course a matter of judgment at the time. Here Kant can be quite conservative. It may be that the faction one should support is not the most progressive of the factions involved, but because it is the faction that stands the greatest chance of re-establishing of central legal order it should be given preference. With the renewal of legal order one can then work for a gradual move to a more republican form of government. In so far as it corresponds to a union of republican states seeking lasting peace it should be fully respected.

Another factor that would have to be taken into account in involving one's state in the civil disorder of another territory is the need for each state to see itself as a member of a potentially ever expanding peaceful union of republican states. Thus in considering involvement one should seek the affirmation of members and potential members of this union. Although in today's world the United Nations is not the perfect embodiment of Kant's peaceful federation, it has some of the characteristics of such a federation so its authority ought not totally to be overlooked.

Is it true, Marshall asked, that Kant holds that philosophers who provide war council are debasing themselves? Not so. Kant appends an ironically entitled Secret Article to the second edition of his *Perpetual Peace*. In that article he requires that heads of states who are considering war should first of all consult the views of philosopher. By this Kant does not mean that high policy circles within governments should have philosophers as members. Far from it. What he has in mind is that governments should encourage the freedom of expression in their countries so that philosophers are able to give their opinions on pressing political and military matters in an unrestricted way. They should be allowed a public voice. As part of this arrangement Kant thinks that philosophers should steer clear of taking policy decisions. Kant is opposed to Plato's view that philosophers should rule. Philosophers should be carefully heard, both by the public and those who govern on its behalf. As I interpret it, he envisages a kind of bargain between rulers and philosopher. In return for being able to comment freely in a scholarly manner on all issues of the day – and that discussion being carefully heeded by rulers – philosophers should hold back from being actively involved in policy making and seeking to lead public political action.

Van der Linden's review of the book, which disputes the interpretation I present, suggests that 'just war theory in the form of international humanitarian law has reduced at least some of the horrors of war.' Does this mean there is merit to just war theory that a Kantian should appreciate? To this I reply that international humanitarian law is indeed a wonderful innovation of the twentieth century. And the creation and recognition of international courts that deal with crimes against humanity that has now occurred go well beyond Kant's wildest dreams. They are evidence that the world is moving in a Kantian direction toward an international order regulated wholly by law. But I think it is mistaken to assume that there now exists a firm form of international humanitarian law which permits or encourages the waging of just wars on humanitarian grounds. It is true that the UN commissioned an influential report by the Australian diplomat Gareth Evans (chapter

6) which recommended drawing from just war theory when the international community was considering humanitarian lapses around the world. But as I have tried to show, attempting to tie humanitarian assistance to just war theory represents a mistake, and certainly one cannot draw support from Kant's writings to justify such a link. Kant envisages a world sovereign authority emerging only after a long process of political and legal integration through federation. Until that process of peaceful federation is complete (and Kant is not very sanguine about its total achievement) he appears to think that the world should hold back from direct military intervention in the name of such a would–be world sovereign.[3]

Although limited, a Kantian interpretation might permit us to intervene in some cases but this would not, for instance, have led to support for intervention by fascist Italy and Nazi Germany in Franco's offensive against the republican government in the 30s in Spain. Where does a Kantian draw the line? We can see that when Kant comes to considering military involvement in the affairs of a another territory he looks for physical contiguity (how immediately is your state threatened by the disruption); secondly he looks at the chances of restoring legal order which favours republican rule; and thirdly he looks for the support/cooperation of the developing peaceful federation of republican states to determine whether action may be justifiable. Clearly in the instance of the Spanish civil war intervention by Fascist Italy and Nazi Germany was ruled out on all three grounds. Neither country was an immediate neighbour, nor was the Fascist cause in Spain in favour of republicanism, indeed the fascists were fighting to extinguish the republican government. Equally both interventionist countries were opposed to the League of Nations – the only international organisation that at the time bore any resemblance to Kant's ever-widening peaceful federation.

When it comes to the 2012–15 events in Libya and Syria the same considerations have to be taken into account, and they have different, more complex implications. The argument for physical contiguity was not strong in the case of Libya: many of the states that were most actively involved (e.g. Britain and France) in intervention against Gaddafi's forces were not neighbouring states. However, it does seem that the powers intervening were in favour of the creation of a more stable legal state and did also prefer a representative/republican model of government. They also had an eye to the support of other states with republican/representative modes of government in trying always to comply with UN resolutions. On the whole also their intervention was requested by representatives of those forces who in the end were involved in an all-encompassing civil war.

What can one say about the situation in Syria from a Kantian perspective? Is it clear that the central power of the state has disappeared and the whole country is enveloped in civil war? Has central legal authority disappeared? It is difficult to say if both conditions are fully satisfied. Israel is a highly significant neighbouring state that may feel greatly endangered by the developments in Syria. But are these fears shared by the Jordanians and the Turks? In all probability yes, but Turkey and Jordan are a good deal less likely to intervene. Arguably the Syrian state is seriously abusing some of the rights of its citizens in the troubled areas – but does this provide sufficient grounds for military intervention by other states? Civil war has certainly broken out in some parts of the country but is this sufficiently widespread for us to say that any semblance of central authority has disappeared? Clearly there is no international consensus about what is going on or what might be done to prevent further crises in the region. Assad's government may survive and may present the least worst option in establishing stability.

I should like to think that the cautious 'Kantian' approach on intervention I outlined above has so far prevailed and this has borne some dividends in relation to the more consensual approach that the UN Security Council has adopted. I think the attitude that Kant suggests that outsiders adopt in relation to such tense and violent internal conflict, namely, of sympathetic concern that a just resolution be achieved by the peoples and states concerned, applies now more than ever.

In chapter 7 I argue contemporary just war theory is Hegelian rather than Kantian in its view of the state. Hegel's political philosophy is more suited to just war theory (although he himself rejected the idea that any absolute standard of justice applied amongst states) since it gives priority to the sovereign state. Nevertheless there is a developing tendency to seek to present a theory of just war that is drawn from interpretations of Kant's writings. Brian Orend (a student of Walzer) is a significant representative of this school, but there are other Kantian scholars that have suggested that war might be rightfully waged from a Kantian perspective. These include Susan Shell, Thomas Hill, Alyssa Bernstein as well as van der Linden. The final three mentioned have paid more attention to the question of humanitarian intervention than to the broader question of which wars are just. Although the predominant tone of contemporary just war theory is Hegelian since the focus of its ethic is the well-being of the national state, Kantian arguments – which focus primarily on the dilemmas of the individual (be it the politician, the citizen or the ordinary person) – are not overlooked. And in so far as the Kantian arguments are presented in their most authentic form they represent a significant challenge to the Hegelian trend.

So to what extent am I prepared to subscribe to the Kantian line that we should be striving to bring about the conditions of perpetual peace? Marshall feared that this might appear too timid an approach to world conflicts. Is the problem with the Kantian approach that it overlooks the possibility that there are greater evils than war? However, the Kantian line is that upholding law requires, if one is to be thoroughly consistent, to seek to bring about a condition of lasting peace everywhere. We need to begin in the way we need to continue. Kant sees all levels of law as interlinked. For Kant the doctrine of right concerns three interlocking spheres: the domestic or internal, the international and the cosmopolitan (which concerns all individuals on the earth). You cannot in his view fully enjoy justice in any of the three spheres unless it is also enjoyed in the two spheres as well. So you cannot be considered properly free if your state does not interact with other states on the basis of a respect for republican freedom in each and second, if you are treated with hostility upon entering another state.

I find it difficult to believe that there are greater evils than war. This is especially so since the development of weapons of destruction has reached the point where their use might easily destroy the human race as a whole. I think many of the things we might like to believe are worse than war already amount to war: genocide, for example, is already a war waged against one people and terrorism is self-evidently a nascent form of war. A Kantian does not deny that such dreadful things can and do happen. What a Kantian denies is that the war prosecuted to deal with such crimes is itself virtuous. No one should be morally comfortable about engaging in war. It is a dehumanizing activity.

Taking this stand, that engaging in war always involves an ethical breach, helps to demonstrate why the view that Marshall advanced is not acceptable. Once political leaders start saying they are striving to bring about perpetual peace it may appear the resistance to going to war from a Kantian perspective is overcome. Marshall pointed out the paradox that striving for perpetual peace along Kantian lines may have the perverse effect of actually producing more war. However, this would be to misinterpret Kant. It would indeed represent an irony if the attempt to bring about perpetual peace led to more, rather than fewer wars. But no state is charged individually with the compulsory goal of creating perpetual peace. The last thing Kant has in mind is a military crusade by powerful states trying to bring about perpetual peace. When he speaks of how the end of war might be brought about in *Perpetual Peace* he places emphasis on how a large and powerful state may play a vital role in the process, but not through the use of arms but rather through its rigorously legal demeanour both internally in possessing and upholding a republican constitution and externally in relation to other states by adhering to the principles that will make possible a worldwide peaceful federation of like-mined republican states. It is the power of the example that is crucial here and not the example of power.

Kant can be seen as a countervailing force to Hobbes in international relation. There is a contrast between Hobbes focus on sovereignty and Kant's emphasis on cosmopolitanism. What this contrast amounts to is this. Hobbes is a remarkably subtle political philosopher. His systematic writings on politics such as the *Leviathan* have to occupy all political philosophers. I have argued in *Kant's Critique of Hobbes* (2003) that Kant engages seriously with the main precepts of Hobbes's political philosophy. Kant indeed accepts a substantial number of Hobbes's conclusions about the human condition – albeit Kant sees those conclusions differently. Kant, I argue, looks for an alternative to Hobbes's conservatism/pessimism about our situation. Kant concentrates greatly on providing an alternative to what he sees as Hobbes authoritarian tendencies. In particular, Kant wants to allow for criticism with the state and also that through the mechanism of what he calls publicity this criticism should be heard and attended to by those in authority. Kant wants to take the focus away from Hobbes's Leviathan model of government to a republican form. For Kant it is crucial that we can see ourselves (through our representatives) as the author of those laws under which we live.

The contrast I draw between sovereignty and cosmopolitanism in my subtitle to *Kant's Critique of Hobbes* is this. Cosmopolitanism is an alternative to Hobbes' one-state-on-its-own viewpoint. In looking at this contrast it is important to bear in mind that by stressing cosmopolitanism Kant by no means wanted to abandon state sovereignty. But he understands sovereignty in entirely different way from Hobbes. Hobbes in his construction of the *Leviathan* focuses on depicting an all-powerful force that can dominate the politics of a society. Arguably the time of the publication (1651) of the *Leviathan* marks the birth of the modern sovereign state and the advent of the so-called Westphalian system in international relations, where politics is dominated by national states and their interaction. Hobbes seeks to construct the state in such a way that it is safe both from internal and external enemies. Notoriously to achieve this he denies the right of criticism to the subject of the state. Moreover Hobbes believes that the people as a whole should be kept out of the political process. He thinks our freedom can best be safeguarded by a centralized state where power is in the hands of one individual or a body of men.

As a result of the all-powerful state he constructs, which is beholden to no other body or state, Hobbes depicts the international sphere as a 'state of nature' similar to the condition that prevails amongst human individuals before the state comes into being. In depicting the international condition in such a tense and hostile manner Hobbes' purpose is not to transcend it but rather to bolster the individual state in such a way that it does not fall victim to the perilous conditions in which it finds itself. For Kant this represents the starting point of his political philosophy. The condition Hobbes describes may well be an accurate account of the relations amongst individuals and states but it is for Kant a condition to be overcome. Here I agree with Kant that we should aim to overcome both the individual state of nature and the international state of nature through the recognition of the rule of law. Indeed, the Kantian view is that both can only be achieved together. Hobbes stops at the border of states in seeking to establish a secure order, for Kant this will not work. In order to safeguard law and peace internally you must also aim for lasting peace and the rule of law amongst states. The acceptance of non-war like means for resolving disputes amongst states and the recognition that non-foreign nationals also enjoy rights within our state are not simply a desirable added extra for law, but essential to it.

Can we see Marx's radical theories developing out of this cosmopolitanism? Is Marx more indebted to Kant than Hegel? Strangely in contrast to his voracious reading of Hegel there is very little evidence that Marx devoted a great deal of his studies to reading Kant's work. In many ways this is a pity since – mainly because of his duel with Hegel – Marx finds himself dealing directly and indirectly with many of the epistemological and moral problems that troubled Kant. There is mention of the categorical imperative in one of Marx's earlier articles. So it seems certain as with any other student of German philosophy in the nineteenth century Marx would have been aware of many of the central tenets of Kant's thinking. And it's possible he thinks of his proletarian internationalism as a more effective and concrete way of realising Kant's cosmopolitan aims. It would be very satisfying if philosophy and reality could coalesce in the way that Marx believes and that the working class could bring with its political advance peace and freedom. But the connection could only be accidental. I think Kant is right in believing that for peace and freedom to be realised world-wide you need the ethical cooperation of people everywhere – regardless of their class background. It may well be that the life circumstances of working people may make more disposed towards republican political progress, but this in itself does not guarantee that supporting working class political movements will necessarily bring about such an improvement.

Finally, we spoke of the neo-liberal discourse that still seems prevalent in the public sphere. Can we see this as this changing now? Are the sorts of consideration you are identifying in Kant becoming more visible? Can we see movements like the Occupy protests and the Arab Spring as demonstrating new possibilities, or are they bringing false hopes? As the unprecedented leadership of the United States by its first non-white leader comes to a close can we conclude that we have entered a new and better era? Much as I'd like to think that events like the Arab Spring and the success of the Occupy movement portent a new and badly needed change in the discourse of our times. But is it too early to tell. Neo-liberalism needs challenging and no doubt will ultimately suffer the fate of all dominant ideologies in being discredited, but I don't see that it is imminent. What does appear to be happening is that its dominance is being challenged. And I think that the careful reading of Kant and the application of his principles can play an important part in this process. There is a gradual realisation that people have to play a more significant part in their own government. If you leave law-making and governing entirely to other people, and don't seek to influence their reasoning you are likely to get misgoverned, at best, and oppressed at worst.

I think this kind of awakening occurred in the late sixties: then there was a call for greater participation and involvement in ruling on the part of subjects. But possibly a difference that is to be detected in present developments is the awareness that this widening of government and opening of channels to the public has to be a continuous process. I think the radicals of the 60s were influenced too much by the model of revolution: the idea that politics can be improved by a once and for all cleansing process where those at the bottom of society became its leaders and removed the previous ruling class. This model has now been discredited, instead there is a call for a more gradual and continuous transformation that takes on the form of metamorphosis rather than a complete overthrow of existing institutions and practices. I think those who described the transformation in Central and Eastern Europe in the 1990s came close to describing what I have in mind with their ironic phrase the 'Velvet Revolution'.

Acknowledgements

I would like to express my thanks here to the British Academy for a grant of £2,000 which considerably eased the process of gathering material from German libraries in the final stages of the research. Colleagues in the Department of International Politics, Aberystwyth, provided exceptionally valuable advice and criticism in constructing and presenting the argument. My profound thanks also go to my family, in particular to my wife Jennifer, for the support they have given me in completing this book.

The book is dedicated to our two grandchildren, Aoife and Oisin. They have provided a wonderful distraction from the military problems of our age.

Introduction

Kant, politics and international theory

Kant stands almost unchallenged as one of the major thinkers of the European Enlightenment who influenced directly and indirectly all the subsequent major figures in philosophy from Hegel to Wittgenstein and modernists (such as Habermas) and post-modernists (such as Lyotard) alike. He is best known as an ethical theorist and, above all, as the theorist of knowledge who composed the extraordinarily impressive *Critique of Pure Reason* (1781). Kant has also developed a standing as a political philosopher of some note, now sufficient to join the canon in the history of political thought alongside figures like Hobbes and Locke, and Rousseau. Articles on Kant's political theory nowadays proliferate in political science journals and he is increasingly seen as a political thinker who addresses the central problems of our age. His work is particularly highlighted for the way in which it draws together considerations of traditional political theory, focused on the internal functioning of the state, and considerations of international political theory, focused on the relations among independent sovereign states.[1] This interest was given a tremendous impetus at the turn of the century by the 'democratic peace thesis' put forward by Michael Doyle[2] and further developed by writers like Francis Fukuyama[3] and Bruce Russett.[4] Kant was widely cited as an inspiration for this thesis which brought out in an impressive way the relevance of his thinking for international politics. The important contribution that Kantian thinking might make to international law has been illuminated, albeit with less recognition, by the publications of authors such as Fernando Teson and Leslie Mulholland.

The beginning of the twenty first century saw Kant's political and international theory enter the *Zeitgeist* in an unprecedented and often controversial way. Largely Kantian thought has had a quiet and unseen influence on political developments in the western world. Kant has had his enthusiasts amongst academics, lawyers and political leaders, but this has not led very many wishing to identify themselves openly with Kantian ideas. However, the end of the Cold War brought with it an enthusiasm for democratic ideals and their supposedly pacifying effects, which openly and directly connected itself with Kant's political thinking – particularly his tract on *Perpetual Peace*. Attention centred on the republican mode of government which Kant advocated in the first preliminary article of that book, and also in a secondary way on the federation of free states that Kant hoped would develop from the growth of republican states. Because Kant's republican ideal rested upon governments elected by citizens and a separation of powers between legislature and executive and executive, legislature and judiciary it was identified as fundamentally similar to the form of rule enjoyed by the leading western democracies. Thus through the popularization of Kant's political theory western societies were able to indulge themselves in a form of self-congratulation which appeared to vindicate the mode of government established by their founders and forerunners. This celebration was not entirely empty because those central and eastern European peoples who freed themselves from one-party communist rule turned to the western model of representative government with a division of powers in establishing their own post-communist systems of government. Also the evidence is fairly overwhelming that such representative governments, i.e. those that come nearest to meeting the requirements of a Kantian republic, almost without exception have not gone to war with one another.

By the time of the bi-centenary of Kant's death (which took place in 2004) Kant's name was ineradicably associated with what has become known as the democratic peace thesis. The event was marked by the appearance of the then German Foreign Minister Joschka Fischer in Kant's birthplace Kaliningrad (formerly the East Prussian city of Königsberg, but ceded to the Soviet Union in 1945 as a warm water port) and his placing flowers at the tomb of the philosopher, which lies out on the outside wall of the now partially restored cathedral. By 2004 Kant had impinged upon the popular consciousness – not only as the principal source of the democratic peace thesis, but also amongst some critics and sceptics as a source of western hubris and imperial overreach in trying to put the world to rights in Kosovo, Afghanistan and Iraq. Kant has simultaneously earned the reputation of both being an advocate of peace and a source of universalistic political ambitions that inevitably lead to war between the west and 'the rest'. This study situates itself at the heart of this controversy between the Kantian disposition that aims in a consistent and principled way towards eternal peace and the supposed contrary Kantian disposition that leads to excessive interference in the affairs of non-democratic states (and so to eternal war). I shall attempt to steer a course between the Scylla of Kant as the unquestioning supporter of western democratic rule and the Charybdis of Kant as the dogmatic universalist who has no feel for national and cultural differences. Indeed, I shall try to demonstrate that looking closely at what Kant has to say about politics and the permissibility of war detaches him from both caricatures (of rigid democratic peace theorist on the one hand and blind, insensitive universalist on the other). Kant has a progressive political theory which is sensitive to historical and cultural differences that has yet fully to be understood and reckoned with.

Thus Kant's influence as an Enlightenment thinker is extending beyond the traditional fields of ethics and epistemology. He is not now primarily seen as the moral philosopher who coined the phrase 'the categorical imperative', nor simply as the philosopher of mind who brought about a 'Copernican Revolution' in the theory of knowledge. Kant's philosophical thinking on politics has become central to the understanding of contemporary international relations. Kant has an important contribution to make to the debate on just war thinking. The ethics of war is a major concern in Kant's political philosophy – just as it is in the writings of one of the founders of modern international law Hugo Grotius – and has already been the subject of one full length study by Brian Orend in his *War and International Justice: A Kantian perspective* (2000). Deeply influenced by the writings of Michael Walzer on just war, Orend makes a bold effort to establish that Kant also can be counted amongst those theorists who belong to the just war tradition. However, I believe there is a need to challenge the approach taken to Kant in this work and the literature on 'Kant's just war theory' that has flowed from it. Although the book and the response to it have served to draw attention to Kant's contribution to international relations thinking, they have in my view taken the understanding of Kant's political philosophy in a false direction. One of my major concerns is to re-establish Kant's reputation as a critic of just war thinking.

This new study is intended not only to present a different point of view from Orend, but also to bring the ideas of Kant's critical philosophy as a whole to bear on one of the leading political and legal questions of our age: under what circumstances, if any, is recourse to war legally and morally justifiable? This issue was strikingly brought to the fore by the 2003 war in Iraq. It was hotly debated both at an international level in the forum of the United Nations Security Council and at a national level in the Assemblies, Congresses and Parliaments of western states. Many thought the decision on the part of the leaders of the United States, Britain and a coalition of other states to go to war against Iraq without the consent of the United Nations Security Council prejudiced not only the standing of the United Nations as a world political body, but also placed in jeopardy international law. Here I am not directly concerned with establishing the rightness or wrongness of this second Gulf War, but the debates surrounding it offer us an opportunity to clarify and illuminate the ethical, political and legal issues that lie behind a declaration of war.

The book should neither be regarded simply as a contribution to the burgeoning literature on just war theory nor, least of all, as a fresh supplement to the tradition of just war thinking. Primarily this work is intended *as a critique of that tradition* and a suggestion for how international law and international relations can be viewed from an alternative perspective that aims at a more pacific system of states. Instead of seeing just war theory as providing a stabilizing context within which international politics can be carried out, as many theorists do,[5] I regard the theory itself as contributing to the unstable context which is the present international condition. The just war tradition is not in my view construed as the silver lining in a generally dark horizon but rather as an integral feature of the dark horizon of current world politics. Kant was one of the first and most profound thinkers to present this understanding of just war reasoning and remains a crucial starting point for a critical theory of war today. I look closely at the sections in Kant's work where he discusses the ethics and legality of war, attempting to bring out carefully the ideas he seeks to convey. I focus closely on possible ambiguities and even contradictions in his discussion of this question and attempt to bring out one consistent standpoint.

The book is set out in eight chapters. Chapter 1 deals with 'the Motif of war in Kant's Critical Philosophy'. This sets the scene for the discussion in Chapter 2 of 'the Problem of Kant and Just War Theory'. In Chapter 3 I look at *Perpetual Peace* and the case made there against just war theory, contrasting it with the apparent approval for the theory shown in the *Metaphysics of Morals*. This chapter places the two works in strong opposition to one another. Chapter 4 takes us to Kant's main work on legal and political theory, the *Metaphysics of Morals*, and looks at the case for continuity between the approach to war in *Perpetual Peace* and that advocated this principal work. Chapter 5 attempts a synthesis of the two previous chapters. Under the heading 'Bringing the Argument together' it seeks to show how it is possible to avoid being a sorry comforter in dealing with the international state of nature bequeathed us. Chapter 6, 'Kantian perspectives on foreign intervention', looks at a further sphere in which just war theory is still very much present – particularly in the field of humanitarian intervention. Chapter 7 brings us to the question that looms large in the background to our discussion of Kant's complex views on war, namely, where does Kant theory lie in relation to contemporary just war theory? The final chapter 'The Critique of Just War Theory' provides a brief summary of the conclusions of the book.

I turn now to a brief summary of each of the chapters, focusing on their main themes.

Chapter 1 The Motif of War in Kant's Critical Philosophy

Kant's approach to just war theory has to be understood in the context of his philosophy as a whole. This chapter examines how the problem of war represents an important theme in Kant's critical system in its entirety. The chapter surveys the uses to which the concept of war is put in Kant's major writings such as the *Critique of Pure Reason* and *The Critique of the Power of Judgment*, and the role it plays in his many short essays and articles such as 'The Idea of Universal History with a Cosmopolitan Purpose' and 'The End of all Things'. This chapter will set the scene for the discussion of the problem posed by just war thinking for Kant's philosophy.

Chapter 2 Kant and Just War Theory: the Problem Outlined

This chapter considers how the problem of just war theory arises in Kant's philosophy. It examines briefly the work of recent contributors to Kant scholarship who argue that Kant can be seen as deploying a modified just war theory, and contrasts this with the previously dominant view that Kant thoroughly distances himself from such thinking famously describing its principal adherents Grotius, Vattel and Pufendorf as 'sorry comforters'. This divergence in views represents a dilemma for Kant scholarship that this study attempts to resolve in the subsequent chapters. I seek to resolve the dilemma through a close examination of the key texts, *Perpetual Peace* and the *Metaphysics of Morals (Part One: The Doctrine of Right)*, where the apparent conflict arises.

Chapter 3 *Perpetual Peace* and the Case against Just War Theory

The practitioners of just war theory in Kant's day are described as 'sorry comforters' in *Perpetual Peace* (1795), and the possibility of ever pursuing war in a way that is compatible with right is thoroughly called into question. The relevant passage seems to distance Kant markedly from the just war tradition in political philosophy and international law, and it would also seem to contain the warning that putting together theoretical justifications for when a state might rightly go to war would, instead of limiting war, add fuel to the flames of any conflict by providing a ready-made pretext for politicians to turn to armed measures. War and justice are here placed at opposite poles – and both philosophical and moral attempts to unite the two are, it seems, bound to fail. There is almost a hint of despondency and disillusionment in the way in which Kant speaks of the theoretical endeavours of his predecessors in international law. It may be the task of lawyers to give such advice to leaders when those leaders are contemplating war, but philosophers seriously concerned with advancing the good of humankind should not consider debasing themselves by providing the kind of counsel that Grotius, Pufendorf and Vattel give in their manuals on the law of nations. Here I focus on the contrast that is presented by the treatment of just war thinking and thinking about war in *Perpetual Peace* with their treatment in early modern international law or the law of nations, and the just war tradition in particular.

Chapter 4 The *Metaphysics of Morals* and the Case for Just War Theory

However, when Kant looks in detail at the position of war in international law in the first part of the *Metaphysics of Morals*, the Doctrine of Right (published two years later than *Perpetual Peace* in 1797), he appears to take a different tack to his earlier rejection of the 'sorry comforters' and seems to endorse the idea that war can be employed as a legitimate means of resolving disputes amongst states. He suggests several conditions under which this might be so, and recognises that as a matter of fact states do attempt to resolve conflicts in this way. The terms that Kant uses in the *Rechtslehre* (Doctrine of Right) appear to accept that there is a right in the law of nations to go to war, given that nations have not formed full civil relations amongst each other. There is not only the threat to peace that is brought about by changes in the balance of power but also positive acts of aggression where Kant appears to consider a hostile response legitimate.

Thus, in this chapter I look at Kant's treatment of war in the Doctrine of Right and *Perpetual Peace* in a contrary way to my discussion in the previous chapter, emphasising the continuity between the two. Two different strategies of doing this are pursued. First of all it is suggested that the apparent moral permissibility of war canvassed in the Doctrine of Right extends also to *Perpetual Peace* and, secondly, that the objections to traditional just war theory apparent in *Perpetual Peace* continue to be maintained (in a modified form) in the Doctrine of Right. Here the contemporary re-interpretations of Kant (particularly those of Brian Orend in his book *War and International Justice* and Susan Shell in her article 'Kant on Unjust War') that imply that he has a just war theory are closely examined in the light of what is said in the original Kant texts, and the notion of Kant's legal pacifism developed from a Habermasian perspective is tested in relation to the idea of the permissibility of war outlined in the Doctrine of Right and reflected also in *Perpetual Peace*.

Chapter 5 Bringing the Argument together

Even though there are discrepancies between the Doctrine of Right and *Perpetual Peace* in the views they adopt of the possible legitimacy of war, they are far from being wholly incompatible with one another. In this chapter I attempt to present a developmental (and arguably coherent) account of Kant's thinking that preserves his antipathy to modern just war theory at the same time as exploring thoroughly his analysis of possible grounds for war under the international law of his day. In this context the problems of the 'unjust enemy', the '*potentia tremenda*' and the declaration of war which arise in the Doctrine of Right are closely considered. In the first two instances Kant appears to put a strong case under current international right for engaging in punitive and preventative wars. Here they will be presented as limiting cases, which not so much provide grounds for engaging in war but rather demonstrate starkly the need to reform international law. For it is international right with an international state of nature that permits war, and it is this condition Kant wants to overcome.

Chapter 6 Kantian Perspectives on Foreign Intervention

Is it possible that Kant's notion of a reformed international law as first outlined in *Perpetual Peace* and his cosmopolitan doctrine lend themselves to an interventionist outlook towards states that threaten the international system? This is a particularly thorny question that has been raised by recent just war theory, especially where this intervention involves the use of military force. Some recent commentators on Kant have suggested that Kant's republican peace theory implies that under certain circumstances it is right to intervene to ensure that human rights are respected. Roger Scruton has argued this in the case of Iraq and Fernando Teson has presented a more general line of reasoning for intervention to safeguard human rights. We shall also consider here arguments that Jürgen Habermas presented for intervention by NATO in the internal Serbia conflict over the province of Kosovo. However, although Kant is committed to a cosmopolitan outlook which pays heed to the abuse of rights in all parts of the world, this does not automatically translate into support for forcible intervention in the affairs of other countries to right wrongs. Kant wants to regard states as the principal agents through which human rights (or in his terms our 'innate right') should be defended, and only where sovereign power within a state collapses does he see grounds for outside involvement. Thus, this chapter will oppose strongly the extension of just war doctrine into the sphere of humanitarian intervention.

Chapter 7 The Hegelian Premises of Contemporary Just War Theory and their Kantian Critique

This chapter aims to situate Kant's views on the justifiability of war in the context of early twenty first century debates on just war in the west. The ideas of several prominent just war theorists, such as Michael Walzer, Jean Bethke Elshtain and James Turner Johnson are canvassed and compared with those of Kant. This is done through the prism of Hegel's political and international theory, which is presented as the typical standpoint from which today's just war theory is elaborated. Hegel's perspective is chosen because Hegel prioritizes the nation state as the focus of political loyalty for individuals and also takes the view that war (perhaps in a progressively less damaging form) is a permanent feature of the international system. From a Kantian perspective these are undesirable and indeed dangerous conclusions to draw since both international law and the survival of the human race are endangered if we presume the permanence of war and the lack of feasibility of an international peace league. For Kant the requirement for the federation of peaceful states is implicit in law itself. There is no certainty in the rule of law unless gradually a peaceful world civil society is formed. Law he regards as an interlinking system from the domestic sphere to the international sphere and its final, cosmopolitan dimension. This is denied by the Hegelian perspective, and so also by most contemporary just war theory. So Kantian thinking must take up the challenge of Hegelian thinking on the international system and its contemporary just war derivative. This is attempted in this chapter.

Chapter 8 Conclusion: the Kantian Critique of Just War Theory

The paradox exhibited by Kant's writings on war is that war stands morally condemned at the same time as he accepts that it is none the less necessary to confront its existence as part of the historically inherited human condition. The problem is how to exit the warlike condition we have inherited without resorting to war as a means of achieving this. Kant's view is that the appropriate way to get beyond the just war tradition is to aim at the reform of international law. Just war theory is a symptom of the contradictions brought about by an inadequate system of world law. The major difficulty for Kant with just war theory is that it accepts the flawed system of international law created by the Westphalian system of sovereign states. In so far as post 1945 is concerned it can be argued that a new system of world law has come into being, involving an element of federation through the United Nations and various other regional arrangements, there is now greater hope for the Kantian perspective to prevail.

   This investigation seeks to reaffirm Kant's conclusion that those who present principles of just war within the context of international law are 'sorry comforters' who too lightly condemn humankind to a future of ever recurrent war. Although there are many laudatory aspects to just war theory, particularly in building up a case against frivolous causes for war and in countering human rights abuses during wartime, in the main the theory fails because it seeks to establish something as just and legal which can never be fully so. A Kantian perspective looks beyond just war theory to a better system of world politics and a binding order of international law. Engaging in war, and planning for possible engagement in war, represent a non-ideal form of thinking about world politics; and whilst Kant believes that the ideal theory of right should engage with the non-ideal, it has to be careful neither to be overwhelmed nor wholly absorbed by it.

1
The Motif of War in Kant's Critical Philosophy

Introduction

The main focus of this book is Immanuel Kant's account of war and the controversies that have arisen from its interpretation. This interest draws us naturally to the principal writings in which Kant addresses war and international relations: *Perpetual Peace* and the second part of the *Metaphysics of Morals* in the Doctrine of Right. These were late publications (1795 and 1797 respectively) that represented the working out of the implications of his critical philosophy. The central chapters of this book deal with the relationship between his views on war and its declaration in the two works. However, despite this necessary emphasis on two of Kant's final publications, we have to be aware that Kant's views on war were not simply the outcome of a later interest in concrete issues of world politics; rather they developed over a long period in his intellectual life and are, above all, a reflection of the main ideas of his novel critical account of philosophy, which received its fullest and most authoritative expression in the *Critique of Pure Reason* (first edition 1781; second revised edition 1787).

The purpose of this chapter is to set Kant's thinking about war in the context of his philosophy as a whole. I suggest that war plays an important role in his thinking in general, and I outline the dialectic of war that he portrays in his mature philosophical works. In my view we cannot evaluate fully how Kant deals with the questions of the justness of war and the role that war might play in the development of human history, which arise with the fullest force in *Perpetual Peace* and the *Metaphysics of Morals*, without assessing how the notion of war enters into his transformative criticism of modern metaphysics, which occurs not only in the *Critique of Pure Reason* but also in the two other works of his triptych-style philosophical *oeuvre*: the *Critique of Practical Reason* (1788) and the *Critique of the Power of Judgment* (1790). I believe there is a motif or theme of war that runs throughout these works and also is evident in Kant's shorter publications, very many of which appeared in the journal of his friend Johann Biester *Berlinische Monatsschrift* such as the essay 'What is enlightenment?' (1784). It is this motif that I want to examine and highlight here as the indispensable background to the evaluation of Kant's mature ideas on war. War for Kant is not simply a problem for international relations; it is a problem that lies at the heart of human existence.

War constitutes a major problem for Kant's critical system of philosophy. This is the system of philosophy which emerged in the *Critique of Pure Reason* (1781) and was developed in two further *Critiques* and the doctrinal writings of the 1790s. He abhors war above all human failures; yet he cannot deny that it is a prominent part of human social and political life. Although perhaps not as politically and socially troubled as the seventeenth century, war was none the less a highly significant feature of eighteenth-century European life. As a citizen of Königsberg in Prussia, Kant was witness to the reign of Frederick the Great, who for most of his time as monarch was either engaged in or preparing for military conflict. One of the earliest incidences of the citing of war – as opening 'a dark abyss' where all 'the afflictions of the human race are evident' – in Kant's Collected Writings (*Gesammelte Schriften*, 2: 40), occurs at a time (1760) when Königsberg was occupied by Russian troops.[1] From both a general philosophical perspective and a moral perspective war is wholly out of keeping with Kant's critical stance, which requires that human differences be settled through reason and agreement. However, the historical context in which he wrote was anything but amicable and peaceful; instead of providing an atmosphere in which social and political conflicts were resolved by open debate and the verdict of reason, the historical context was unstable and occasionally very hostile.

The dilemma concerning Kant's attitude to war comes out in a striking way in his comments in the essay 'Idea for a Universal History with a Cosmopolitan Purpose' where he presents his startling claims about the 'asociable-sociability' or the 'unsocial-sociability' (*ungesellige Geselligkeit*) of the human individual. Kant takes a highly ambivalent stand in relation to Aristotle's assertion that the human being is by nature a political animal. Although Kant does not entirely agree with Thomas Hobbes's view that we are by nature nothing of the sort,[2] he cannot bring himself to assent to the view expressed by Grotius that we are distinctively social beings. For Kant there is the constant tension between our tendency to want to be ourselves, and so free from the limiting influence of others, and our tendency to seek the attention and approval of others in order to bolster our self-esteem. 'Human beings have an inclination to associate with one another because in such a condition they feel themselves to be more human, that is to say, more in a position to develop their natural predispositions. But they also have a strong tendency to isolate themselves, because they encounter in themselves the unsociable trait that predisposes them to direct everything only to their own ends and hence to encounter resistance everywhere, just as they know that they themselves tend to resist others' (8: 21/7).[3] This dialectic in human nature does not unduly alarm Kant though. He thinks it is a means by which the human race is made to develop its talents, often directly against our individual inclinations. 'Without those characteristics of unsociability, which are indeed quite unattractive in themselves, and which give rise to the resistance that each person necessarily encounters in his selfish presumptuousness, human beings would live the Arcadian life of shepherds, in full harmony, contentment and mutual love' (8: 21/7). Conflict, risk and social disharmony may from a historical perspective be good for human individuals because they awaken an awareness of their capacities and talents and oblige them to put them to positive use. Culture and its advancement are often a consequence of the competitiveness and natural antagonism of humans. War is in good part a product of this natural antagonism amongst human beings, and can only properly be countered by the development of a civil society which places our natural irascibility within the restraining context of the rule of law.

There is then, from Kant's perspective, a beneficial side to the enmities that lead to war. These enmities play their role in the imposition of culture and its development in the human species. But Kant does not regard warlike antagonism as the permanent fate of the human race. Our political apolitical nature has to be harnessed if it is not to lead to the permanent hampering and ultimate obliteration of the human species. We cannot live in a condition of 'wild freedom for very long' (8:22/8). At the individual level we have to move to the civil condition to realise the benefits of our competitive and irascible spirits. Although Kant believes we are destined to attempt to move out of the condition of unrestrained freedom amongst states at an international level, he anticipates that it will occur slowly only and possibly only after an enormous number of setbacks.

To seek to understand more fully Kant's appreciation of the dialectic of war we have to turn to Kant's *Critique of the Power of Judgment* and in particular to the section on teleological judgement. In the absence of a cosmopolitan system of peace 'with the obstacles that ambition, love of power, and avarice, especially on the part of those who hold the reins of authority, put in the way of the possibility of such a scheme, war is inevitable. Sometimes this results in states splitting up and resolving themselves into lesser states, sometimes one state absorbs other smaller states and endeavours to build up a larger unit' (5: 433/300/40).[4] Whilst Kant does not underestimate the fear and damage a war can cause both physically and psychologically, he does not see its occurrence as grounds for losing hope about the human race in general. In a similar way to our unsociable sociability, which he highlights in the essay 'Idea for Universal History', the propensity of states to engage in war is here also taken to have a positive aspect. 'War, just as much as it is an unintentional attempt on the part of human beings (prompted by unbridled passions), is also a deeply concealed, perhaps intentional attempt of the most supreme wisdom, if not to establish, then at least to prepare lawfulness along with the freedom of states and thereby the unity of a morally grounded system of states. And despite the most horrible sufferings it imposes on the human race and the perhaps even greater sufferings brought on by the condition of constantly being prepared for it during peacetime, war nonetheless constitutes another motivating force (while the hope for a people's happiness in a state of peace become more remote) for developing, to the highest degree possible, all the talents that serve culture' (5: 433/300/96). War can be seen as having a providential dimension in that as a consequence of the dire threat it poses to the lives of individuals and peoples it presents them with an imperative to make the fullest use of their capabilities and resources. Culture develops both in its dimension as skill (mastering ever more complex technical tasks) and its dimension as discipline (mastering our natural inclinations).

The ingenuity of Kant's thinking on the idea of teleology in human history – and the role that the dialectic of war plays in it – can be indicated by reflecting on recent historical experience. Extrapolating Kant's argument to the twentieth-century and twenty-first-century context draws our attention to the extraordinary inventiveness that war and the threat of war have brought about in the most powerful and wealthy states of our times. Many of our most significant technological innovations have come about because of the striving of those employed in defence industries and research to produce even more effective, even more destructive weapons – and the equally strong compulsion to create means for ensuring our survival in case of the use of such weapons against us. The exploration of space in the twentieth century took place against the background of the most extraordinary weapons race between two superpowers. Perhaps human ingenuity and inquisitiveness played a role in the development of space travel and exploration, but one of the dominating impulses was surely the search for military and strategic advantage. Nonetheless this competition to be at the head of innovation and success in space exploration produced countless improvements for the human race as a whole. Without satellites that orbit in space around the earth and the capacity to deliver them there, human communications would be severely hampered. The instantaneous transmission of information and images around the world that we now take for granted would have remained a dream.

This of course raises the issue of what precisely is the standing of the teleological judgement that Kant proposes in relation to war and the course of world history. This is a complex question. First, there is the question of the overall status of a teleological judgement as outlined in the *Critique of the Power of Judgment* that reflects the position of the work in relation to Kant's critical philosophy as a whole. A teleological judgement is one that suggests that an event or an object has a functional role or worth. And, secondly, there is the particular question of how we are to assess how this kind of judgement relates to our experience of the phenomenon of war. With regard to the first question it is useful to bear in mind that Kant does not see teleological judgement as structuring what we experience in the way that the deployment of the categories by our understanding does in the *Critique of Pure Reason*. Kant sees the categories of our understanding as constituting or generating what we observe. Teleological judgement is, for him, in contrast *reflective* rather than *determinant* or *constitutive*.[5] By this Kant means that such a judgement can play a legitimate heuristic (or teaching) role in giving rise to propositions about how we might see aspects of the human world developing, but we cannot take these propositions to be concretely true (as depicting any kind of inner essence of our world). The teleological judgement on war is a stimulus to our thinking as we try to expand our knowledge and draw moral conclusions for action about war.

We are entitled to view human history providentially from a subjective moral human point of view. From this viewpoint war can be taken as a spur to improve our moral capacity and to seek to avoid the endless repetition of unsatisfactory and damaging behaviour. Thus, secondly, we can see war as having beneficial consequences not because that is necessarily factually always the case (this is something we cannot know), but because this helps satisfy a legitimate interest of human reason. This interest of reason is to discern whether or not the obligatory recognition and acceptance of duty in our personal and social life – which is the aim of the free human being and so is an obligation from which at all times we cannot escape – might not be without beneficial consequences with regard to the way of the world. Although we cannot take the good outcomes of our dutiful actions as the motive for our actions, we none the less cannot be indifferent to their effects.

The providential impact of war does not end solely with the picture given in the *Critique of the Power of Judgment* of the impetus it gives to the growth of our talents and culture. Seen as a reflective judgement that is intended to frame our moral life, Kant claims in the essay 'On the Common saying that this may be true in theory but does not hold in practice' that he is 'permitted to assume that, since the human race is constantly progressing in cultural matters (in keeping with its natural purpose), it is also engaged in progressive improvement in relation to the moral ends of its existence. This progress may at times be interrupted but never broken off.' As Kant sees it, he does not 'need to prove this assumption; it is up to the adversary to prove his case' (8: 308–9; 88/62).[6] The outcome of this progressive improvement must be a condition of lasting peace. 'Just as omnipresent violence and the duress that arises from it must ultimately bring a people to the decision to subject itself to the constraint that reason itself prescribes as a means, namely, public laws, and enter into a state constitution, so too must the duress of constant wars in which states seek to diminish and subjugate one another ultimately bring them, even against their will, to enter into a *cosmopolitan* constitution. Or, if such a state of universal peace (as has likely happened several times with overlarge states) is itself even more dangerous in that it brings about the most horrible despotism, this duress must force states into a condition which is admittedly not a cosmopolitan commonwealth under one head, but nonetheless a legal condition of a federation according to a commonly agreed international right' (8: 310–11; 63/90). Kant takes a very long perspective on history here, going back it appears at least to Roman times. Rome may have been one of those 'overlarge states' that degenerated into despotism.

The dialectic of war that Kant observes is not confined in its impact solely to military and security concerns. Just as relentless as the pursuit of war in the life of states is the increase in the costs and damage incurred by participating in them. Though states may engage in war for gain, Kant notes that profit is the least likely outcome. 'The increasing culture of the states, along with their growing tendency to aggrandize themselves by cunning or violence at the expense of others, must make wars more frequent. It must likewise cause increasingly high expenditure on standing armies, which must be kept in constant training and equipped with ever more numerous instruments of warfare. Meanwhile the price of all necessities will steadily rise, while no-one can hope for any proportionate increase in the corresponding metal currencies. No peace will last long enough for the resources saved during it to meet the expenditure of the next war, while the invention of national debt, though ingenious, is an ultimately self-defeating expedient' (8: 311; 90/63–4). 'Sheer exhaustion' will lead states to reform themselves internally into less warlike entities and gradually move towards the creation of an effective international right. The prevalence of war brings with it the risk of states bankrupting themselves in the attempt to remain competitive, armed and prepared for war. The need for raw materials and arms with which to prosecute war drives up the price of these commodities. As the price of commodities increases currencies devalue – so the whole external trade of a country can be placed in danger whilst living standards simultaneously fall. Security and military pressures precipitate a general economic collapse. The dialectic of war is thus a dialectic of human civilisation.

The imaginative nature of this Kantian judgement about war is evident here. Not all that he says may ring true of the trend of events; however it is the overall picture of both the apparent worsening of international affairs and their (compelled) improvement he wants to convey that most captures our attention. War and the psychological make-up that leads to it is a major issue for Kant's philosophy. He tackles the social and political conditions that lead up to war in his practical philosophy, and the human bent of mind (its tendency towards excessive ambition and dogmatism) that provides one of the main bases for warfare is tackled in his theoretical philosophy. Kant's belief appears to be that we have the capacity as a species to overcome war, but also the propensity always to be drawn into it. It pays therefore to look more closely at the manner in which the topic of war comes up over the whole extent of his published writings.

The incidence of war in Kant's writings

Important background knowledge for appreciating Kant's attitude to war can be derived from the incidence of the occurrence of the idea in his philosophical writings. Here we are of course concerned with significant mentions of the idea and not simply passing remarks of a descriptive or historical character. The purpose of this section is to survey this important background knowledge to give the reader a firm understanding of the manner in which Kant approaches the problem of war. Andre Simari cites fourteen instances in Kant's collected works where the topic of war and peace comes to the fore.[7] They provide an interesting point of orientation in this inquiry since he not only enumerates the contexts in which the topic arises but also provides a thoughtful interpretation of the relevant texts. Here I put this thoughtful inventory into a wider philosophical framework to enable us to develop more systematically the argument about the status of war in Kant's system.

Simari begins with two of Kant's pre-critical writings: Kant's response to the remarkable Lisbon earthquake of 1755, whose effects had been felt over a large part of the globe which had led to widespread doubts about the future of the human race; and his later reply to Edmund Burke's *Observations on the Feeling of the Beautiful and Sublime* (1764), where Kant weighs up the aesthetic dimensions and apparent merits of war. In the essay on the Lisbon catastrophe which had resulted in the deaths of thousands, Kant considers in what respects events such as the earthquake can be regarded as acts of God either testing or judging the human race. Kant regards war as a catastrophe similar to the earthquake as a pestilence that affects the human race, and he completes his essay by praising the ruler that seeks to ward off the 'misery of war'. Such a leader is a 'charitable instrument in the gracious hand of God.'[8]

An interesting claim he makes in the later *Observations* demonstrates his ambivalence towards the adoption of a military ethos. He notes that 'bold acceptance of danger for our own, our country's, or our friend's rights is sublime.' This seemingly positive comment has to be set side by side with the more negative remarks that immediately follow: 'The crusades and ancient knighthood were adventurous; duels, a miserable relic of the latter arising from a perverted concept of chivalry, are caricatures (*Fratzen*)' (2: 214–5/56 modified).[9] The third incidence of war's mention takes us into the critical system, with a consideration of Kant's deployment of the concept of war in the 'discipline of pure reason in polemical use' (A752/B780) in the *Critique of Pure Reason*. This incidence bears close examination because Kant reveals here his antipathy to war as a form of human conduct for the first time in a systematic way. He speaks here of the analogy that can be made between the endless controversies of philosophy in his time with the violent disputes Hobbes saw as a hallmark of the state of nature. Just as Hobbes saw the Leviathan state as the means of resolving the endless warring of individuals in the state of nature by instituting lawful coercion, Kant sees his critique of pure reason as a means of bringing peace within metaphysics. As we shall see later, this sets the scene for an integration of his negative assessment of war (and his concern eventually to root it out) into his overall approach to philosophy. The next important mention that Simari notes is in the article 'Idea for a Universal History with a cosmopolitan purpose', which appeared in the *Berlinische Monatsschrift* in November, 1784. Here there are several significant dimensions to Kant's use of the term, both bringing out the useful functions that can be said to be served by war as well as its highly destructive material and social consequences. The fifth mention of war and peace Simari brings out is in a similar context, in the essay 'Conjectures on the Beginning of Human History', which also appeared in the *Berlinische Monatsschrift* but two years later in January 1786. The 'Conjectures' provide us with some of the strongest statements on the evil that war represents for the human race in Kant's writings, yet at the same time depicting it at our present stage of development as 'an indispensable means' towards our further advancement (8: 121/ 232).[10] By 1795 Kant argues less visibly for this positive side of war and even more radically for its elimination.

The sixth point at which Simari notes the emergence of the topic of war and peace is the *Critique of the Power of Judgment* published in 1790. We have already seen evidence of how in this text the topic of war is treated in its most systematic way in Kant's philosophy. The discussion occurs in two sections of the work: the first where Kant relates war to aesthetic judgement (5: 262–3), and the second which is devoted to 'teleological judgement'. Since the treatment of war is ultimately most strongly conditioned by this second facet of Kant's critical theory of judgement the second occurrence is the more significant (5: 332–3). Arguably all the later uses of the term are under the influence of the treatment of war presented in this section. The seventh point in his writings, at which Kant deploys the term extensively, according to Simari, is in *Religion within the Boundaries of Mere Reason*. Here Kant compares the state of nature with a state of war in dealing with the hypothesis that 'the human being is by nature evil' (6: 32/55) and notes the attitude of savages (such as the Arathapescaw and Dog Rib Indians of North America) of his day who regard 'bravery in war' as 'the highest virtue' (6: 33/56).[11] War is also considered in *Religion* as a condition to be overcome – not only in the form of the external rivalries and antagonisms that lead to hostilities amongst peoples and states, but also as a condition of hostility within individuals which prevents them from attaining the highest ethical good. Simari's chronological survey takes us next to the previously mentioned essay 'On the Common Saying: "this may be true in theory, but it does not apply in practice"'. This essay appeared in the *Berlinische Monatsschrift* in 1793 and the topic of war is taken up in the third section of the article where Kant deals with 'the relationship of theory to practice' in international law (8: 307/87).[12] This section of the essay is written against the popular philosopher Moses Mendelssohn who had propounded a cyclical theory of history which portrayed the human race as never getting better but also not ever getting worse. According to this view distinct human individuals can progress, but not the human race as a whole. Kant takes objection to this view, so his treatment of war in the article is intended to show that although war indicates a flaw in the human condition it is not a flaw to which we are always fated to succumb. Contrary to Mendelssohn's pessimism and resignation, Kant holds that at the same time as we expect the worst of human individuals we should also concentrate on the possibility that this apparent constant wrongdoing may still issue in improvement. For each state that might find itself a victor in a war there will always be others that find themselves defeated. As the experience of defeat becomes as widely known as that of victory, the leaders of states may gradually gain the wisdom that will lead them to avoid war. The Second World War may, for example, have proved a positive experience for the USA (despite the enormous casualties sustained) but the Vietnam War of the 1960s and 1970s was anything but a positive experience for the nation. In contrast with the waste and destruction that war brings in its wake cosmopolitanism will become an ever more attractive option (8: 310/90). Both at the domestic level and the international level, Kant expects through its own harsh experience the human race will gradually feel compelled to abandon the condition of war.

The ninth incidence in the survey of the occurrence of the term in Kant's writings demonstrates the wider philosophical significance which the idea of war has in Kant's thinking. This occurs in the essay 'The end of all things' which appeared in the *Berlinische Monatsschrift* in June 1794. In the essay Kant good-humouredly expresses his love and respect for the Christian religion and derives from it a vision of the moral 'end of all things', which contrasts with the doom laden vision of others. 'Bloody wars igniting over the earth' should not be seen as 'omens of the last day'. He prefers the vision of an end of all things given by a 'heroic faith in virtue' to one that is dominated by unseen and unimagined 'terrors' (8: 332/199).[13] Drawing on *Religion within the boundaries of mere reason* he emphasises as much attention should be given to the disposition to be good in human nature as the disposition to evil in considering theology from the standpoint of practical reason. In harmony with his other writings, 'The end of all things' demonstrates that Kant believes that we should not give in at any time to the spirit of war. As is only to be expected, *Perpetual Peace*, which forms the tenth text to which Simari draws our attention, is central to the consideration of the role of war in Kant's critical system. Although each page of the book could be made a point of reference, it is interesting to note that the main themes of Kant's treatment are evident from his earlier writings and the synthesis upon which Kant most strongly relies is that presented in the *Critique of the Power of Judgment*. Those main themes are the juxtaposition of the destructiveness, arbitrariness and meanness of war with its apparently salutary and progressive effects. The conflict between the two diametrically opposed effects of war is mediated by a teleological judgement that allows us to reflect critically upon the condition of international anarchy and to create space for a politics of reform that may bring a higher level of civilization. This teleological judgement does not represent so much of a prophecy about the possible future of the human race as a moral challenge to seek to bring about a better future.

Simari points to four further, not insignificant, occurrences of the topic of war in Kant's philosophy, three of which broadly fall in line with the approach set out in *Perpetual Peace* (12, 13 & 14), and one which brings us back to the comprehensive philosophical significance of the topic (11). In the essay 'Announcement of the imminent conclusion of a treaty for perpetual peace in philosophy' published in the *Berlinische Monatsschrift* December 1796,[14] Kant returns to a theme that had occupied him in the *Critique of Pure Reason*. Responding to some recent philosophical controversies he suggests that it may be time to seek to bring order to philosophy by agreeing some fundamentals. He accepts that it is an inevitable tendency of human beings to enter into disputes with one another over philosophical issues, and this can admittedly develop to such a point that philosophers take up arms against one another forming schools that fight one another like 'army against army' (8: 414). In contrast with this bellicose scene Kant thinks his critical philosophy through its continuous vigilance against transcendent speculation and its emphasis on our capacity for freedom (8: 416) presents the opportunity for a lasting peace. Although Kant's article was prompted by the polemics of J.G. Schlosser against his critical philosophy, there is room to believe that Kant took wholly seriously his suggestion that what above all would assure perpetual peace in philosophy was a resolve never to tell lies – most especially when one has pious intentions. Here

Kant includes in lying not simply when one presents as true what one knows to be untrue, but when one presents as a certainty what one 'is conscious is none the less uncertain' (8: 421–2). Philosophical argument should not simply aim at getting the better of those who dispute our views but rather at expressing what we think is certain and true. Peace and sincerity are deeply connected for Kant.

The final three incidences of the appearance of war in Kant's writings that Simari cites are: *The Doctrine of Right* (1797); *The Contest of the Faculties* (1798); and *Anthropology from a Pragmatic Point of View* (1798). *The Doctrine of Right* as is to be expected engages directly with the problem of war: first, as a condition endemic in the international system and one for which rules have been developed in international law; but also, secondly, as a condition in the system to be overcome through the development of a 'universal union of states (analogous to the union through which a people becomes a state)' (6: 350/ 171).[15] Contrary to the views of the world-wise politician, those of a military disposition and the international jurists hired to represent the rights of states, Kant insists unequivocally here that 'war is not the way in which anyone should pursue his rights'. 'Moral-practical reason within us pronounces the following irresistible veto: *There shall be no war*, either between individual human beings in the state of nature, or between separate states' (6: 354/ 174). The theme of overcoming war through the development of new peaceful forms of the state and interstate relations is taken up in *The Contest of the Faculties* where Kant discusses the evidence of progress that can be found in one of the key events of his time, the French Revolution. Evidence of that progress is for him not to be found primarily in the events themselves but in the reactions of the spectators who look on. What is to be praised in the event is not 'a phenomenon of revolution but of the evolution of a constitution governed by natural right. Such a constitution cannot itself be achieved by furious struggles – for foreign and civil wars will destroy whatever statutory order has hitherto prevailed – but it does lead us to strive for a constitution which would be incapable of bellicosity, i.e. a republican one' (8: 87–88/ 184). A republican constitution is one dictated by reason where the citizens' representatives make the laws and the citizens themselves get to decide on whether or not war should be declared. Engaging in war is not the best way of bringing about improvement in the political order. In today's parlance, 'Regime change' should not be sought from outside through military intervention but should rather be allowed and peacefully be encouraged to occur in an evolutionary manner from within the relevant society. Thus, although a paradoxical outcome of war is frequently that political improvement may come about, war should not be consciously entered into with this end in mind. The *post hoc* teleological argument should not be used as an *a priori* ground for waging in war.

Simari directs our attention in *Anthropology from a Pragmatic point of view* to two interesting observations about war and warlike behaviour which illustrate the subtlety of Kant's philosophy on the topic. In the section on the 'highest physical good' Kant lists three vices – laziness, cowardice and falsity – and suggests that of the three, laziness is the worst. As vices they are qualities that we should try to root out in our character, but seen from a developmental standpoint, not even laziness can be seen as entirely evil because certain pauses in our concentration and labour are necessary for recovery and health. In a similar vein, cowardice and falsity can be seen as having positive consequences under certain circumstances. Were it not for the calming effects of cowardice, for example, the bellicose bloodthirstiness of men would soon surface (7: 276), just as without the propensity to duplicity in our character which leads to plots against the authorities being undermined by informers, whole states would have been brought down. The propensity to aggression is something Kant believes should be held back as much as the propensity to revolt. The second reference in the *Anthropology* brings us to a theme that emerges in the section on teleology in the *Critique of the Power of Judgment*. Kant once more looks at the apparent perversity in the human condition which seems to require that harmony grow out of discord. Some of our other natural impulses (such as the love of life and its consequent, the urge to procreate) can hold back our contrary tendency to violence. Arising from this conflict amongst our impulses an opportunity is given for our culture to improve, and the ideal of a lasting peace can take hold. (7: 277) Culture is advanced through the conflict amongst men, both in the competition that exists within societies and the disunity amongst states. The human race seems only to advance at great cost to our enjoyment of life. Kant glimpses a purposeful development here: it appears as though the tendency towards discord was implanted in the human race so that it would indirectly and with great suffering lead to the gradual perfection of the species. Here again then war can be seen as part of the 'plan of nature', which is the 'means of a higher, to us undiscoverable wisdom' (7: 322).

Of course Simari's fourteen instances of Kant's use of the term 'war' necessarily represent a selective list, but it does provide a useful vantage point for our enquiry. As I have suggested, his list helps us to focus our discussion both by allowing us to group together certain similar deployments of the term and by giving us a strong hint as to what might be the most significant amongst them. There are underlying themes to Kant's treatment of war that are symptomatic of the major concerns of his critical philosophy. As I indicated earlier, the treatment of war in *The Critique of the Power of Judgment* appears to provide one key turning point in his treatment of the topic and, as we might expect, *The Critique of Pure Reason* is also central in establishing the context. Finally the various political writings of the 1790s such as *Perpetual Peace* and *The Contest of the Faculties* bring war into the sharpest focus both as the main obstacle to political justice and stability and as the most important spur to bringing it about. We see also that the stilling of the guns of war not only has a moral and political significance but also a symbolic significance for philosophy as a model of debate for it to follow.

Having now completed this preliminary survey of the role that war plays in Kant's philosophy, we can turn to the major issues of substance that arise from Kant's approach. These issues of substance relate to the interpretation of the dialectic of war. How are the positive and negative dimensions to war that Kant detects to be reconciled? I deal with this question first in relation to the *Critique of the Power of Judgment*; secondly in relation to the 'guarantee' that is provided in *Perpetual Peace*; thirdly in relation to the interpretive strategy that lies behind the *Critique of Pure Reason*. By looking at these topics we shall be able to determine more precisely how strongly Kant believes in the end of war.

A Clash of Judgments

Up to this point, in mentioning *The Critique of the Power of Judgment* I have focused upon the second part of the book, which deals with the critique of teleological judgment. However, this glosses over an important tension in the work in the way in which it deals with war because in the first part of the book, the critique of the aesthetic power of judgement, a different picture of war is given. This tension in the treatment of war is to be found in most, if not all, of Kant's detailed treatments of the topic.[16] This is the tension between the apparently beneficial consequences of war in some contexts and respects and its generally deplorable moral implications and effects. This tension arises in a particularly stark way in *The Critique of the Power of Judgment*.

In discussing the 'dynamically sublime in nature' in the critique of the aesthetic power of judgement, Kant makes this remarkable comment about military conflict: 'Hence however much debate there may be about whether it is the statesman or the general who deserves the greater respect in comparison to the other, aesthetic judgement decides in favour of the latter. Even war, if it is conducted with order and reverence for the rights of civilians (*buergerlichen Rechte*), has something sublime about it, and at the same time makes the mentality of the people who conduct it in this way all the more sublime, the more dangers it has been exposed to and before which it has been able to assert its courage; whereas a long peace causes the spirit of mere commerce to predominate, along with base selfishness, cowardice and weakness, and usually debases the mentality of the populace' (5: 262–3/146).[17] It is important to bear in mind that this represents an aesthetic judgment which forms part, but not the whole of Kant's final practical-moral judgment on the impact of war. However, it is clear that Kant does not dismiss the ordinary normative judgment that a nation may make of its conduct in war and the value that might be placed amongst its population on having 'fought a good war' or having made great sacrifices for a noble cause. Kant openly recognises here that war might be good for the character of an individual and people.[18] Bravery and commitment to a cause are better than cowardice and indifference because they demonstrate that we value human, social purposes higher than natural purposes of survival. We value our worth as a human being which is accorded to us by rational thought above the worth of naturally given objects like 'goods, health and life' (5:262/145). Sublimity is attached to this capacity to be independent of the power of nature, becoming 'conscious of being superior to nature within us and thus also to nature outside us (insofar as it influences us)' (5: 264/147).

Kant suggests that this awareness of the sublime in relation to war can be seen in the most primitive of societies. 'For what is it that is an object of the greatest even to the savage? Someone who is not frightened who has no fear, thus does not shrink before danger but energetically sets to work with full deliberation.' The protagonist in war sets himself above nature putting a higher value on honour and bravery than life itself. 'And even in the most civilized circumstances this exceptionally high esteem for the warrior remains, only now it is also demanded that he at the same time display all the virtues of peace, gentleness and compassion and even proper care for his own person, precisely because in this way the incoercibility of his mind by danger can be recognised' (5: 263/146). Citizens of an advanced society will recognise the sublimity of military virtue as a value that goes beyond the mere defence of the state – it is the preparedness to risk death in the service of a greater cause that evinces the respect. Individuals defy their own natural instinct for survival in pursuit of an aim shared by a community. Military martyrdom has its own dark attraction which is brought out by the idea of the dynamically sublime.[19]

This seems a very positive gloss on war and would present a very startling picture if it were Kant's last word on the matter. Kant appears to accept that there is greater sublimity to war than peace, and war may unleash more creative energy than its opposite.[20] But Part two of *The Critique of the Power of Judgment* takes a different tack in presenting war as an element in teleological judgment. In section 83 'On the ultimate end of nature as a teleological system' Kant takes the view that the 'human being not merely, like any organized being' is a 'natural end', 'but is also the ultimate end of nature here on earth' (5: 429/297). In the hierarchy of functions that can be observed in the natural world, the human being from Kant's perspective stands at the apex as a natural being that can also set purposes for itself. As the sole rational beings on the planet it is wholly justifiable that we subordinate the rest of nature to our ends. But this does not entitle the human species to subordinate nature to itself in a wholly arbitrary way. We are the lords of nature only as moral subjects (noumena), as beings who possess 'a supersensible faculty' and a law of causality 'together with the object that it can set for itself as the highest end (the highest good in the world)'. (5: 435/302) The human species can be seen as the 'highest end of creation' from an ethical standpoint, wherein we act in accordance with the categorical imperative in all its dimensions, setting the good will before us as the model to follow.

Now it is into this ethical teleological picture that Kant tries to fit the occurrence of war. How can war, which gives such clear evidence of the perversity, cruelty and destructiveness of human beings, be seen as fitting into a picture of the achievement of the 'highest good in the world'? War amongst human beings has emerged as one of the apparently unavoidable, almost mechanical, outcomes of nature but its patent immorality seems to fly in the face of the highest purpose that can be imputed to nature. How is it that humans, who are arguably the ultimate purpose of the existence of the world, can be so calamitously engaged in destroying their fellow human beings? An answer to this question would be that the teleology that Kant imputes to nature is not a static perspective; it is rather a dynamic process. We are the final ends of nature expressly from a practical-moral perspective; taken as natural or phenomenal beings it is something that has always to be developed within us. The human species is not immediately what it ought to be. Just as with the single individual who does not at birth possess all the full human abilities and capacities, so with the human species our full range of abilities and capacities has to be developed over the ages. The human species has to go through a process of maturation to realise its full purpose. War is an outcome of the process of trial and error that the human species has to undergo to become conscious of its potential and its ability to fulfil that potential. We have to be slowly prepared 'for a sovereignty in which reason alone shall have power'. War is integral to 'the evil that is visited upon us partly by nature, partly by the intolerant selfishness of human beings' which at 'the same time calls forth, strengthens, and steels the power of the soul not to be subjected to those, and thus allow us to feel an aptitude for higher ends, which lies hidden within us' (5: 433–4/301).

If we follow Kant's story in *The Critique of the Power of Judgment* then until such time as we have a global civil condition, war both *honours* and *dishonours* us. War honours us insofar as it demonstrates a capacity in human individuals and peoples, through their bravery to set goals – however disputable from the standpoint of right and morality – that are beyond nature; but it also dishonours us since the activity destroys what is supposed to be the final end of nature: human individuals. The argument in the section on teleological judgement tries to make the best of this predicament. We learn by our failure to create an international political structure 'in which the abuse of reciprocally conflicting freedom is opposed by lawful power' that a worldwide 'civil society' is required (5: 432/300). Indeed Kant suggests that 'a cosmopolitan whole' is immanent within the historically developed world system of states. This is a very striking idea and it has to be seen from both a reflective and regulative perspective. From the reflective perspective it represents a judgment on past human history that seeks to bring out the conditions and structures that may make possible harmony amongst states. Examples of such conditions would be the growing interdependence of nations based on the development of interactions through travel, trade, written and spoken communication. The gradual evolution of a system of international law would also be seen an example of such a condition. The reflective judgment allows the individual to bring together a picture of progress. The regulative principle that this gives rise to, namely that a cosmopolitan whole is possible, can be deployed by practical reason. Although no factual truth can be imputed to this assertion the principle can, nevertheless, provide support for actions that seek to bring such a world-wide community into being.[21] The message of the teleological argument is that peace and order do not have to be brought to the historically inherited world political arrangements from the outside but they can be developed – and they do develop – from what is at hand. The inevitability of war is both tragic and instructive for the human race. That it appears to occur regardless of its illogicality and the terror it brings in its wake is read by Kant as evidence of a higher purpose that needs to be realised to take us beyond war. But this higher purpose is not a transcendent one that goes beyond the human individual: it is one that is implicit within humanity itself. 'Pure reason, as a practical faculty, i.e. as a faculty for determining the free use of our causality by means of ideas (pure concepts of reason), not only contains a regulative principle for our actions in the moral law, but at the same time also thereby provides a subjectively constitutive one, in the concept of an object that only reason can think and which is to be made actual by means of our actions in the world in accordance with the concept. The idea of a final end in the use of freedom in accordance with moral laws thus has subjectively practical reality. We are determined *a priori* by reason to promote with all of our powers what is best in the world, which consists in the combination of the greatest good for rational beings in the world with the highest condition of the good for them, i.e., the combination of universal happiness with the most lawful morality' (5: 453/318). As rational beings we ought to avoid war and so even in war we need to detect a way beyond it. The human world we inherit from past generations may not have rooted out war and its causes but we have a duty to continue the task of eliminating it. Our vocation as a race is to seek to overcome our warlike habits, but at the same time each generation has to begin with the same basic raw material: our finite, fallible, human nature that has a propensity towards evil. This is the dilemma Kant tackles in the *Doctrine of Right* and, above all, in the supplement on the 'Guarantee of Perpetual Peace' in his book *Perpetual Peace*.

The 'Guarantee' of perpetual peace

That Kant presents a book on the topic of eternal or perpetual peace in a period of such turmoil in Europe – in the immediate aftermath of the French Revolution – is testimony to the extent to which his predominant motif in depicting war in his philosophy is to live up to his moral conclusion that war is 'the greatest of all evils' and that there should be no more war. But this demise of war is to come about in a way that reflects the complexity of his critical system and the actual intricacies of historical, social and political development. Arguably *Perpetual Peace* is as much an essay in historical anthropology and sociology as it is a philosophical sketch of the doctrine of right. Certainly the philosophical sketch is supported by a very close analysis of human and social behaviour. Kant lectured repeatedly on anthropology to his students and his *Anthropology from a Pragmatic point of view* was one of his last published writings.[22] He draws on this knowledge in putting together his arguments about war in *Perpetual Peace*.

The section on the 'Guarantee' probably deals with one of the most controversial aspects of Kant's essay and certainly brings to the fore his concerns about war. On the surface Kant seems here to be providing an out and out prediction about the future of the human race. He argues that even if the moral and political principles he outlines in the essay are not consciously adhered to, the unguided antagonistic path of human history will none the less lead in the same direction. Kant has a progressive philosophy of history and it seems that he is bringing it to bear on his political philosophy simply to get the outcome he desires. This progressive philosophy of history is, as we have seen, strikingly outlined in the 1783 article 'Idea of Universal History with a Cosmopolitan Purpose' and, evidently, Kant takes its conclusions as a point of departure for his doctrine of public right and perpetual peace. In his philosophy of history Kant regards the human species as a natural scientist might do so: as subject to the laws of nature outside its control. Human actions are seen as the consequences of prior facts and events. In his philosophy of history Kant leaves behind the moral realm where we are regarded as potentially self-moving and we are demoted to the phenomenal or natural realm where our actions are regarded as determined.

The philosophy of history tells us there is a guarantee provided by 'nothing less than that great artist nature' (8: 360/440). 'In her mechanical course we see that her aim is to produce harmony amongst human beings, against their will and indeed through their discord' (8: 361/440). It seems here that we are almost in the realm of magic. Kant appears to be suggesting that even if the human species does not voluntarily take up the rules he outlines in *Perpetual Peace* they will still be brought into line by nature, or even 'the profound wisdom of a higher cause' (8: 362/440). Religion, fate, nature and fortune are all brought together on the side of the good. Quite frankly, this seems too good to be true. Although not quite so contentedly presented as Aristotle's teleological view of human existence, there appears to be an overconfidence about Kant's view of history which seems disturbing. He appears to be conjuring up improvement from an apparently supernatural cause.

But Kant does try to dispel the apparently mysterious effect. Although the scientific, anthropological point of view leads in the direction of unavoidable progress through conflict and war, we cannot with certainty accept this conclusion. The scientific, anthropological point of view is that of theoretical reason, and true to the conclusions of his critical philosophy Kant argues that we cannot accept the totalizing ambitions of a purely reflective reason. 'Human reason in questions of the relation of effects to their causes must remain within the limits of possible experience' (8: 362/441). So from the standpoint of the observation of human history it would be wrong to conclude that its deadly conflicts naturally tend towards improvement and the ultimate attainment of perpetual peace. The scientific frame of mind, applied on its own to history, provides no ultimate guarantee of peace. This scientific frame of mind has to be combined with practical reason to provide this sought-for assurance: 'We do not observe or infer this providence in the cunning contrivances of nature, but, as in questions of the relation of the form of things to ends in general, we can and must supply it from our own minds in order to conceive of its possibility by analogy to actions of human art. The idea of the relationship and harmony between these actions and the end which reason directly assigns to us is transcendent from a theoretical point of view; from a practical standpoint, with respect, for example, to the ideal of perpetual peace, the concept is dogmatic and its reality is well established, and thus the mechanism of nature may be employed to that end' (8: 362/441). The phrasing is very complex here, but the implication is very plain. Although we can claim no absolute validity for the supposition of progress from a factual or empirical point of view, we can nevertheless from a moral point of view employ the supposition in order to help bring about improvement. Most striking is the way in which Kant uses the term 'dogmatic' to refer to the way in which we are entitled to suppose the idea of progress in the practical realm. One of the main purposes of Kant's critical philosophy is to undermine dogmatism in terms of human knowledge, but here Kant is advocating a kind of dogmatism, albeit one that is distinct from a theoretical dogmatism. We are entitled to this dogmatism in relation to our aims in acting. We have to suppose perpetual peace is the inevitable outcome of natural mechanisms in human society when attempting to act in accordance with justice. Yet we cannot assume that this progress is in fact an inevitable outcome when we dispassionately observe human society.

There seems to be a conflict here between Kant's theoretical scepticism and his moral dogmatism, which is a theme not only of the section on the 'Guarantee' in *Perpetual Peace* but also of his whole philosophy. On the one hand Kant is arguing that we have to assume the world is improving according to a natural mechanism and, on the other, we are warned against assuming there is such a natural mechanism. What are we to make of this? The idea is certain to puzzle those who come to Kant's philosophy for the first time through his writings on politics and international relations and so are not acquainted with his critical system and with Kant's teleological arguments in the *Critique of the Power of Judgment*. We can only understand this complex, dialectical argument if we are aware that for Kant practical reason has a far greater objectivity than theoretical reason. The consequence of taking as dogma a hypothesis of theoretical reason is bound to be a contradiction. Because we are dealing with ideas which cannot be verified by any possible experience, one supposition is just as good as its opposite. However, if we take as dogma a supposition of practical reason – such as the regulative principle of progress – it can secure reality or objectivity as part of our motivation. We can take it as a maxim in acting that we seek to avoid action that may lead to war. Practical reason can also discriminate between opposed hypotheses. Where a hypothesis runs contrary to morality it excludes itself as a possible basis for acting since, as Kant sees it, immoral suppositions cannot be consistently acted upon.

Kant's 'guarantee' of perpetual peace has a very ambivalent standing in his treatment of war. Kant explicitly makes clear that he is not putting the guarantee forward as an empirical proposition. If someone comes forward with evidence to suggest the human race may not be progressing – by suggesting for instance that war is inherent in human nature – Kant would argue this would leave his practical-moral argument unaffected. The role of the guarantee is not incontrovertibly to demonstrate actual progress but rather to strengthen our resolve to work for progress. At an empirical level Kant would argue that his supposition of progress cannot be disproved, and at a moral level he would argue the supposition was essential to lend completeness to our moral vision. The guarantee of perpetual peace is then a kind of story we tell ourselves when we engage with the world as politicians, philosophers and citizens. It is almost as though Kant sees his story of inevitable progress as a kind of ideological nourishment for the moral practitioner in politics. In some respects, the story can provide consolation when immediate moral gains are not realized and encouragement for greater efforts when things are going well. The point of the story is not to claim that things are definitely improving but rather to encourage us always to help bring about improvement through our actions.

The crucial aspect of Kant's guarantee is the moral certainty that it is intended to provide. Kant is quite prepared to be sceptical about the epistemological standing of the assertion that the human race is, despite its violent episodes, progressing; but we have to have no doubts in terms of our moral motivation. Indeed, 'nature guarantees perpetual peace by the mechanism of human passions. Certainly she does not do so with sufficient certainty for us to predict the future in any theoretical sense, but adequately from a practical point of view, making it our duty to work toward this end, which is not just a chimerical one' (8: 368/445). There is an extraordinary liberality of spirit towards the human race at work here. Kant argues that we can never give up the sublime vision of lastingly peaceful world – not primarily as a scientific hypothesis about the course of human life, but as an imaginative construction underlying our free action. We have to commit ourselves to the regulative principle of progress towards a worldwide federation of free states.[23] In his view, any other assumption about the course of the world would prevent us from being self-determining individuals. We can only do the right thing on the assumption that ultimately the whole of human society will become a sphere of effective justice and morality.

Criticisms of Kant's guarantee miss the mark, then, if they focus on attempting to disprove empirically the assumption of progress. Kant's progressivism is not a mere factual progressivism. The abysmal history of the twentieth century (however dreadful the picture) cannot shake Kant's generous estimate of our potential. Those who are tempted to discard Kant's political philosophy because of the apparent failure of the human race to better itself, evident in its continued engagement in war, have misunderstood Kant's meaning. Although Kant clearly is pleased where events seem to support his supposition of improvement, his argument does not wholly depend on the accumulation of such evidence. Kant is simply suggesting how our autonomy obliges to look upon the world: not with the assumption that progress *is* taking place but with the assumption that progress *may* occur. The future is unknowable, but it is none the less our duty to aim at improvement.

The examples he brings forward of spurs to human progress are arguably intended in this light. He is looking at the past to show that improvement is possible, even though it may not always or even consistently occur. This perhaps explains the curiously negative way in which Kant outlines his guarantee of perpetual peace. Each line seems to take it for granted that improvement may not occur and stresses the obstacles that stand in its way. For Kant progress occurs as much against our will as with our blessing. There are three conditions which nature imposes on us (and war is central to two of them) that initially make progress possible:

1. She has made it possible for human beings to live in every region of the world.
2. She has driven them by war into even the most inhospitable regions in order to populate them.
3. By the same means (war) she has forced them into more or less lawful relations with each other (8: 363/441).

As a moral philosopher Kant is utterly opposed to war, yet he sees that it can bring improvement in its terrible wake. War is always wrong 'as it produces more evil men than it takes away' (8: 365/443). But war has far greater effects than those who first prosecute it imagine. According to Kant, it is war that first drove people to inhabit the less hospitable parts of the globe. The human race would by far prefer to live in warm or temperate climates where the fruits of nature grow most abundantly and the labour of cultivation is least demanding. But through war tribes were pressed to bring into cultivation less productive lands and seek to domesticate more diverse creatures. Our hostility towards each other leads to ever greater inventiveness in the production of weapons. As we develop our skills in inventing and producing new weapons our general intelligence and skill increases. The improvement we might have attained through greater application and diligence is forced out of us by necessity. The competition amongst peoples prevents idleness and complacency. Oddly because of the prevalence of war in human society this begets rules to govern relations amongst states. First those rules govern relationships that are assumed to be hostile amongst states and peoples, but gradually through the emergence and acceptance of these rules another frame of mind is engendered where the assumption of predominantly peaceful arrangements arises.

As well as war there are two other key forces which ensure people are divided and come into conflict with one another. Those forces are language and religion. That religions separate people presents Kant with a problem, since in his philosophy of religion he regards religious faith as something which unites the human race. But this is religious faith within the limits of pure reason.[24] As Kant sees it the various historical forms of religion are but various forms of appearances of this one valid religion. But because they are historically and culturally determined forms they can serve to drive individuals apart and even lead to war. Each sect believes it worships the one true God and regards the other as pagan or heterodox. Such disputes belong, as Kant sees it, to the infancy of the human race. They are as lamentable as they are inevitable – until the human race attains a condition of enlightenment.

Kant seems to be right about the divisive powers of religion and language. They do seem to present almost insuperable obstacles to peace. The Middle East is in continuous turmoil and the two factors which above all appear to divide the parties in the conflict are religion and language. The Israelis want to preserve a Hebrew state in the face of Arab nationalists who wish to create a Palestinian state. The gulf seems deepest between the most religiously orthodox Jews and the Muslim fundamentalists amongst the Arabs. Similarly, a kind of civil war took place in Northern Ireland between the late 1960s and the early years of this century between Protestants (who wished to preserve a unified British state, still tied to an official Protestant religion) and Catholics (who wished to create an all-Irish state where Catholicism had an institutionally favoured position). The problem seemed wholly intractable until the marked improvement that has been observed in recent years. Language and religion seem also to have torn Yugoslavia apart, with the Eastern Orthodox Serbs at war with the Catholic Croats and the Muslims in Bosnia.

Here then seem to be many of the greatest obstacles to the perpetual peace that Kant advocates. But Kant presents these obstacles as part of nature's secret plan to force us to live in harmony with each other! Realist political thinkers must accept that Kant takes fully into account the unfavourable aspects of human history that stand in the way of the realization of his plan for lasting peace. It would seem unlikely that Kant believed that the threat posed to peace by divisions of religion and language would easily or immediately be overcome. It seems plausible that he contains them in his 'guarantee' because he wanted to demonstrate that even the most difficult barriers to peace cannot be seen in an entirely negative light. Here we have to recall (and stress) that what Kant wants to establish is that no reading of history can entirely rule out the possibility of improvement. And even in the Middle East, Northern Ireland and Bosnia improvement has fitfully and occasionally surprisingly quickly taken place. As Kant mildly puts it, 'These differences involve a tendency to mutual hatred and pretexts for war, but the progress of civilization and human being's gradual approach to greater harmony in their principles finally lead to peaceful agreement' (8: 367/444). This is not a despotic peace achieved by the weakening of all the participants in the conflict that would undermine human freedom. Rather it will be a peace 'produced and maintained by their equilibrium in the liveliest competition' (8: 367/444).

The guarantee of perpetual peace brings out perhaps more clearly than any other of Kant's writings the two-edged, paradoxical aspect of war that is such a theme of his critical philosophy. The guarantee represents a prime example of Kant's deployment of teleological judgement as developed in the third *Critique*. On the one hand war appears as an integral part of the human species' existence – a hallmark of its limited, abrasive and self-centred qualities – on the other hand it is seen as a hallmark of our adaptive, creative and even cooperative qualities. For war amongst states to occur requires the mobilisation of huge numbers of people for a unifying social and political cause. This propensity to mobilize for war can, under favourable circumstances and with good political leadership, be turned into a mobilization for peace. And should the human race fail properly to make this transition from armed hostility to a worldwide civil society governed by laws then further war will be the consequence. War sets limits on itself. Until such time as the human race matures sufficiently to impose on itself a regulated peace, war will remain an expedient for arbitrating, if not settling, disputes. War occurs, but Kant is in no doubt that in a properly ordered human society it should not occur.

Critique of Pure Reason

The *Critique of Pure Reason* is central to determining the role of war in Kant's critical system. As the major work of his system of philosophy it determines the place of the key concepts in his philosophical thinking. The book is a major survey of the nature and limits of human knowledge. In this chapter I have been concerned to argue that war is an important theme of Kant's critical philosophy, so in approaching his major work I want to stress that I am not just looking for simple analogies between the way in which Kant deals with conflict within philosophy and the larger social and political problem of war, but rather for concrete discussions of war and its implications in terms of human conduct. War as a human institution presents a stark antithesis – if not the starkest antithesis – to the way in which a properly disciplined human reason should conduct itself. His prime object in the *Critique of Pure Reason* is to establish what such a disciplined reason should look like. In reviewing the way in which the history of philosophy has developed up to his time, with its controversies, confusions and downright errors, Kant comes to the conclusion that in future the operations of pure reason have to occur openly, wholly without bias and must be accessible to universal assent. In the preface to the second edition of the *Critique* he laments, however, that 'in metaphysics we have to retrace our steps countless times, because we find that it does not lead where we want to go, and it is so far from reaching unanimity in the assertions of its adherents that it is rather a battlefield (*Kampfplatz*), and indeed one that appears especially determined for testing one's powers in mock combat; on this battlefield no combatant has ever gained the least bit of ground, nor has any been able to base any lasting possession on his victory' (Bxv). The history of metaphysics is seen as unsatisfactory because it resembles too much human history in general. Philosophers engage with one another as though in deadly combat. Although up to his time Kant sees metaphysics as a arena of combat that has led to a mere stumbling around amongst its protagonists, his proposal is that a properly limited metaphysics should take on a more fruitful, less ambitious and so less antagonistic form. Whereas reason respects and seeks to debate with and to persuade the other, war seeks to destroy the other (the enemy). And in its mock battles metaphysics has followed its actual counterpart in bringing about irreconcilable divisions and enmity. This antagonistic pattern has brought metaphysics into disrespect, making its claim to be a reliable source of knowledge seem empty. Kant wants to repair this position by putting forward a means for arbitrating its endless disputes and suggesting ways in which reason can be deployed metaphysically without controversy. Thus one of the key aims of Kant's theoretical philosophy is to move metaphysics from its current war footing. Philosophy properly conducted should not be divided into mutually hostile camps. Just as within the political world, law and peace should reign within philosophy.

Instead of the image of the battlefield Kant proposes for philosophy the image of the court of justice: 'One can regard the critique of pure reason as the true court of justice for all controversies of pure reason; for the critique is not involved in these disputes, which pertain immediately to objects, but is rather set the task of determining and judging what is lawful in reason in general in accordance with the principles of its primary institution.' The critique of pure reason should be seen as a kind of tribunal which is set up to investigate the claims of metaphysics and the use it makes of our human cognitive faculties. We have to reflect fully on the nature of the demands of metaphysics and our mental abilities before setting forth on our ambitious philosophical expeditions. The ground rules for how properly to engage in metaphysics have to be laid out and agreed by all participants before we set out to bring about substantive metaphysical results.

The antagonistic, warlike attitude with which dogmatic philosophers have engaged one another has to be set aside if philosophy is to proceed successfully. 'Without this, reason is as it were in the state of nature, and it cannot make its assertions and claims valid or secure them except through war. The critique, on the contrary, which derives all decisions from the ground-rules of its own constitution, whose authority no one can doubt, grants us the peace of a state of law, in which we should not conduct our controversy except by due process. What brings the quarrel in the state of nature to an end is victory, of which both sides boast, although for the most part there follows only an uncertain peace, arranged by an authority in the middle; but in the state of law it is the verdict, which, since it goes to the origins of the controversies themselves, must secure a perpetual peace. And the endless controversies of a merely dogmatic reason finally make it necessary to seek peace in some sort of critique of reason itself' (A751–2/B779–80). The contrast between the outcome of a war that is decided by violence and the outcome of an authentic legal process could not be starker. Kant attributes the warlike tendencies of previous metaphysics to the dogmatism of some of its main exponents. Dogmatism in metaphysics arises not from the deployment of dogmatic procedures themselves (there is a place for such procedures in all philosophical enquiries) but rather in the adoption of 'the dogmatic procedure of pure reason, without the antecedent critique of its own capacity' (Bxxxv). Kant sees his predecessors in philosophy, such as Spinoza and Leibniz, as embracing an over-ambitious view of the capacities of human reason and its ability to dictate for nature and the human world the form that they should take. That rival systems emerged from the use of pure reason – which engendered deep conflict – should have alerted philosophers to their limitations. Instead of which the errors which occurred inflamed the controversies even more and ultimately brought philosophy itself into disrepute.

The operations of the critique of reason – which Kant prefers – where reason itself comes to the fore are therefore defined in contrast to the conditions that prevail in a condition of war. War and reason are seen as continually at odds with one another. The arbitrary violence that reigns in war is the direct antithesis of the clear, open and fair processes of reason.

'Reason must subject itself to criticism in all its undertakings, and cannot restrict the freedom of criticism through any proposition without damaging itself and drawing upon itself a disadvantageous suspicion. Now there is nothing so important because of its utility, nothing so sacred, that it may be exempted from this searching review and inspection, which knows no respect for persons. The very existence of reason depends upon this freedom, which has no dictatorial authority, but whose claim is never anything more than the agreement of free citizens, each of whom must be able to express his reservations, indeed even his veto, without holding back' (A738/B766).

This passage demonstrates the extent to which Kant regards his critique of reason as a social and political process. The critique does not simply proceed in a way that is analogous to comparable social and political processes – it is in itself such a process.[25] His critical philosophy seeks to gain the unanimous support of its readers. No reader is forced to accept Kant's conclusion: he invites readers to participate with him in the investigative procedure, and if readers are not fully convinced then they are entirely free to dissent – even if their worries are not shared by other (even all other) members of the audience.

Kant returns to this theme of the pacifying aims of his own critical philosophy, as we have seen, in one of his final publications 'Announcement of the imminent conclusion of a treaty for perpetual peace in philosophy'. Although there is a playful element to the title of the article, which first appeared in the *Berlinische Monatsschrift*, Kant does fear the development of a military ethos amongst philosophical schools, who instead of seeking common ground attempt to annihilate one another in mock battle. The dogmatists threaten to annihilate all philosophical life with their certainties while the sceptics endanger philosophy in a different way by 'putting to one side everything' that animates a lively reason – and the moderate school which seeks to find a halfway point between the two extremes by discovering the 'stone' of wisdom in 'subjective probability' ends up not being philosophy at all (8: 415). In this article he presents a very simple two-step solution to the problem of philosophical warmongering. These two steps are: first, that philosophers should stick to what is true in what they say (and here he admits that most philosophers do aim at this); secondly, (and here he seems to suggest there is the most scope for improvement) they should avoid presenting with certainty conclusions whose truth they are unsure of. There can be no higher authority than reason itself. It is only through open debate and not through oracular assertion that philosophy can best be advanced. In being modest in claims about what we can know the philosopher shows due self-restraint. This self-restraint that brings about lasting peace in philosophy mirrors the self-restraint and discipline that have to be shown and are necessary for bringing about peace among nations.

Conclusion

From a practical perspective much of Kant's moral and political philosophy is focused on overcoming bad habits of mind to which we are all prey. This is because we are both rational beings and natural beings and our natural, sentient side impresses upon us non-rational affects. Countering these affects is a difficult task and in Kant's view it requires that we adopt a systematic metaphysics of morals to aid us in the task. Kant is a rationalist and universalist who makes the assumption that human individuals share common patterns of thought and, if they are to communicate effectively with one another, the cognitive faculties of reason and understanding must be identical in each of us. At the psychological level Kant assumes a broad similarity in the way our minds work and at an intellectual level a precise resemblance in the way they must work. Many misguided ideas and customs have to be cleared out of the way if we are to attain lasting peace in philosophy and politics.

Thus, a critically delimited metaphysics and a moral politics coalesce in pursuing a similar goal and the means of attaining that goal.[26] A critical metaphysics sets its sights on removing the cause for outright hostility amongst philosophers. Just as there should be no war in the political realm there should be no war in the philosophical realm. From the standpoint of the critical philosophy there can be no need for warring factions in philosophy once the limits of human reason are properly recognized. By demanding too great a finality in our theoretical enquiries dogmatic philosophers are led to irresolvable disputes and irreconcilable antagonisms. By rejecting the pursuit of such finality in metaphysics philosophers can engage with what is attainable – rules of conduct in the practical sphere which form the basis for morality and right. In a complementary manner to the overcoming of war in the philosophical realm, peace at a political level involves the worldwide recognition and acceptance of the best methods of resolving differences. Here also the focus is upon appropriate rules of conduct.[27] At the domestic level a republican constitution within a state allows individuals to pursue their happiness in their own way in a manner that is compatible with the rule of law. Each person is free to follow his or her own material ends so long as this does not hinder or harm others in the pursuit of their material ends. The proper balance between individuals within states has to be matched from Kant's critical perspective with a proper balance in relations among states. The focus in the resolution of war is upon the form and structure of relations amongst individuals and states: it is a matter of right. International law has to be transformed from a symbol of the need for states to govern their relations amongst each other in a civil way into a working institution, respected and observed by political leaders and their subjects. A gradually expanding federation of republican states is the necessary counterpart to a representative government elected by citizens at home. This means that individuals not only enjoy rights within the borders of their states but also beyond those borders when they visit other states and territories. Each individual has the right not to be treated with hostility when visiting. No one can be treated as though they were a wrongdoer simply through seeking to present themselves in a territory that is not their own. By adhering to the principle of hospitality states and their subjects will live up to a rule required by reason. The cosmopolitan goal of politics is identical with the cosmopolitan epistemological interest of the critical philosophy.

Here we can unmistakeably see Kant's commitment to resolving the disputes of philosophy through discussion and open debate when he speaks of his method in the *Critique of Pure Reason*:

> If you grasp at means other than uncoerced reason, if you cry high treason, if you call together the public, which understands nothing of such refinements, as if they were to put out a fire, then you make yourself ridiculous. (A747/B775)

This is supported by a vision of philosophy which is of course a strictly academic discipline, respecting unreservedly the rules of logic and the proper provision of evidence, yet one that is also systematically connected to our vital moral interest in the highest good in the world:

> Until now, however, the concept of philosophy has been only a scholastic concept, namely that of a system of cognition that is sought only as a science without having as its end anything more than the systematic unity of this knowledge, thus the logical perfection of cognition. But there is also a cosmopolitan concept (*Weltbegriff-conceptus cosmicus*) that has always grounded this term, especially when it is, as it were, personified and represented as an archetype in the ideal of philosopher. From this point of view philosophy is the science of the relation of all cognition to the essential ends of human reason (teleologia rationis humane) and the philosopher is not an artist of reason but the legislator of human reason. (A439/B867)

Seen from this perspective, the ending of war is not an end that lies to one side of the objectives of philosophy but one that is at the core of its concerns. Bringing philosophy under the rule of law is but one aspect of the overall aim of bringing human society under the sway of a critically delimited reason.

2
Kant and Just War Theory: The Problem Outlined

> The right of nations is a right in the condition (*iuridice*) of war, that is of the lack of public justice, and there is no other principle appropriate to it than that all the actions of the nation (Volk) in regard to others stand solely under the stipulations under which the creation of public justice is possible, that is, a union of nations.
>
> Kant (19: 598)[1]

Introduction

We have seen how the idea of war forms a key theme for Kant's philosophy as a whole. It enters his theoretical philosophy – in his theory of knowledge in the *Critique of Pure Reason* – as the model of human interaction most to be avoided, since the outcome of war is never determined by reason alone; it enters his practical philosophy as the paradigm case of the breakdown of human relations most to be feared and shunned; it enters his aesthetic thinking as a form of human behaviour that epitomizes the dynamically sublime; and it enters his teleological thinking as a key example of how the negative and dispiriting aspects of human experience can be turned to the advantage of the species. Each one of these uses of the idea of war is highly contentious; none the less the overriding pattern is one of a rejection of war as an acceptable *future* form of human behaviour. War can be seen as a form of interaction that lies between that of the lives of savages and the lives of genuinely human individuals. The abiding impression given of war by Kant in the main writings of his critical philosophy is of war as a mode of conduct that has to be overcome. In none of his references to war does he appear to take for granted its presence and persistence in human society: each mention of it alludes to it as a transitional or episodic process, and one by no means inevitable for the human race. From the practical perspective he thinks it imperative that we view war as an occurrence that has ultimately to vanish from our common lives, just as from the theoretical perspective he regards the warlike attitude as one which denotes the collapse and defeat of reason.

The most difficult thing to fathom with Kant's treatment of war in his critical philosophy is that, after condemning it from the standpoints of all but the aesthetic perspective, he nevertheless finds space to *praise* war's socializing and humanizing effects. Seen from the standpoint of the moral condemnation of war this may appear a perverse way of looking at things. But it is something we might expect from Kant's rejection of outright pacifism – we have somehow to understand that although war is a blot on the human character it is also a necessary phase in the development of the species. Given the stage we have so far reached in human history, war is not without its positive consequences for the human species. In commending these positive aspects of war Kant is neither recommending war as the best means of achieving those aims nor recommending the persistence of war as the way in which to attain these positives in the future. He is simply attempting to stress what is good within the bad. Clearly the pressure which peoples are put under by the experience of war leads them to cooperate, to innovate, and to demonstrate resolve and bravery. War has given an immeasurable boost to human productivity and technological innovation. War sharpens our reactions all round and also leads us to consider more carefully our social and political arrangements. Above all, the experience of war drives us to overcome war. These are undeniable positives that war generates, but it is a sad reflection on the character of the human race that thus far in its development war has been required to bring about these improvements. If only the human race had been more capable of improvement and reform without the need for war!

Kant's understanding of human nature, though, makes clear that this perfection was not to be expected of the human being. We are not the kind of beings who are always going to do what is right. Observation of the human species, and his acquaintance with his own and others' psychology, leads Kant to the conclusion that we are both animal beings that are driven by instinct and inclination and rational beings that are potentially capable of being motivated by reason. The interaction of these two forces or aspects of the human character can be seen very clearly in human society and history. It is evident in Kant's understanding of our 'unsociable-sociability' as highlighted in his essay 'Idea for a Universal History' (8: 21/7). This phrase captures in an exceptionally clear way the ambivalence of the human character: our capacity on the one hand for justice, great nobility and sacrifice, and on the other for meanness and ignobleness. According to Kant, there is inherent in each individual a propensity to radical evil. This is a propensity (*Hang* – tendency)[2] which will always be present, and each generation of human individuals will feel it with the same force as the previous one. Yet, although Kant recognises this propensity to radical evil in human nature he does not come to the same pessimistic conclusions as political philosophers such as Hobbes about human conduct, war and international relations. The essential difference is that the Hobbesian conceives the human individual in a solely deterministic way and Kant conceives the human individual in a simultaneously determinist and voluntarist way.[3] Hobbes, as a mechanical materialist, denies the human individual has a free will, whereas one of the central concerns of Kant's philosophy is our free will and the autonomy we may consequently strive to enjoy. Thus for Kant we are neither wholly evil by nature nor driven by mechanical forces, as Hobbes sees it, to seek self-preservation above all else; we are voluntarily drawn to evil by our own freedom to prioritize our choices. Evil is a path we are prone consciously to take and for that reason Kant thinks 'it must be equally possible to overcome this evil, for it is found in the human being as acting freely' (6: 37/59).

This propensity to evil is particularly evident in war. Indeed Kant finds in war the most compelling evidence of 'a corrupt propensity rooted in the human being' (6: 33/56) and he holds that it is undeniable that 'civilized peoples stand in vis-à-vis one another in the relation of raw nature (the state of constant war)' (6: 35/57). However the paradox is that through war Kant hopes the human race will bring itself round to more civilized ways. This hope is not expressed solely in terms of an expectation that human individuals will suddenly allow the laws of morality to determine their actions but also (and largely) in terms that war will ultimately undermine itself. The idea is that a historical learning process will take place where the human race will gradually seek to eliminate its mistakes. Although as individuals we cannot aspire to the full realization of our human powers, it is possible that as a species we can do so. Through a harsh process of trial and error the human species may learn gradually to exercise its freedom in ever more virtuous ways. We will never wholly overcome our propensity to evil, but we may slowly become more skilled in counteracting its effects. In his teleological understanding of history Kant aspires to see morality and strategic thinking (both at an individual and a state level) coalesce in the conclusion that there should be no more war.

What also is evident in Kant's treatment of war in his major critical works is the respect in which he holds public law as a means of resolving disputes amongst individuals and states. The respect for law runs very deep in his critical system. As we have seen he presents his first *Critique* as 'the true court of justice' where all the issues with which our reason is assailed are decided (A751/B779). Those issues are decided by the fair and consistent application of rules which are open to the scrutiny and criticism of all. Human reason is in no need of defence through belligerence and antagonism: public debate and the preparedness to respect the rule of law in the deployment of reason are sufficient for it to hold sway. The same respect for the rule of law is equally (if not even more) evident in Kant's practical philosophy, where the cornerstone of his moral thinking is the idea of a categorical imperative which requires us to 'act only in accordance with that maxim through which you can at the same time will that it become a universal law' (4: 421; 73). From this idea Kant derives the related notion that we should never treat others solely as means but always also as ends. As is only to be expected, community and harmony are at the heart of Kant's notion of morality, which is summed up by the idea of a 'kingdom' or dominion of ends which is 'a systematic union of various rational beings through common laws' (4: 433; 83). Respect for law is also at the heart of Kant's political philosophy, so much so that Kant sums up the role of politics as the 'carrying out of the rule of law (*ausuebende Rechtslehre*)' (8: 370; 338). Thus moving beyond the rule of law to the judgment that can be brought about by the prosecution of a war would for Kant take us beyond the realm of true politics. The arbitrary nature of the outcome of a war amongst states can never be entirely shaken off. War is only accorded indirect approval in Kant's critical writings as a means of moving human society away from the tyranny and imperative of war and towards the only lasting condition fit for a society of rational beings: continuous peace.

All in all Kant's view of war in his critical philosophy is that it is a pathological aspect of human experience. The term pathology derives from the Greek words 'pathos' – disease and 'logos' knowledge or treatise. Literally it means the study of a disease. To me this conveys accurately the way in which we should approach war from a Kantian perspective. Although Kant grants that war has always been part of the human condition, he refuses to recognise it as a normal part of human life. As he puts it in his comments on Achenwall's *Juris Naturalis* 'the so-called state of nature' where it occurs 'is actually amongst rational beings pre-natural (*praenaturalis*); thus war is an extraordinary condition (*status extraordinarius*) which is only allowed as an occasion of necessity (*casus necessitatis*)' (19: 601).[4] In some respects war is like physical diseases that affect the human race: always potentially present and not always necessarily curable. However, its status is different from natural diseases such as tuberculosis or poliomyelitis: since the cause of war is to be found in human behaviour itself, it is potentially wholly eradicable. Thus Kant's critical outlook cannot persist alongside the acceptance of the complete normality or inevitability of war. From a practical standpoint war has to be approached as a curable disease. This is, as we shall see, what lies behind his depiction of the just war theorists of the modern period as 'sorry comforters'.

Just War theory

Given Kant's highly complex view of war as we have just outlined it, the central question we shall be addressing in the first part of this book: is Kant an opponent or a supporter of traditional just war theory? Traditional just war theory maintains that the right to go to war is an integral part of international law, and that there is a discourse shared by political leaders, military leaders and theorists of international law that encapsulates what the tradition maintains. Just war theory has a rich history, going back at least to Roman times and figuring systematically in Augustine's *City of God* and developed in its classical form in the philosophy of Aquinas. Aquinas distinguished conditions under which a just war might be possible, which are often referred to as right authority; just cause and right intention.[5] The first refers to the legitimacy of the ruler declaring the war; the second to the justice of the occasion for war; and the third to the motives which govern the way in which the war is conducted. A distinction that became a part of the modern theory of just war was that between *jus ad bellum* and *jus in bello* where the former refers to the correct evaluation of the condition prior to war and the latter to the manner in which the war is conducted.[6] The object was to delineate the right conduct for both. Just war theorists attempt to specify as accurately as possible those precise conditions that make a war morally right and so legally acceptable. A leading example of a twentieth-century just war theorist is Michael Walzer, who in *Just and Unjust Wars* tries to establish that 'nothing but aggression can justify war.'[7] According to modern just war theory, each sovereign/independent state is the final judge of what constitutes a threat to its security and each state is free to determine independently when its capacity to defend itself is threatened and so when it needs to declare war.[8] Just war theory has formed a part of international law from the inception of the discipline – with ever greater attempts at precision in determining what might be a 'just cause' being made – although its status and application have always been hotly disputed.[9]

This book highlights, as I have already indicated, Kant's celebrated depiction of three of the best known proponents of just war theory in the early modern period: Hugo Grotius (1583–1645), Samuel Pufendorf (1632–94) and Emmerich de Vattel (1714–67) in *Perpetual Peace* as 'sorry comforters' and his apparent dismissal of their arguments that attempt to justify war under international law.[10] It asks whether this satirical phrase represents his considered view on the subject and whether or not there might be some inconsistencies in his position that prevent him from being regarded as an unequivocal opponent of the theory. Evidence for this possible inconsistency is the recent development of accounts of just war that draw primarily from Kant's arguments in the Doctrine of Right in the first part of the *Metaphysics of Morals*, but also draw attention to Kant's rejection of pacifism both in *Perpetual Peace* and in the Doctrine of Right.[11] In this chapter we pursue this issue by looking at the background to just war theory in international law in Kant's day. Grotius, Pufendorf and Vattel were the major figures in that discipline.

International law or the law of nations was already an important aspect of legal and political philosophy in Kant's time. Because of its connection with natural law, which was the main focus of political and legal philosophy in prior centuries, the law of nations was as much studied and discussed as internal political and legal issues. Certainly for Kant's immediate precursors Gottfried Achenwall (1719–1772)[12] and Christian Wolff (1679–1754)[13] all questions of political and legal philosophy were dealt with under the heading of natural law. Within the framework of natural law the law of nations was regarded as a logical extension of the domestic legal and political spheres. For philosophers such as Wolff and Achenwall natural law underpinned both internal law and international law. This was a common assumption for the period: Thomas Hobbes and John Locke[14] similarly saw the law of nations as derivable from natural law.

The continuity between internal and external law was a feature of Roman law which greatly influenced the development of legal and political thinking in the middle Ages. Thomas Aquinas, who absorbed the pagan philosophies of Ancient Greece and Rome into Christian thinking (with special emphasis on Aristotle), gave to natural law an important function in linking eternal law, divine law and human law.[15] Compared to international law in the twenty first century eighteenth-century international law was indeed underdeveloped, but it was far from being a novel endeavour. In writing on international law there was as much (if not more) for Kant to draw upon in the work of his contemporaries as there was in writing on two of the key dimensions of his domestic political theory: social contract theory and constitutional law.

Early modern international law and the legalisation of war

Here I depict international law in the period immediately prior to Kant as *Grotian* international law. I find the term useful since it denotes the formative influence of the Dutch jurist and political philosopher, Hugo Grotius, upon the development of modern international law and so also upon an understanding of the role of international law that persists to this day. It is an understanding of international law that attempts to normalize war as a part of the international system. Law and armed conflict amongst states are compatible for the Grotian. Hugo Grotius's *On the Law of War and Peace* (1625) presents the case for a voluntary law binding upon independent states in the European context. It was an understanding of law that was suited to the political system emerging in Europe at the time, which was partially codified in the 1648 Treaty of Westphalia. Grotius regarded war amongst the independent sovereign entities as permissible under certain circumstances, yet he devised a system of rules for states which he believed was largely binding. Despite the latitude given for war Grotius held that states were part of a developing natural community.

The question concerning the justness of war for Grotius has to be considered in terms of what God has willed. God's will is the origin of all law for 'what God has shown to be his will, that is law.'[16] However, the will of God is revealed 'not only through oracular and supernatural portents, but above all in the very design of the Creator, for it is from this last source that the law of nature is derived.'[17] Here Grotius turns to the Roman philosopher Cicero to support his argument. Cicero had recommended that even the study of the stars and the heavens was of benefit from the standpoint of justice because they revealed the workings of the mind of the 'supreme Ruler'.[18] Grotius believes strongly in the rationality of the natural order we can observe around us. 'Since God fashioned creation and willed its existence, every individual part thereof has received from Him certain natural properties whereby that existence may be preserved and each part may be guided for its own good, in conformity, one might say, with the fundamental law inherent in its origin.'[19] Grotius's method of argument diverges markedly from that of Kant here who sees phenomena not so much as revealing a divine consciousness but rather as evidence of the shaping of human consciousness. Human awareness with Kant imparts rationality to the observed object and does not simply testify to rationality external to it. Kant is also, in contrast to Grotius, extremely careful about the attribution of functionality or teleology to nature. He does not share Grotius's direct and optimistic approach of attributing an immediate factual purpose to nature.

For Grotius, 'he, who wills the attainment of a given end, wills also the things that are necessary to that end. God wills that we should protect ourselves, retain our hold on the necessities of life, obtain that which is our due, punish transgressors, and at the same time defend the state, executing its orders as well as the commands of its magistrates.' There are certain rules that follow incontrovertibly from our existence as natural beings that require the society of beings of the same kind and need to be observed. 'But these divine objectives sometimes constitute causes for undertaking and carrying on war. In fact, they are of such a nature that it is very often impossible for us to attain them without recourse to warfare'. War is depicted then as an unavoidable part of our natural condition. Another way of putting this is to say that for Grotius orthodox international relations implies the occasional outbreak of war. 'Just as a certain natural conflict is waged, so to speak, between dryness and moisture, or between heat and cold, so there is a similar conflict between justice and injustice. Indeed factual evidence clearly shows that there are in existence many men of a bloodthirsty, rapacious, unjust and nefarious disposition, traitors to their native lands and disparagers of sovereign power – men who are strong, too, and equipped with weapons – who must be conquered in battle (as Tacitus puts it) in order that they may be brought to book as criminals. Thus it is God's will that certain wars should be waged; that is to say (in the phraseology of the theologians) certain wars are waged in accordance with God's good pleasure.'[20]

Grotius thoroughly rejects any pacifist interpretation of Christ's teachings propagated by some of the Christian Church's early followers. Grotius acknowledges that it was Christ's teaching that we should love our neighbours, but when those neighbours turn out to be thieves and criminals they can be rightfully punished. In his view, it is not true that both sides in a war commit sin. He draws the conclusion from the teachings of the 'Holy Writ', obeying 'the guidance of nature' and in being 'influenced in some degree by 'the example or by the pronouncements of famous men' that 'some wars are just for Christians, against Christians, from the standpoint of all law.'[21]

Grotius indeed pressed the paradoxical position that the binding nature of the law of nations is in evidence in war itself. First, it is evidenced by the reference to only a restricted number of just causes permitting the resort to arms and, secondly, by the prohibitive rules that come into force in war itself. *Jus ad bellum* and *jus in bello* are for him key parts of international law. Thus a hallmark of the Grotian position as I depict it here is that there is no contradiction in law and war coexisting with one another.[22] It was an understanding of international law that went side by side with a competitive system of states, armed and prepared to do battle with one another to preserve their vital interests, but at the same time mindful of the damage that could be caused by unrestricted war to the persistence of the whole system. It is a view of international law that is not without its progressive dimension. As Georg Schwarzenberger astutely puts it: 'Growing forces of public opinion with tendencies towards nationalism, liberalism and pacifism could only increase the attractiveness of an approach, such as that of Grotius, that was safe on the essentials of establishment policies but could be used selectively whenever convenient in diplomatic exchanges, adversary proceedings, and, on suitable occasions even in faint support of public yearnings for better things to come'.[23] Grotius thinks that the effects of warfare can be mitigated, encompassed and regulated within international law. As we shall see, this is an assumption that Kant sets out to challenge and to overturn with his own critical view of international law.

Emmerich de Vattel, one of the most fluent and interesting writers on international law in the eighteenth century, employs a similar line of reasoning in bringing international law and just war together. He is the only one of the three figures portrayed as 'sorry comforters' who was Kant's contemporary. Vattel was steeped in the same natural law literature as Kant. A minor civil servant and diplomat, Vattel used the generous time he appeared to have at his disposal to study thoroughly natural law and its derivative law of nations. Vattel shared with Kant a strong Prussian connection, being born in Couver, Neuchatel which was a Swiss principality which became the personal property of the King of Prussia in 1707. Vattel's father, a protestant clergyman and a prominent figure in his denomination, was made a nobleman by the King in

1727. Vattel studied at Basel where he became acquainted with Samuel Pufendorf's legal and political philosophy before going later to Geneva to study metaphysics and law.[14] As with Kant, Vattel's early theoretical development was influenced by the writings of Leibniz and Wolff who both enjoyed considerable sway over philosophy in the middle of the eighteenth century. Vattel, like Kant, strove to shake himself free of the hold over his thoughts exercised by Wolff, but is less radical than Kant in starting afresh.[25] Vattel begins, in his principal work *The Law of Nations*, from what he takes to be indubitable facts to demonstrate that war in the international system is from time to time inevitable. 'Were men always reasonable, they would terminate their contests by the arms of reason only: natural justice and equity would be their rule, or their judge. Force is a wretched and melancholy expedient against those who spurn at justice, and refuse to listen to the remonstrances of reason: but, in short, it becomes necessary to adopt that mode, when every other proves ineffectual. It is only in extremities that a just and wise nation, or a good prince, has recourse to it'.[26] It is the injustice of others and the lack of a common judge that leads to war. 'The right of employing force, or making war, belongs to nations no farther than is necessary for their own defence, and for the maintenance of their rights. Now if anyone attacks a nation, or violates her perfect rights, he does her an injury. Then, and not till then, that nation has a right to repel the aggressor, and reduce him to reason. Further, she has a right to prevent the intended injury, when she sees herself threatened with it. Let us say in general, that the foundation or cause of every just war is injury, either already done or threatened.'[27] Vattel sees himself as setting out reliable and stable principles of law, principles that nature dictates – but they rapidly develop into variable and unpredictable principles once he acknowledges that each nation will see its predicament differently. And it is the independence of each sovereign state that is paramount for Vattel. For example, he maintains in the first instance that 'war cannot be just on both sides'.[28] He holds that it is illogical that both parties can be in the right: 'they may be considered as two individuals disputing on the truth of a proposition; and that is impossible that two contrary sentiments should be true at the same time.' Thus accepting that war can be justly declared within the framework of international law should lead to no conflict. However it may happen 'that both the contending parties are candid and sincere in their intentions; and, in a doubtful cause, it is still uncertain which side is in the right. Wherefore, since nations are equal and independent and cannot claim a right of judgment over each other, it follows, that in every case susceptible of doubt, the arms of the two parties at war are to be accounted equally lawful, at least to external effects, and until decision of the cause.' Thus Vattel's line of reasoning leads to imprecision and insecurity instead of precision and stability in the application of international law. And he compounds this effect by noting that the lack of clarity about the justness of the two sides does not 'deprive other nations of the liberty of forming their own judgment on the case, in order to determine how they are to act, and to assist that party that appear to have right on their side.'[29] Only if we make the extremely generous assumption that the combatant that has justice on its side will attract the most material support from onlooking nations can we place any faith in the view that Vattel's approach will lead to a legally satisfactory conclusion. Accepting, as does Vattel, that nations unilaterally have the right of prosecuting wars leads to a highly fluid and flexible version of international law.

The problem of Kant and Just War theory defined

Brian Orend and Susan Shell are two prominent commentators who strongly believe that Kant can be regarded as being positively disposed to a just war theory. Orend devotes his book *War and International Justice: A Kantian Perspective* to the thesis, and Susan Shell in an article in *Kantian Review* 'Kant on Unjust War and "Unjust Enemies": reflections on a pleonasm' tries 'to show that Kant is less averse to the use of force, including resort to pre-emptive war, and far more attuned to possibilities for political catastrophe, than he is often taken to be.'[30] Orend acknowledges that the prevailing view of Kant (at the end of the twentieth century) was that he had no just war theory, citing W.B. Gallie, Georg Geismann and Fernando Teson as commentators who take this view. Orend even scrupulously recognizes that 'there is a bevy of quotes in the Kantian corpus to support this reading'.[31] But for Orend these numerous quotes do not outweigh the evidence for the contrary view that Kant embraces just war thinking. In stark contrast to the view I shall be advancing here, Orend makes the argument in his book that 'the weight of the textual evidence points clearly in favour of a pro-just war reading of Kant, and that any view to the contrary can only be sustained by a partial and selective reading of the texts.'[32] Since Orend's reading of Kant on the question is heavily biased towards the key sections in the *Metaphysics of Morals* in which Kant deals with war and international law, he in effect privileges the 1797 publication at the expense of the better known *Perpetual Peace*. The emphasis in Susan Shell's article is similar. She focuses in her commentary upon the principal paragraphs devoted to the law of nations in *Metaphysics of Morals* (pp. 53–61) to claim that 'preventive warfare in good faith, that is, without actively hostile intention to claim more, in principle, than one allows to other, is, it seems, permitted.'[33] Both Orend and Shell then give primary credence to Kant's statements on international law and war in the *Metaphysics of Morals* and present his depiction in that work of the current doctrines of international law as a clear declaration of Kant's own views.

My argument here is that the account that Kant gives of permissible war under the auspices of international law in the *Metaphysics of Morals* is logically subordinate to the critique of war as an instrument of international politics given in *Perpetual Peace*. Kant is not (as Shell suggests)[34] an advocate of pre-emptive or anticipatory wars under the aegis of international law critically understood. I take the account in *Metaphysics of Morals* which accepts *inter alia* the 'right' to go to war 'for active violations' and to deal with a 'menacing increase in another state's power' (6: 346) in large part as a caricature showing what the position was under the law of nations in Kant's day (and to a large extent even now). I argue the outcome for the discussion in *Metaphysics of Morals* is that the traditional position on war in international law is incoherent. Thus to get a clearer understanding of Kant's critical outlook, the initial part of the discussion in *Metaphysics of Morals* where he appears to endorse defensive wars should be read in close continuity with the later two sections that subject the war ethos of traditional international law to severe critique. Although *Perpetual Peace* (1795) was published before *Metaphysics of Morals* (1797), I suggest that the account of war provided in *Perpetual Peace* should be regarded as Kant's most fully worked out treatment of the question of just war. Thus his remarks about the 'sorry comforters' (*leidige Troester*) Hugo Grotius, Pufendorf and Vattel in *Perpetual Peace* apply to any attempts to harness a coherent account of international law to a legal justification for war. It is traditional international law that morally vindicates wars of self-defence (and pre-emptive varieties of it) and not Kant.[35] At best such wars for Kant are excusable.

There is undoubtedly a marked divergence between the account given of war and the possible grounds for its justification in the Doctrine of Right at the beginning of *Metaphysics of Morals* and the account given by Kant in *Perpetual Peace*. In *Perpetual Peace* Kant finds war in most of its aspects morally reprehensible, and thinks no place should be found in a properly structured international law for its legitimization. In contrast, the discussion of war and its possibility in the section on international right in the later *Metaphysics of Morals* appears to accept the inevitability of war, and to acknowledge that states under international law seem to be in possession of a right to declare it unilaterally. Of course in *Metaphysics of Morals* Kant expresses puzzlement why states should be in this position, and it needs a great deal of both coaxing and reconstructing of his words to show that he positively accepts a 'right' to go to war – however, we have to grant that some of Kant's phrases indicate a readiness to put up with hostilities, and even a warming to the possibility where it comes to dealing with a particularly belligerent country that has a predominance of power.

The contrast between the two works might be attributable to the different times and contexts in which Kant wrote and published them. This would be one way of dealing with our problem. Arguably *Perpetual Peace* might be presented as the work which includes the most mature of Kant's thoughts about the issue of war – even though *Metaphysics of Morals* was published later than the shorter *Perpetual Peace* – because *Metaphysics of Morals* may well in part have been written over a much longer period and incorporated sections that Kant may feasibly have penned well before 1795. Kant had been planning a *Metaphysics of Morals* and so a systematic exposition of the Doctrine of Right from as early as 1756, and thirteen years later Kant wrote to Herder that his metaphysics of morals should be completed by the end of that year.[36] There is some suggestion also that the final text of the work 'had been put together from various manuscripts'[37] that may well have been completed and different times. If this is so, then *Perpetual Peace* might be regarded as the more authoritative of the two accounts (at least of Kant's thinking in the 1790s), so that what is written in *Metaphysics of Morals* should always be seen in its light. This is an interpretation towards which I am drawn here because Kant devoted so much of his time to *Perpetual Peace* and it went through two editions very rapidly in 1795 and 1796 (with a translation into French). No doubt this is very difficult to prove, and as Kant would have had an opportunity (which he might not have taken) to update his *Metaphysics of Morals* to align it with his views in *Perpetual Peace*, it may be better to leave it at the suggestion that there is a legitimate case for at least regarding both *Perpetual Peace* and *Metaphysics of Morals* as authoritative accounts by Kant of his views on war and justice and so requiring us to discover within them one golden unifying thread. Can we do this though? – here the divergence between the two texts is arguably so marked that we have somehow to account for two different and authoritative views on war in Kant rather than one coherent view.

Of course, Kant is not wholly consistent in the opinions he expresses in his published writings. It is possible to discover other marked discrepancies between what Kant says in his shorter, more popular writings and his more systematic texts. This certainly seems to apply to the views on independence which Kant advances in the essay 'On the common saying: this may be true in theory, but does not apply in practice' (1793) and the views he expresses on the same topic in *Metaphysics of Morals*. In this instance there seems to be a development and arguably a greater sophistication in the account of independence given in *Metaphysics of Morals* as compared to the earlier published views in 'Theory and Practice'. The distinction that stands out between the two is that in the earlier essay no mention is made of the notion of the passive citizen that is deployed in an interesting manner in *Metaphysics of Morals*. The 'Theory and Practice' essay seems to work on the assumption that there is only one division with citizenship: full citizenship where one is accorded the vote and non-citizenship where one is not eligible to vote on the grounds that the individual is not his 'own master'. At best these non-citizens are members of the commonwealth but not independent members. 'Those who are not entitled to this right are still, as members of the commonwealth, subject to compliance with these laws and thereby enjoy protection in accordance with them, not, however, as citizens but as co-beneficiaries of this protection'. (8: 294)[38] the picture is different in *Metaphysics of Morals* where the non-independents are upgraded into 'passive citizens' who enjoy freedom and equality as human beings but they do not have the right of the active citizen 'to manage the state itself' and 'to cooperate for introducing certain laws'(6: 315/458). Here there is a clear discrepancy between the view of the earlier published article and the later published book. And arguably there is an improvement in the presentation in the book since there is a greater fluidity in the relationship between passive and active citizen as compared to the relationship between the citizen and non-citizen. The distinction in *Metaphysics of Morals* seems more easily to allow for movement between the two categories (at least as the male individual grows up or gets a more prestigious/less dependent way of earning a living). The later published work arguably shows a greater sensitivity towards the situation of the less favoured individual than the article.

This appears to suggest then that Kant may possibly have regarded his articles in the *Berlinische Monatsschrift* as earlier less complete drafts on which he might later wish to elaborate. But can the short work *Perpetual Peace* be put into the same category as these articles, to be seen as a first draft for the later and fuller account of international law in the *Metaphysics of Morals*? If this were the case, the sweeping criticism made of just war thinking in *Perpetual Peace* might be seen as superseded by the more moderate position presented in arguably the more authoritative account given of war in the *Metaphysics of Morals*. Here I argue that we cannot see the relation of the two publications in this way – first, because the latter is a book in its own right and not an occasional article; secondly because *Perpetual Peace* takes us into issues of the application of the principles or right that are beyond the scope of the *Metaphysics of Morals* and so is more explicit on some questions only touched upon in the longer work; and thirdly because *Perpetual Peace* must have been one of Kant's most eagerly awaited publications, for which both his scholarly and public audience would be at its widest, it seems highly unlikely he would wish to present them incomplete (or 'work in progress') thoughts.

Sharon Byrd and Joachim Hruschka take a different approach in their commentary on *Kant's Doctrine of Right*. Like Orend and Shell they appear to accord to *Metaphysics of Morals* a higher authority than *Perpetual Peace* in determining Kant's approach to war. In their commentary they 'assume that the statements Kant made on legal philosophy before the *Doctrine of Right*, namely in his lectures in 1784, in *Theory and Practice* of 1793, in *Perpetual Peace* of 1795, and in his short comments in many other works, are steps toward the system of legal philosophy that unfolds in the *Doctrine of Right* of 1797. They are steps towards his system, but they do not already contain the system itself in a nutshell.'[39] In their view the less prohibitive account of war presented in the *Doctrine of Right* is the systematic point of view that Kant is only hinting at in his earlier writings. Accordingly they regard it as 'conceivable that Kant makes mistakes while groping toward the system he later develops to perfection.' These are 'mistakes he too would have called mistakes from his later point of view.'[40] Thus where there is a conflict between what Kant says in *Perpetual Peace* and the *Doctrine of Right*, the standpoint in the latter represents Kant's true position. Byrd and Hruschka sharpen the conflict between the publications to the point where they argue that 'in *Perpetual Peace* there is no right to wage war, whereas Kant assumes precisely the opposite in the *Doctrine of Right*.'[41] Whilst not employing the term 'just war', Byrd and Hruschka endorse an interpretation of Kant that would permit his inclusion amongst just war theorists. In particular, they appear to endorse the exceptionally destabilizing idea that Kant allows for wars to be waged to force other states into peaceful federation of states or what they describe as 'a juridical state of states'.[42] By taking this view they open the way for Kant's doctrine to be deployed by those enthusiastic proponents of the 'democratic peace' thesis of the early twentieth century who wish to extend the democratic system to new territories by force if necessary. We shall come to this topic in a later chapter where I shall seek to demonstrate the implausibility of this interventionist application of Kant's ideas.

In contrast to Byrd and Hruschka, there is every reason to believe, as Mary Gregor indicates, that 'thematically *Toward Perpetual Peace* takes up where *The Doctrine of Right* ends.'[43] Gregor sees the shorter book as building upon the more schematic outlook presented in the book on right. Thus despite the shorter book appearing before the treatise on right, Gregor maintains it has a similar systematic priority. This seems most plausible, since the problem of war is dealt with in only ten sections of the *Doctrine of Right* in the context of Kant's reception and interpretation of orthodox international law as found in the school books of his day. In contrast Kant devotes the whole of *Perpetual Peace* (112 pages in its second 1796 edition) to the problem and seeks to provide a response to it which reflects the full import of his critical system. Gregor takes the view that we shall explore in the fourth chapter of the book, namely that *Perpetual Peace* and the *Metaphysics of Morals* can be seen in continuity with one another. We turn first though to the apparent distinct conflict between the two works in their handling of the justice of war.

Conclusion

In this chapter we first considered how Kant's overall approach to war colours his reception of international law and its dilemmas. We then went on to consider the treatment of war in two prominent representatives of international law in Kant's time: Grotius and Vattel. We show how these writers both construct and embrace a just war theory. Thirdly, in highlighting the main theme of this book: Kant's approach to just war theory, we contrasted Kant's equivocal view of the legality and morality of war with Grotius's and Vattel's affirmative views. Finally we indicated that our most likely answer to the question of whether or not Kant can legitimately be regarded as an exponent of just war theory was negative. In the following chapters on *Perpetual Peace* and the doctrine of right in the *Metaphysics of Morals* we shall indicate why this is so.

3
Perpetual Peace and the Case against Just War Theory

The nature of the contrast: *Perpetual Peace* and the *Metaphysics of Morals* compared

This chapter examines the case for regarding *Perpetual Peace* and the *Metaphysics of Morals* as entirely at odds in their treatment of just war theory. In *Perpetual Peace* Kant can be regarded as being generally hostile to any just war doctrine, whereas in the *Metaphysics of Morals* he can be interpreted as being a good deal more supportive. It asks if it is possible to portray the polemic against Kant's forerunners in international law as 'miserable' or 'sorry' comforters in *Perpetual Peace* as out of character with Kant's wider reception of the tradition. From this perspective is it possible to present the *Metaphysics of Morals* as displaying a more constructive reception of the tradition? If the line of argument followed by Sharon Byrd, Joachim Hruschka, Brian Orend and Susan Shell is correct then something like this must be possible. Because Kant is neither a realist who holds that world politics is above morality and law, nor a pacificist who holds that war in general is morally unjustifiable, Orend concludes he 'must be a just war theorist.'[1] If we are to accept Kant as a thinker who integrates just war thinking positively into his philosophy, the remarks he makes about Grotius, Pufendorf and Vattel in *Perpetual Peace* have to be interpreted as untypical, and the positive remarks he makes about the right to go to war in the *Metaphysics of Morals* have to be interpreted as deriving from his systematic philosophy of international right.

Kant makes his comments on the just war theorists, as we have noted, in the gloss he provides on the Second Definitive Article in *Perpetual Peace*. In these remarks he gives the background to his reasoning in advocating in that article a federation of free states as the basis for a sound world politics. He wants to explain why he holds that international law should in future be based not solely on the principles of the sovereign equality and independence of all states but also upon 'a federalism of free states' (8: 354/325). In taking this view Kant is not retreating from the principles of the equality and independence of states in international relations, but seeking to put them in the context of a principle he regards as philosophically prior, namely the necessary interdependence of legally founded states. A sovereign state based upon law cannot exist on its own (unless it is a world state which can only be conceived as occurring in far off future times) but has also to depend on the existence of similar sovereign states. Thus Kant does not like the implications of the use of the principles of equality and independence with regard to states when those principles are treated in isolation in international politics. He thinks particular care has to be taken in connecting the principles with the parallel principles of equality and independence as they apply to human individuals, both before the creation of civil society (in a state of nature) and after under a civil constitution. The analogy between the individual state of nature and the state of nature amongst states is important for Kant in determining his attitude to international relations, but in a very complex way. The transition between the warlike, pre-social condition and the peaceful (ordered) social condition which occurs with individuals has significant implications for the transition Kant would like to see at the international level from a condition of ever threatening (possible) war to a condition of lasting peace, but there is also a striking discontinuity.[2] Whereas the transition from the individual state of nature to the settled civil commonwealth can and should if necessary occur by force (and historically often has), the transition from an international state of nature to a settled civil condition cannot and should not occur by force. Sovereign states have outgrown the condition where they can be coerced by others,[3] but this does not make the condition of nature that exists between them any more acceptable than the natural condition their subjects found themselves prior to the creation of a sovereign. Leaving the international state of nature requires that sovereigns have to commit themselves to the rejection of war as a legitimate method of resolving disputes.

These are Kant's remarkable comments on the permissive nature of modern international law and its complementary doctrine of just war theory:

> In view of the malevolence of human nature, which can be seen unconcealed in the free relations of nations (whereas in the civil

condition under civil laws it is greatly veiled by the government's constraint), it is surprising that the word right could still not be altogether banished as pedantic from the politics of war and that no state has been bold enough yet to declare itself publicly in favour of this view; for Hugo Grotius, Pufendorf, Vattel, and the like (only sorry comforters) – although their code, couched philosophically or diplomatically, has not the slightest lawful force and cannot even have such force (since states as such are not subject to common external constraint) – are always duly cited in justification of offensive war, though there is no instance of a state ever having being moved to desist from its plan by arguments armed with the testimony of such important men'. (8: 355/326)

This passage seems to distance Kant markedly from the just war tradition in political philosophy and international law; it would also seem to contain the warning that putting together theoretical justifications for when a state might rightly go to war would, instead of limiting war, add fuel to the flames of any conflict by providing ready-made grounds for politicians to turn to armed measures. The tone of this passage would seem to suggest that war and justice are at opposite poles and both philosophical and moral attempts to unite the two are bound to fail. There is almost a hint of despondency and disillusionment in the way in which Kant speaks of the theoretical endeavours of his predecessors in international right. He appears to imply a downright dislike of the attempt by these practitioners of international law to provide direct advice to political rulers on the kinds of policies they should follow. It may be the task of lawyers to give such advice to leaders when those leaders are contemplating war, but philosophers seriously concerned with advancing the good of humankind should not consider debasing themselves by providing the kind of counsel that Grotius, Pufendorf and Vattel give in their manuals of international law.

One of the notable features of modern just war theory is its combination of theoretical speculation and policy advice. Just war theorists are not solely concerned with a detached analysis of the causes of war and the moral arguments that can be brought in favour or against any specific recommendation of war. Generally just war theorists regard themselves as providing profitable advice to rulers. Many believe it is important their words are heeded and followed by those who make political decisions. Just war theorists see themselves as addressing those who count in the decision to make war. In this context it is interesting that Jean Bethke Elshtain, in her recent book *Just War Against Terror*, refers to her project in the subtitle as 'the burden of American power in a violent world'. This indicates clearly her sense of involvement in the war process. Like Elshtain many just war theorists imagine themselves as participants in the cabinet making the political decision and in the briefing rooms of military leaders as they set out their campaign. Alex Bellamy traces the just war tradition back to what Michael Walzer describes as the 'war convention' which 'shapes our judgment on military conduct'.[4] Parties to this war convention are not merely the jurists and moral philosophers who work on the stipulations of the agreement but also political leaders, diplomats, strategists and military leaders who will be involved in their implementation. The convention, in Bellamy's words, 'provides a justificatory framework; a meaningful language that soldiers and politicians use to legitimate their actions and that friends, foes and bystanders alike use to evaluate those claims'.[5] Bellamy sees the war convention generated by just war theory as inclusive: 'actors from a range of diverse cultural backgrounds can communicate their normative judgments about war'.[6] Just war theory is not oriented solely towards reflection; it does more 'than provide a framework for judgment. It can also constrain and enable certain types of activity.'[7] Thus with some reservations it can be said that 'armed forces and political leaders are inhibited from acting in ways that cannot be justified by reference to the war convention.' The wide constituency at which just war theory aims seems to include primarily those involved in the practice of war. Citizens on the whole are held at bay. The main audience is the professional one. At best it seems that just war theorists permit citizens to comment as bystanders and spectators.

Kant does not, however, follow this line of argument. He considers his relationship to the policy adviser and the political and military leader as that of the critic. He neither wants to step into the cabinet room nor the military bunker. He casts his account of *Perpetual Peace* as a reflective philosophical argument that it is intended to stimulate debate amongst philosophers and citizens and to provide an agreed framework between citizens and politicians within which foreign policy can be pursued. In introducing his topic at the beginning of *Perpetual Peace* Kant refers to the satirical sign above a public house in Holland which depicted perpetual peace with a picture of a graveyard. The nub of the joke could equally be humankind in general that could only strive for eternal rest in that condition, or the leaders of states ('who never tire of making war') or philosophers 'who dream that sweet dream' of perpetual peace. In referring to his topic in this way Kant puts the philosophers at odds with the heads of states and locates his book as the work of a 'theoretical politician' or an academic, one whom the head of state is glad to look down upon as an impractical visionary. Kant wants to take the practical politician at his word in this regard: believing that the academic treatise of the philosopher can have no direct impact on what goes on in the world, the head of state should allow the philosopher to speak freely. Indeed Kant believes the philosopher 'can be allowed to fire off all his skittle balls at once without the worldly-wise statesman needing to pay heed'. (8: 343/317) The philosophy of war and peace is directed not at any policy in particular but rather to the public discussion of war and political deliberation about war in general.

For Bellamy in contrast 'the Just War tradition fulfils two roles. It provides a common language that actors can use to legitimize recourse to force and the conduct of war and that others can use to evaluate those claims. It can also inhibit actions that cannot be legitimated. The Just War tradition is a protracted normative conversation about war that has crystallized around a number of principles.'[8] Kant's philosophy of war can, it seems, be deployed partially to fulfil the second of the roles that Bellamy outlines since Kant is very concerned to put in the spotlight arguments for the use of force in international politics; however it would seem wholly unsuited to fulfilling the first role. Kant is no doubt an important participant in the 'protracted normative conversation about war' but his contribution should not be understood as a means of legitimizing the recourse to war. Some wars may be more legitimate than others from a Kantian perspective, but none is fully recommended in a legal or moral sense.

What is a sorry comforter (*Leidige Troester*)?

Georg Cavallar provides a very helpful insight to the meaning of the phrase 'sorry comforter' (*leidige Troester*) in his discussion of Kant's global commonwealth in *The Rights of Strangers*.[9] The phrase takes us to the heart of the issue of the acceptability of war in Kantian theory. Cavallar argues that the term *leidig* has two 'meanings in eighteenth-century German. It may either mean *beschwerlich* (troublesome, but also tiring) or *unangenehm* (unpleasant, inconvenient). Thus Kant either wants to tell us that the doctrines of the mentioned natural lawyers are in fact only subtle justifications of more wars, and as such unconvincing. Or he intends to stress that their treatises are inconvenient in so far as they remind ruthless power politicians of the demands of morality, and cause occasionally some pangs of remorse'. In Cavallar's view, Kant's text plausibly 'supports both interpretations'. On the one hand Grotius,

Pufendorf and Vattel can be 'conveniently cited' as Kant indicates to justify an offensive war and, on the other hand, the political leaders' 'very abuse of the language of rights and duties indicates that there is a "dormant, moral predisposition" in humans – a sense of justice... which cannot be eradicated.'[10] War is a field of enquiry where philosophers have to be very careful about the opinions they give. Kant is extremely anxious to avoid the fate of the early modern writers on international law in being used as an authority in order to declare a war. Yet, on the other hand, he acknowledges that these writers performed a service in trying to keep alive the idea of the law of nations even when such a law was under threat. Kant is moved by the depressing view of the human condition given by thinkers like Vattel and the distress they show at the harm caused by war. As Vattel puts it, 'whoever knows what war really is, whoever will reflect upon its terrible effects and disastrous consequences, will readily agree that it should not be undertaken without the most urgent reasons for doing so. Humanity revolts against a sovereign who, without necessity or without pressing reasons, wastes the blood of his most faithful subjects and exposes his people to the calamities of war, when he could have kept them in the enjoyment of an honourable and salutary peace.' The sovereign who gets the judgement of war wrong bears a heavy responsibility, and Vattel hopes that sovereigns are fully aware of this. 'The violence, the crimes, the disorders of every sort which accompany the confusion and the license of war are a stain upon his conscience, and are laid to his account, since he is the original cause of them.' A wrongly undertaken war is both a crime against its victims and the sovereign's subjects who suffer without necessity. Vattel is most sensitive about the consequences of war and wants rulers to share the same perspective: 'would that his feeble picture might touch the rulers of Nations and create in them, with respect to their military undertakings, circumspection in keeping with the serious consequences of their acts.'[11] Just as much as Vattel recognizes the occasional absolute necessity of war he deplores it and its consequences. But this tragic perspective is not Kant's.

Kant's use of the Biblical term of 'sorry comforters' tells us a great deal about his frame of mind in judging such traditional justifications for deciding to go to war. Kant disagrees with the natural lawyers' tolerant attitude towards the presence of war in the European state system and the relations of those states with societies elsewhere in the world. As Cavallar points out, Kant is at odds with the predominant tradition in international law which regards war as part of the permanent pattern of events in international politics.[12] Thinkers like Pufendorf and

Vattel 'took up the Hobbesian contention that the transnational state of nature cannot be compared with and is more tolerable than the natural condition among individuals. This is in agreement with their assessment of war as a kind of lawsuit, as the continuation of legal procedures by different means.' This idea of war as taking the form of a lawsuit can be found in the law of nations 'from Grotius to Smith'.[13] In the book *Die europaeische Union –von der Utopie zur Friedens- und Wertegemeinschaft* Cavallar goes into greater detail in his discussion of Kant's use of the phrase 'sorry comforters'. He cites what are two very likely sources for Kant's use of the phrase. The first is Johann Georg Hamann's *London Writings* and the second (also in connection with Hamann's writings),[14] perhaps more significant, chapter 16 in Job, Old Testament. In the first example Hamann speaks of his religious and intellectual crisis whilst in London when he could no longer turn to his books for inspiration. Such is his despondency that he refers to those books as only 'sorry comforters'. In the second example, chapter 16 of Job, the author speaks of his friends efforts to console him (and lessen his grief) when he faces catastrophic loss of his whole family by depicting him as a sinner and frivolous waster who has rightly brought the wrath of God upon himself. The accusations of sin and license turn out to be false so there is particular irony in Job's depiction of his companions as 'sorry comforters'.[15] Intending to offer him help in a situation for which he is not fully responsible they undermine him further. They burden him unnecessarily by attributing all his ill-fortune to his own folly. Worse than not offering a cure for the situation they make a false diagnosis of his ills. Job is indeed conscious of his own culpability for the evils that befall him, but he is also aware that not everything was his to control.

It is of course still a matter of theological controversy what precisely the implication of Job's fate[16] is, but it is unlikely that Kant would have (indirectly) appealed to the story without there being some connection with the thesis he wished to advance in *Perpetual Peace*. In Kant's story about the comforters of international law we have to substitute for Job and his tragic dilemma the whole human race, and to a lesser extent its responsible rulers. It would appear that the doctrines of Grotius, Pufendorf and Vattel were attributing the entire blame to the human race's sinfulness for the continued occurrence of war, without distinguishing between those things the human race had the power to bring about and those things that were beyond its powers. Arguably in their tracts on international law Grotius, Pufendorf and Vattel were worsening the predicament of the human race rather than effectively tackling it. They shared with Job's friends the false appreciation of the wrong that is under consideration. Just as the comforters failed to understand fully Job's misfortune, the sorry comforters of international law failed to understand the blight that affected international relations and was made evident in war. We can surmise that Kant believed that Grotius, Pufendorf and Vattel were taking for granted the presence of war in international society (as evidence of our inherent evil) rather than questioning it and asking how it might be removed.

We can gain from Kant's article 'On the Miscarriage of all philosophical trials' an appreciation of his understanding of Job's condition. Kant certainly takes Job's part against his two apparently well meaning friends who seek to offer consolation: 'Job's friends declare themselves for that system that explains all ills in the world from God's justice, as so many punishments for crimes committed; and, although they could name none for which the unhappy man is guilty, yet they believed they could judge *a priori* that he must have some weighing upon him, for his misfortune would be impossible according to divine justice. Job – who indignantly protests that his conscience has nothing to reproach him for in his whole life; and, so far as human unavoidable mistakes are concerned, God himself knows that he has made him a fragile creature – Job declares himself for the system of unconditional divine decision. "He has decided," Job says, "He does as he wills".' Kant is not impressed by the line of reasoning adopted by either side: 'There is little worthy of note in the subtle or hyper subtle reasoning of the two sides; but the manner in which they carry them out merits all the more attention. Job speaks as he thinks, and with the courage with which he, as well as every human being in his position, can well afford; his friends, on the contrary, speak as if they were being secretly listened to by the mighty one, over whose cause they are passing judgement, and as if gaining his favour through their judgement were closer to their heart than the truth' (8: 265; 25).[17] It is in this light, then, that Kant sees the reasoning of the sorry comforters in international law, the supporters of the just war tradition. Kant regards them with the same suspicion as Job's friends, whom he sees as conveying 'more of an appearance of greater speculative reason and pious humility' than the old sage. Those friends pride themselves on their insights into the way of the world, and the orthodoxy of their beliefs, and Kant grants that they might appear to be more persuasive than Job before a 'court of dogmatic theologians, before a synod, an inquisition,' and 'a venerable congregation' (8: 266; 26). The comforters are depicted as going with the tide of current opinion whereas Kant praises Job for his sincerity and honesty. Although Kant finds much to praise in the just war theorists of his day, the indirect allusion to Job in *Perpetual Peace* indicates a profound misgiving about their role. Perhaps he would say of them as he says of Job's friends: 'Their malice in pretending to assert things into which they yet must admit they have no insight, and in simulating a conviction which they do not in fact have, contrasts with Job's frankness – so far removed from false flattery as to border almost on impudence – much to his advantage' (8: 266; 26). It may be then that Kant finds Grotius, Pufendorf and Vattel too sweeping and rash in the judgements they make upon the human race.[18] Their certainty that the human race will always be drawn to violent conflict and war is not one he can share. They make a judgement about the human species that takes us beyond what we may legitimately draw from experience, and at the same time they take attention away from the moral effort we should make to avoid war even if we do not know whether this is ultimately possible. The 'sorry comforters' of just war theory pride themselves on their acquaintance with the way of the world and contrast it with the presumed naivety of those who seek security without war.

All these things might be read into Kant's use of the term 'sorry comforters' to depict his most important predecessors in international law. Hamann like Kant was a Koengisberg citizen. He and Kant corresponded about philosophical and political issues. Thus it is likely that Kant would have known of Hamann's London Writings.[19] The phrase would have conveyed to Kant a deeply felt despair at advice being offered in an apparently well-meaning spirit. Arguably Grotius, Pufendorf and Vattel let down the ideas of right and law – by presenting as lawful militaristic strategies that only deepen the problems of international politics, and they let down philosophy by allowing their doctrines to be cited by counsellors advising political leaders. As Kant sees it, it is not the task of philosophers to seek to gain the (privileged) ear of rulers, but rather the duty of political leaders to pay attention to the unbiased researches of philosophers. Thus Kant would rather not be seen as providing advice to leaders as to when war is acceptable than lose his status as an independent commentator on their policies. Grotius and his followers have allowed their advice to underpin and follow power whereas Kant wants only that power should follow advice independently given. Kant thoroughly disagrees with the view that implies that war can be seen as part of legal normality:

> The way in which states pursue their right can never be legal proceedings before an external court but can only be war; but right

cannot be decided by war and its favourable outcome victory... yet reason from the throne of the highest legislative power, delivers an absolute condemnation of war as a procedure for determining rights and, on the contrary, makes a condition of peace, which cannot be instituted or assured without a pact of nations amongst themselves, a direct duty. (8: 355–6/327)

Kant leaves us in no doubt in *Perpetual Peace* that the legal doctrine of just war is a thoroughly incoherent one to which he cannot subscribe:

The concept of the right of nations as that of the right to go to war is, strictly speaking, unintelligible (since it is supposed to be a right to determine what is right not by universally valid external laws limiting the freedom of each but by unilateral maxims through force); one would have to mean it is quite right if human beings so disposed destroy one another and thus find perpetual peace in the vast grave that covers all the horrors of violence along with their authors. (9: 356–7/ 328)

It seems difficult in the light of this to subscribe to the view of Brian Orend that Kant must have a just war theory.

Just War Doctrine and the *Metaphysics of Morals*

In the *Critique of Pure Reason* – in the section on the dialectic of pure reason – Kant presents the antinomies of pure reason. The antinomies are two diametrically opposed arguments that lead to an apparent deadlock in their conclusions. Two examples of the antinomies are: first, the argument about the existence of God (fourth antinomy), and, secondly, the argument about whether or not the universe has a beginning at any point of time in the past (first antinomy). Kant produces powerful cases in his presentation of the antinomies for both sides of the debate. The case for the existence of God is put as powerfully as the case against his existence. On reading the dialectic for the first time a student might just as easily be convinced of the truth of the one side of the antinomy (the thesis) as the other (the antitheis). Our procedure here will to some extent mimic Kant's approach to the antinomies in the first *Critique*. I have already put the case for regarding *Perpetual Peace* as entirely opposed to just war doctrine. Here in order to move the presentation along dialectically – in a similar fashion to Kant – I shall seek to demonstrate that the account of war in Kant's doctrine of right in the

Metaphysics of Morals is entirely at one with the views of conventional just war theorists. Thus at this stage in our discussion it will appear that there is a marked contradiction in Kant's presentation of the problem of war. We shall now look at Kant's doctrine of right in this light.

It is entirely to be expected that an account of the role of war in the law of nations in the late eighteenth century would be one that would accord considerable latitude to states in engaging in war. Early modern and modern international law grew out of the natural law tradition. Exemplified by Hugo Grotius's philosophy, that tradition dealt with war as arising out of the conditions of individuals in the state of nature. It was often thought enough to show that there was a right for the individual to defend himself when under mortal threat in the state of nature to prove that a similar permission applied to states. Achenwall, Kant's immediate predecessor in the natural law (and law of nations) tradition derives the right to engage in war in two places in his natural law textbook. He does so first of all at the level of individual interaction in the state of nature and then secondly at the level of state interaction towards the conclusion of his book. He points out that the discussion at the interstate level rests upon the treatment presented in the earlier interpersonal level. Thus the acceptance of the right to go to war was orthodoxy in the law of nations of Kant's day. As a younger academic and student Kant would have been keenly aware of this. In the earlier part of his career Kant was an adherent of the Leibniz–Wolff school of philosophy and appears to have retained a high estimation of Christian Wolff's work even later when he formally rejected many of the main tenets of the school. Wolff (who was an extraordinarily prolific writer) published in 1754 his *Principles of Natural and International Law*, in which he makes the right to go to war an integral part of the doctrine of international law. Wolff is well known for his idea of the *civitas maxima* or the 'great republic' or the great society. [20] According to this view there is a society amongst states – appears to come into being through its own contract. As Wolff puts it: 'this society which is created for the general welfare is called the greatest state (*civitias maxima*), whose members are, so to speak citizens, the individual members'.[21] This great republic has laws of its own which include the laws of war. The only rightful cause for war is, according to Wolff a wrong (*Unrecht*) already done or intended. For armed hostilities to be justified he suggests that war must be the only way of making good the wrong for it to be undertaken. General usefulness is not a sufficient ground for war (paragraph 1171).[22] Thus in Wolff's great republic there can be no wars in the national interest. Accordingly although there is no great bellicosity in Wolff's account of the law of nations, he does give evidence of a spirit of realism that permits him even to recommend the use of poisoned bullets, spies and assassination when they help bring down an unjust opponent.[27]

There can be no surprise then that in the *Metaphysics of Morals*, in contrast to *Perpetual Peace*, Kant appears to leave the door open to a possible just war theory. Admittedly this door is not left widely ajar, but arguably Kant seeks here not to close it entirely. He states there in a most markedly pro-war passage, Section 56:

> In the state of nature among states, the right to go to war (to engage in hostilities) is the way in which a state is permitted to prosecute its right against another state, namely by its own force, when it believes it has been wronged by another state; for this cannot be done in a state of nature by a lawsuit (the only means by which disputes are settled in a rightful condition). – In addition to active violations (first aggression, which is not the same as the first hostility) it may be threatened. This includes another state's being the first to undertake preparations, upon which is based the right of prevention (ius praeventionis), or even just the menacing increase in another state's power (by its acquisition of territory) (*potentia tremenda*). This is a wrong to the lesser power merely by the condition of the superior power, before any deed on its part, and in the state of nature an attack by the lesser power is indeed legitimate. Accordingly, this is also the basis of the right to a balance of power among all states that are contiguous and could act on one another. (6: 345/484)

Kant speaks of the 'original right that free states have in a state of nature to go to war with one another' (6: 344/483) and in the same paragraph he attempts to outline carefully the conditions under which a law can be legitimately declared from the standpoint of a people who are to prosecute it. The attention Kant gives to the question indicates how seriously he views the chances of war breaking out through the voluntary and legitimate decision of a nation. The arguments he presents in the paragraph could indeed be readily subsumed under the rubric of the 'right authority' principle recognised equally by Aquinas, and the modern just war theory which is derived from his writings.

As well as seemingly accepting the right of states to go to war Kant also acknowledges the existence of 'right in war' or what is often known as the laws of war. 'A state against which war is being waged is permitted to use any means of defence except those that would make its subjects unfit to be citizens; for it would then also make itself unfit to qualify, in accordance with the right of nations, as a person in the relation of states (as one who would enjoy the same rights as others)' (6: 347/485). Open hostilities between well-armed states would then seem permissible under an international law sanctioned by Kant. A war fought under certain limiting conditions is compatible with a state retaining its moral personality in relation to other states in the international system. There are other steps that Kant thinks are permitted by the laws of war. For instance, it is 'permissible to exact supplies and contributions from a defeated enemy, but not to plunder the people, that is, not to force individual persons to give up their belongings (for that would be robbery, since it was not the conquered people that waged the war; rather, the state under whose rule they lived waged the war through the people). Instead, receipts should be issued for everything requisitioned, so that in the peace that follows the burden imposed on the country or province can be divided proportionately' (6: 384/485). Kant even adds a dimension to justice and international law by suggesting that there is a 'right of state after war'. This arises at the 'time of a peace treaty and with a view to its consequences' and consists in the victor laying down 'the conditions on which it will come to an agreement with the vanquished and hold negotiations for concluding peace' (6: 348/486).

These comments suggest that Kant is prepared to enter the uncertain world of international law in the state of nature that prevailed amongst European countries at his time. He clearly pays his respects to the international law taught within the context of natural law that was prevalent in his time. He sets out and closely examines the model of international law found in writers like Grotius, Wolff and Vattel. Kant is not blind to the consequences of the state of nature amongst states that surrounds him. He sees steps within existing international law that can be taken to improve the situation. He argues for instance that prevailing international law rightly does not permit a war to make citizens of another state the slaves of the victorious party (as was often the case in ancient societies). 'The reason there cannot be a war of subjugation is not that this extreme measure a state might use to achieve a condition of peace would in itself contradict the right of a state; it is rather that the idea of the right of nations involves not only the concept of an antagonism in accordance with principles of outer freedom by which each preserve what belongs to it, but not a way of acquiring, by which one state's increase of power could threaten others' (6: 347/485). Here Kant recognizes a difference between the international state of nature and the individual state of nature which precedes the founding of a national civil society. The international state of nature regulated by

Grotian international law places attempts to set limits on the manner in which state power can be deployed to advance the interests of the state. Grotian international law recognises legitimate and illegitimate foreign policy aims and legal and illegal means of pursuing those aims. Kant embraces this framework to enumerate some rules of his own, which are partially to be found in the textbooks of international law of his day. So 'means of defence that are not permitted include: using its own subjects as spies; using them or even foreigners as assassins or poisoners (among whom so-called snipers, who lie in wait to ambush individuals, might well be classed); or using them merely for spreading false reports – in a word, using such underhanded means as would destroy the trust requisite to establish lasting peace in the future' (6: 347/485). Thus Grotian international law provides a basis for some principled relations amongst states that Kant is happy to exploit.

In granting the right of independent states to go to war with one another Kant sees the international legal system of his day as placing limits on the use to which the right is put. He is fully prepared to endorse these limits. In particular he believes modern international law rules out the possibility of war of punishment where one party takes it upon itself to act as the judge of another. 'No war of independent states against each other can be a punitive war (*bellum punitivum*). For punishment occurs only in relation of superior (*imperantis*) to those subject to him (*subitium*), and states do not stand in that relation to each other' (6: 347/485). In this he follows Pufendorf who takes strong objection to the doctrine of Grotius, who encourages wars of punishment. For Grotius 'the justifiable causes for war are three, defence, indemnity and punishment' (p. 51). He extends the right that a sovereign enjoys to punish its own citizens to a right to punish wrongs that are suffered as a result of the actions of other states and their subjects. This is a line of argument that is followed in some contemporary just war theory. Walzer believes, for instance, that all states have the right to punish a state that commits the crime of aggression.[24] But the rejection of the idea of punishment for a state provides another reason for Kant why there can be no war of subjugation: 'a defeated state or its subjects do not lose their civil freedom through the conquest of their country, so that the state would be degraded to a colony and its subjects to bondage; for if they did the war would have been a punitive war, which is self-contradictory.' 'Waging a punitive war' constitutes an 'offence against the vanquished' (6: 348/486). Kant is glad to see that the principles of international law current in his day rule it out.

The kinds of views expressed in Section 56 of the *Metaphysics of Morals* have led Susan Shell to describe Kant as having a robust theory of international politics that allows states to assert their rights against other states, if needs be by war. Shell emphasises the realism in Kant's approach which allows him to be seen not as an outright critic of the just war tradition but as to some extent its supporter.[25] Brian Orend follows a similar line of argument in his book *Kant and Just War Theory*. For Orend Kant '*has* a just war theory. In fact, an argument' is made 'that the weight of the textual evidence points clearly in favour of a pro-just war reading of Kant, and that any view to the contrary can only be sustained by a partial and selective reading of the relevant texts.'[26] Although I diverge strongly in the conclusions I draw, it must be granted that given the current structure at the beginning of the twenty-first century of international relations (and the current way in which international law is founded), there is no doubt that Kant would grant some legitimacy to states that defend their interests in the way laid out in the United Nations charter, Article 51 (which indicates that acts 'of individual or collective self-defence' are permitted 'if an armed attack occurs against a Member of the United Nations'). As things presently stand in world politics Kantians may grant to states this limited permission to go to war in self-defence. But what I want to show here that this granting of legitimacy falls a good deal short of the defence of 'just war' thinking offered by the trio referred to by Kant. Permissible acts that occur on occasions of extreme exigency do not for Kant gain the status of a settled norm for international relations.

The terms that Kant uses in the *Rechtslehre* appear to accept that there is a right in the law of nations to go to war, given that nations have not formed full civil relations amongst each other. There is not only the threat to peace that is brought about by changes in the balance of power but positive acts of aggression where Kant appears to consider a hostile response legitimate. As Cavallar puts it, Kant acknowledges there is 'a right to go to war in the state of nature in the case of an inflicted injury and the threat of overwhelming power'.[27]

In section 56 of the *Metaphysics of Morals* Kant gives this list of further conditions that may make war permissible: 'As for active violations which give rise to a right to go to war, these include acts of retaliation (*retorsio*), a state's taking upon itself to obtain satisfaction for an offence committed against its people by the people of another state, indeed of seeking compensation (by peaceful methods) from the other state. In terms of formalities, this resembles starting a war without first renouncing peace (without a declaration of war); for if one wants to find a right in a condition of war, something analogous to a contract must be assumed, namely acceptance of the declaration of the other party that both want to seek their right in this way' (6: 346/484).

This seems a very dry and factual way of presenting what international law in Kant's day regards as acceptable circumstances for declaring war. In *Metaphysics of Morals* there is little evidence of the polemic unleashed on earlier international lawyers that we find in *Perpetual Peace*. Even though their doctrines are closely scrutinized and found to be wanting, their standing as philosophers and academics is not impugned in the manner we see in *Perpetual Peace*. Kant seems to change his mind in this respect when the *Metaphysics of Morals* is compared with *Perpetual Peace*. On the surface Kant seems to be granting in the former what he firmly wants to deny in the latter: that states may legally go to war to uphold their rights. In *Perpetual Peace* international law is subject to severe censure, whereas in the *Metaphysics of Morals* Kant appears to want to work with it to create a more stable and enduring international order. Which is the truer reflection of Kant's views: the apparent cynicism and despair of *Perpetual Peace* or the seemingly more constructive deployment of an unreformed – yet to be reformed – international law in the *Metaphysics of Morals*?

4
The *Metaphysics of Morals* and the Case for Just War Theory

Introduction: mitigating factors, or is the contrast less stark than it appears?

In the previous chapter we focused closely on the aspects of Kant's discussion of the right to go to war which demonstrated the widest possible divergence between the account in *Perpetual Peace* and the account in *Metaphysics of Morals*. Published (and probably written) at slightly different times they clearly do not in every respect follow the same line of argument. Those writers who suggest that Kant takes a view that favours just war theory tend to emphasize the argument presented in *Metaphysics of Morals* at the expense of the view presented in *Perpetual Peace*. They do so to show that the strong opposition Kant evinces in *Perpetual Peace* to the doctrine of just war, as advanced by the international lawyers of the period, represents an anomaly in relation to his view on war as a whole. But a strong case for continuity can be made between the interpretations offered in the two works, and even (perhaps less strongly) a case for a lack of conflict between the two. Matthias Kaufmann has presented an interesting line of argument on this issue in his article 'What is New in the Theory of War in Kant's *Metaphysics of Morals*?'[1] He acknowledges that 'at first glance, there are many new elements in the *Right of Nations* contained within the *Metaphysics of Morals* when compared to Kant's writings on similar topics.'[2] Kaufmann has particularly in mind here of course the contra just war arguments of *Perpetual Peace*; however he believes the 'frictions are mitigated considerably if we look closely at the key ideas'.[3] Kaufmann emphasizes strongly how Kant structures his argument in the *Metaphysics of Morals* in relation to the existing tradition of the law of nations, particularly the writings of Wolff, Vattel and Achenwall. The treatment of the question of war in

Perpetual Peace is admittedly at odds with this traditional natural law approach – but equally, however, the treatment in the *Metaphysics of Morals* cannot wholly be taken to comply with the established teachings of international law. What is different in the *Metaphysics of Morals* is the claims of the rules already established in international law to govern what Kant takes to be the existing state of nature amongst states are treated seriously. Whereas *Perpetual Peace* dismisses the claims of traditional international law concerning justice before war (*jus ad bellum*) and justice in war (*jus in bello*), *Metaphysics of Morals* looks closely at a number of the claims and tries to follow through their contradictory implications. Since Kant does not regard the international condition to which traditional international law applies as fully legal, it is questionable that he regards any rules that might arise from legal theorizing about that condition as having adequate legal standing.

This question of the contrasting approaches to war in Kant's two major publications on politics and international relations takes us to the heart of Kant's conception of philosophy, and in particular of his understanding of the role of political and legal philosophy. Our judgement on whether or not the doctrine of right radically departs from what Kant presents in *Perpetual Peace* is greatly affected by the way in which we understand how he conceives his task in investigating the philosophy of law. In Kant's day the whole issue was taken up in the context of natural law or right (*Naturrecht*).

Natural law and the right of war

Natural law was a central feature of Enlightenment philosophy. The idea was embraced by thinkers who were quintessential influences on the Enlightenment such as John Locke and Christian Wolff. Up until the end of the eighteenth century all political philosophy was expounded within the framework of natural law. So Kant unavoidably worked within this tradition. But he does not follow the typical pattern of natural law thinking in the *Metaphysics of Morals*. He deploys many natural law ideas in his practical philosophy and presents much of his own doctrine as natural right; yet he does not reproduce the principal feature of previous natural law thinking: an insistence on an actual harmony between the development of nature and the realization of God's will. Indeed in his natural right theory Kant separates the human species from God and the supposed harmonious unfolding of nature, and instead anchors it firmly in human reason alone. Enlightenment and improvement have, for Kant, predominantly to be our own work.

We can only hope for God's grace in aiding us so long as we act as though *everything* depends on us. Thus natural right is presented by Kant as a product of the *human* mind which we have to implement both with and against nature.

At the heart of Kant's original, radical account of natural right is his novel understanding of philosophy. Philosophy has to be presented as a critical metaphysics that sets out limits to our theoretical knowledge, yet provides wide scope to practical philosophy. What we know about the world has to be restricted to what we can take in through our senses, so that pure reason has to be carefully reined in its aims, but how we seek to act must be guided by the ambitions of practical reason. It is thus a mistake to believe that Kant's view of philosophy is dominated by the outlook of scientific knowledge. Kant transcends the subject/object model of knowledge often associated with Cartesian metaphysics. With Kant philosophy has ultimately to present an active relation to human life. Kant of course strongly believes that there is a place in philosophy for the pursuit of theoretical knowledge and this takes on a scholastic form. Within this scholastic framework there are appropriate techniques to be employed, which must be accessible to all and have to be followed by those working in the field. However, he also sees philosophy falling within a larger framework which accords with what he calls a 'concept of the world' (*Weltbegriff*) (A838/B866).

Kant places a lot of weight on the ideal of the philosopher, which in his view lies behind all attempts to philosophize by individuals. According to this ideal what is aimed at, as well as logical consistency (and theoretical veracity), is the good of the world or the 'general happiness' (A857/B879; 701). Quite clearly the human species lies at the centre of this idea of the good, particularly the development of each and everyone's talents and capacities. The ideal philosopher should not be seen simply as an 'artist' of reason but as a 'lawgiver' to human reason (A839/B867; 695). The lawgiving in the theoretical domain sets limits to the deployment of our reason. The mathematician, the natural scientist and the logician are, no matter how excellent their contribution to the progress of philosophy, mere artists of reason. We can only regard them as complying with the archetype of the ideal of the philosopher when they use their researches for the 'essential ends of human reason' (A839/B867; 695). And these essential ends of setting out the system of law by which reason operates are themselves subordinated to the highest or final end, which is represented as the 'entire vocation (*Bestimmung*) of human beings and the philosophy of it is called moral philosophy' (A840/B868; 695). Thus the activity of philosophizing is according to its concept of the world (*Weltbegriff*) part of a hierarchy of thought in which it is subordinate to the laws given in moral philosophy. This does not mean that the philosopher as an artist can be dictated to by the moral philosopher, but rather that how the skills of philosophy are deployed must not contradict the conclusions of moral philosophy.

Thus the philosophy of right, if it is to be pursued in a way which conforms with the ideal of the philosopher, cannot be done in a manner which solely demonstrates skill in the discipline of law – or natural right as it was in Kant's day. The ways in which the rules of international law are set out have indeed to address themselves to the manner in which states actually relate to one another and to facilitate those relations; however, the philosopher of law has to look beyond the merely pragmatic ends of skilfully dealing with the situation as it stands. The rules that regulate the relations amongst states need not only to reflect what is feasible and expedient but also what is required by the unity of reason. Law and morality cannot be taught separately for Kant; an integral part of his project in his *Metaphysics of Morals* is to demonstrate the way in which the doctrine of law can be developed in a manner that is compatible with the central principle of morality, the categorical imperative.

In his later writings (of which the *Metaphysics of Morals* is part) Kant subsumes natural right under the framework of his critical philosophy. He endeavours to give natural right a systematic place within his philosophical corpus. For Kant natural right 'rests only on *a priori* principles' and contrasts with positive law which arises from 'the will of a legislator'(6: 237/393). A right is a capacity for putting 'others under obligation' which accords us an equal liberty with others. Natural laws are binding laws which can be recognized *a priori* by reason and hold for human individuals even in the absence of an actual external law giver (6: 224/379).

Kant taught a course on natural law 12 times from 1767 to 1788.[4] He used Gottfried Achenwall's, *Jus naturae inusum auditorum*, parts 1 & 2, 5th edition (Göttingen 1763; 1750, 1753) as a textbook on the course. Thus Kant was deeply acquainted with the subject matter of natural right in his day. We can surmise that he was also strongly aware of the use to which the idea of natural right had been put in the politics of the time. The idea of natural right historically was heavily intertwined with everyday common sense thinking about politics and society and religious thought. Kant would have seen stark evidence of this in the revolutionary events of the late eighteenth century. Both the American colonists in the newly formed United States of America and the revolutionary politicians of France that deposed their monarch made prominent use of such ideas. As the Declaration of the Rights of Man and of Citizens made by the National Assembly of France puts it: 'considering that ignorance, neglect, or contempt of human rights, are the sole causes of public misfortunes of Government, have resolved to set forth in a solemn declaration, these natural, imprescriptible, and inalienable rights'; it goes on to describe these as the 'sacred rights of men and citizens'.[5] Kant aims to detach the idea of natural right from this rhetoric but at the same time wants to preserve its progressive force and its centrality in public deliberation about government. He chooses the metaphysical path, not on the grounds of its supposed academic complexity but on the grounds of its power to arrive at the conceptual core of the idea of natural right and so to preserve its general (universal) significance.[6]

As a systematic dimension of Kant's critical philosophy natural right is dealt with in the Doctrine of Right of the first part of the *Metaphysics of Morals* (1797). Natural right gives rise to natural laws and positive laws. There he describes natural laws as binding or obligatory laws 'for which there can be an external lawgiving'. They are the type of external laws 'that can be recognized as obligatory *a priori* by reason even without external law giving' (6:224/379). Thus even in the absence of a state, natural laws have to be obeyed without question by human individuals. There can be no legal grounds for disregarding them. In contrast those laws that 'do not bind without actual external lawgiving (and so without it would not be laws) are called positive laws'. For Kant it is possible to conceive of a system of external laws that contains only positive laws, but 'then a natural law would still have to precede it, which would establish the authority of the lawgiver' (6: 224). So as Kant conceives it, any actual legal order must have at its foundation natural right even though it may proceed on the basis solely of statutory right. All external legislation must concur with natural right. Thus natural right is not only at the systematic heart of Kant's practical philosophy, he also sees it at the centre of politics and law. Of course this is not natural right as his precursors, such as Hobbes, see it.

Contrary to what might be implied by the name itself, Hobbes holds that the claims of natural right lead to no settled condition in the state of nature, and it is only with the introduction of the overwhelming political authority of the Leviathan that the laws of nature arising from natural right can come into operation. His theory of natural right derives from his presupposition that all right must be based on each person's entitlement to give the highest priority to his or her preservation: 'The

Right Of Nature, which Writers commonly call Right *Jus Naturale*, is the Liberty each man hath, to use his own power, as he will himself, for the preservation of his own Nature, that is to say, of his own Life; and consequently, of doing any thing, which in his own Judgement, and Reason, he shall conceive to be the aptest means thereunto.'[7]

Kant concurs with Hobbes in the systematic importance he gives to natural right, but his deduction of natural right is of an entirely different order. Hobbes takes a primarily psychological view of the human individual in setting up his conception of political order, which rests on a thoroughgoing materialist philosophy; Kant takes a moral conception of the human individual (grounded in his practical philosophy) which rests upon his transcendental idealism. For Kant natural right deals with the human individual both as a creature of the sensuous, external world and a being of the intellectual, internal world. In terms of the nomenclature of his critical system, natural right deals with the human being as part of both phenomenal and noumenal realms.[8] Right therefore involves mediating considerations of pure moral theory with considerations of an empirical kind such that rational political order can be realised. From his treatment of natural laws it is clear that Hobbes does not ignore the moral side of the human individual in his political philosophy,[9] but in comparison to the significance it has in Kant's political thinking its standing is secondary. From a Kantian perspective Hobbes's account of the appropriate derivation of political obligation places a good deal too much emphasis on empirical as opposed to moral considerations. Arguably with Hobbes it is the empirical that leads and the moral that follows. Kant puts the moral perspective first and seeks to accommodate the empirical perspective within it. For Hobbes the empirical perspective determines the political perspective and that encompasses all morality within it.

Innate and acquired right

Kant divides the study of rights 'as systematic doctrines' into 'natural right, which rest only on *a priori* principles' and 'positive (statutory) right'. The latter form of right proceeds 'from the will of a legislator' and the former only from the deliberations of practical reason (6: 237/393). This leads then to the designation of rights 'as moral capacities for putting others under obligations' which can either be 'innate or acquired right'. Here Kant would seem to be putting his account of right within the framework of natural law, since he refers to 'an innate right (*angeborenes Recht*)' as 'that which belongs to everyone by nature, independently of any act that would establish a right'. This is distinct from an acquired right 'for which such an act is required' (6: 237/393). From this it would appear that acquired right could be separated from natural right as something which pertained only to positive or statutory right. However Kant thinks there is always a part of acquired right that has to be related back to innate right and so forms part of natural right.

We have just the one innate right and that is the right of freedom. This innate or inborn right consists in being free from the constraints that might be imposed by the capriciousness of others. Thus it does not consist in our own right to act in a capricious or arbitrary way. Rather it has to do with the observance of a general law that permits everyone to be unencumbered by the capriciousness of others. Our innate right to freedom is from the beginning tied up with our equality with others. We can only be bound to the extent that others are reciprocally bound. Following from this we have the innate quality of being our own master. This consists in 'asserting one's worth as a human being in relation to others, a duty expressed in the saying "do not make yourself into a mere means for others but be at the same time an end for them"' (6: 236/392). As Kant puts it, innate right is ours on 'the strength of our humanity' (6: 237/393).

Acquired right is not free from the *a priori* basis. Not all law that has become statutory is necessarily compatible with the requirements of natural right. Acquired rights are always subject to the judgement as to whether or not they are in harmony with our innate right. So 'when a dispute arises about an acquired right and the question comes up, on whom does the burden of proof fall, either about a controversial fact or, if this is settled, about a controversial right, someone who refuses to accept this obligation can appeal methodically to his innate right to freedom' 'specified in its various relations'. As well as the qualities of being your own master and being equal with all others, our innate freedom also accords us the status of 'being beyond reproach', since before performing 'any act affecting rights' we can be taken to have 'done no wrong to anyone' (6: 238/394). In addition to presupposing our own legal innocence, our innate right permits us to 'do to others anything that does not in itself diminish what is theirs,' 'such things as merely communicating' our thoughts to them, 'telling them or promising them anything' (6: 238/394).

Kant's treatment of international law (*Völkerrecht*) or the law of nations in the first part of the *Metaphysics of Morals* – the doctrine of right – is remarkably brief. It focuses almost entirely on the question of war: its regulation; its prevention; and its ultimate abolition. Kant does not deal under international law with what might be regarded as the equivalent of contract law at the domestic level. There is, for instance, no section on the law of treaties amongst states or on their regulation. Also he pays scant attention to the matter of customary international law and the regulation of diplomatic relations. It is unclear the extent to which he regards international law as statutory or acquired right and the extent to which he believes it depends solely on natural right. That he presents his doctrine of international law within the context of his attempts to transform natural right suggests that for him its main point of origin is in innate rather than acquired right. Kant seems to believe that statutory right applies primarily within states, and precisely one of the main difficulties of international law is its inability to be applied in a statutory manner. He depicts states as moral persons that owe respect to international law, but up until the present they have not shown sufficient respect for international law to ground it properly by establishing one coercive authority that can implement it for all.

That Kant in the *Metaphysics of Morals* is engaged in transforming the established understanding of law from the ground up tells us a great deal about his approach to existing international law. If Kant is not happy with the way in which domestic law in his time is conceived and implemented – and thinks it should be subject to thoroughgoing criticism and reform – it seems highly unlikely that he is going to find the existing framework of law at the international level appropriate. Kant thinks the laws within states should gradually be reformed in accord with the ideal of innate right, so that the political structures and legislative processes of states should accord more with our equality and freedom; he is implicitly suggesting that the main 'actors' in international relations need also to reform their behaviour and the rules that regulate them. The Doctrine of Right demonstrates a very fluid understanding of law as it was practised in Kant's day. We have to obey existing law but we are not to regard it as complete or wholly satisfactory in any way. Law has to be subject to reform from the top down so that a more independent citizenry can be created. In the essay 'What is Enlightenment?' Kant says that 'one age cannot bind itself and conspire to put the following one into such a condition that it would be impossible for it to enlarge its cognitions (especially in such urgent matters) and to purify them of errors, and generally to make further progress in enlightenment. This would be a crime against human nature, whose original vocation lies precisely in such progress; and succeeding generations are therefore perfectly authorized to reject such decisions as unauthorized and made sacrilegiously. The touchstone of whatever can be decided upon as law for a people lies in the question: whether a people could impose such a law upon itself' (8: 39/20). Kant regards international law as open to reform in the same way. In so far as international law has become statutory through its adoption by the legislatures of the individual states, it should be obeyed in a peremptory way; however its received structures and permissions should not be seen as wholly fixed. They can and ought to be improved in the general process of the enlightenment of peoples. Innate right is a touchstone for reforming international law as much as it is also for domestic law.

Kant's treatment of international law in the *Metaphysics of Morals* is, as I have indicated, abbreviated. Treaties amongst states do not play a role nor are there any discussions of diplomatic relations in his account. These are matters that figure quite extensively in present day texts on international law[10] and were also dealt with at some length in the writings of Kant's contemporaries. In the Prussian Academy edition of the *Metaphysics of Morals* thirteen pages only (pp. 342–356) are devoted to international law or nine paragraphs (§§53–62). If we deduct the four pages that are devoted at the end to his own novel development of cosmopolitan law, we are left with eight pages devoted exclusively to international law. This would seem to indicate that Kant, whilst taking very seriously law in general, did not take too seriously the law of nations as it existed in his day. Arguably his treatment of international law focuses on the subject's area of possible greatest weakness – the occurrence and attempted regulation of war. In contrast to the treatment of international law the analysis of state or national law (*Staatsrecht*) is presented in 31 pages of the Academy edition (pp. 311–342) although this admittedly is done in a similar number of paragraphs (§§43–51). Kant strongly creates the impression that he is happier with the condition of internal state law than he is with the condition of international law. Indeed he apparently wants to warn that the unstable condition of international law may well put in danger the achievements of domestic law.

Kant's treatment of international law can be compared with the account given in a classic of the period, Emmerich De Vattel's, *The Law of Nations or the principles of Natural Law*. It is true that Vattel devotes one of the four books that compose the vast treatise to War, but this is counterbalanced by the three other books – the first of which deals with the domestic law of states, the second with a 'nation considered in relation to other states', and the fourth which deals with the 'restoration of peace and embassies'. In contrast with Kant's treatment, a great deal of Vattel's treatise focuses on what might be taken already to function fully in the sphere of international law. Admittedly war is a central feature of Vattel's account, but it is not the principal feature and is presented as something of an exception to the ideal running of international law. He says strikingly in the preface 'if the conductors of states, if all those who are employed in public affairs, condescended to apply seriously to the study of a science which ought to be their law, and, as it were, the compass by which to steer their course, what happy effects might we expect from a good treatise on the law of nations! We everyday feel the advantages of a good body of law in civil society: - the law of nations is in point of importance as much superior to the civil law, as the proceedings of nations and sovereigns are more momentous in their consequences than those of private persons.'[11] Thus Vattel sees no great problem with the principles spelled out by the modern law of nations but rather finds wanting the policies of those who conduct public affairs who 'pay little regard to the dictates of justice'.[12]

We can arguably detect a note of pride when Kant speaks of the state as a human achievement and the behaviour of some states towards their citizens and other states gives him ground for hope.[13] However, Kant seems to speak with less pride and optimism about the international system and the general conduct of states towards each other. As he puts it in the essay 'On the Common Saying: that may be correct in Theory, but is of no use in Practice': 'nowhere does human nature appear less lovable than in the relations of entire peoples to one another. No state is for a moment secure from others either in its independence or its property. The will to subjugate one another or diminish what belongs to another always exists, and arming for defence, which often makes peace more oppressive and destructive of internal welfare than war itself, can never be relaxed.'(8: 312/309) Most existing states he regards from the standpoint of their internal constitutions and he sees the development of their legal systems as works in progress. Some states give him more grounds for hope (republican France and the USA for instance) and some give him fewer grounds for hope (Britain under Pitt the Younger for instance), but all are preferable to the wild and lawless freedom that preceded them. Compared to the domestic condition of states the international system he presents as being in a far more rudimentary condition. Thus the comparative neglect of international law in his doctrine of right seems to be derived from a lack of confidence in its basic principles as it had be taught and practised up to his time. International law as a whole is, from Kant's perspective in need of critique and improvement. The section on international law in *Metaphysics of Morals*, instead of being an endorsement of modern international law as taught from

Grotius to Vattel, is rather a sketch of how it should be reconstructed. This has to be set against the ringing endorsement that law in general is given in the Doctrine of Right and Kant's other political writings.

In paragraph 61 of the Doctrine of Right Kant indicates that he regards any right of nations which are founded on the present 'state of nature among nations' as 'merely provisional' (6: 350/487). This provisional status is not good news for the human race since it affects not only laws that states may seek to establish amongst themselves but also the laws within states. All laws for Kant are unfortunately provisional until a worldwide civil society is brought into being.

Despite their provisional nature we are bound by all laws and at the domestic level individuals are justly punished who transgress. The problem at the international level is that no compulsory enforcement mechanism has as yet been instituted. In one respect the idea that all right amongst nations is *provisional* can be seen as painting a positive picture of international law as an emerging field of law (which Kant certainly appreciates), but in another respect it is a fairly disparaging view to take of the laws that have emerged, since it reflects the fact that they are only partly effective, binding only those countries that agree to be bound by them. Kant's view is that the human race has to move beyond this condition through countries gradually and voluntarily forming a league of peace. The key factor in the development and observance of international law is the emergence of this peaceful league. The difficult task in the meanwhile is to pursue and maintain the rule of law in the national and the international sphere when the rule of law has not entirely captured the latter sphere.

The question arises as to how Kant sees that this transitional stage – where the idea of international law has gained currency and application so that some laws are routinely observed by a number of states – should be properly managed so that the goal of a fully accepted and practised system of worldwide law should eventually be attained? Here Kant appears to provide an answer that has similar features to Hobbes's response to the apparently unregulated sphere of international law. For Hobbes the laws of nations were to be deduced from the laws of nature that applied to all human individuals. Although sovereigns, like individuals in the state of nature, could not be compelled to obey natural law because of their responsibilities to their subjects, the appeal to the sovereign's conscience in regulating relations amongst nations was not entirely one that was made in vain. Though Kant does not make direct reference to Hobbes he appears to subscribe to a similar idea when he speaks in the Doctrine of Right of the state functioning as a 'moral person'. (6: 343/482) When observed from the standpoint of 'right of states' the state 'is considered as living in relation to another state in the condition of natural freedom'. Thus although the sovereign in the international system is not forcibly bound by international law, it is none the less ethically bound by its requirements. It is in the sense of morality of sovereigns that efforts to create an international community have their purchase, because as well as the right to wage war given by this natural freedom there is also a right for states to 'constrain each other to leave this condition of war and so form a constitution that will establish lasting peace'. (6: 343/ 482)

Kant thus presents then a very mixed picture of international law. He does not rate it highly as it functions in the eighteenth century international order with which he was familiar; however he does see it as having an extraordinary potential. In his day traditional international law was an ally of a fractious, warlike international order. However, if its legal and pacifying aims were taken seriously, then it could provide the cornerstone of a peaceful international system. It is true that each state under Grotian /modern international law can declare war on another when it believes its security is threatened, but equally a strong undercurrent in international law is that each state should be working to bring about a constitutionally binding international settlement. Kant finds all this implicit in the idea of a law of nations. This means that law as it functioned in the international system of his day was shot through with conflict. The claim each state makes to a moral personality obliges it both to guard its interests with force but also to seek a lasting peace with other states. The analogy between the international state of nature and the individual state of nature is not simply a way of depicting the relationship between one imagined condition and one concrete condition – at the international level both are also a concrete reality. Implicit in the idea of the state is first that it is free and, secondly, that it has a moral identity in relation to other states and the subjects of other states. Relations among states are relations of two or more independent moral identities with each other. Without this identity being formed by subjects and states amongst each other, we would not be able to speak of the state. As Kant puts it, in thinking of the 'right of a state' we must also think of a 'right of nations' (6: 311/455). In relating to the state citizens are also necessarily relating to a system of states.

Although *Metaphysics of Morals* is regarded as the more war-prone by some contemporary liberal scholars than *Perpetual Peace*, there are some very powerful statements in *Metaphysics of Morals* that indicate Kant is very discontented with the idea that states have the right to go to war. From paragraph 54 it is clear that Kant (as in *Perpetual Peace*) does not regard the historically inherited condition of international relations as a legal condition. He emphasises there that 'states considered in external relation to one another, are (like lawless savages) by nature in a non-rightful condition' and this is 'a condition of war (of the right of the stronger)' (6: 344/482). In so far as international law condones this situation it undermines itself. Kant regards a law of nations that allows states to go to war with each other as being in contradiction with itself. We might also say that although there are many more states that are representative democracies in the world nowadays in comparison with Kant's time – and so we might expect more progress towards an international order that regards war as the (pathological) exception and not the rule – that the same evaluation still applies. Thoroughgoing legality in international relations would require for Kant going beyond the present arrangements that allow states to declare war on each other in self-defence. The phrasing of Article 51 of the United Nations Charter permitting the right to go to war in defence of their territories indicates that we are still in a pre-legal condition. 'Nothing in the present Charter shall impair the inherent right of individual or collective self-defence if an armed attack occurs against a Member of the United Nations, until the Security Council has taken measures necessary to maintain international peace and security. Measures taken by Members in the exercise of this right of self-defence shall be immediately reported to the Security Council and shall not in any way affect the authority and responsibility of the Security Council under the present Charter to take at any time such action as it deems necessary in order to maintain or restore international peace and security.' Here there is a very uneasy balance between the apparent complete independence of each state to judge when it has been attacked and so defend itself militarily and the apparent authority accorded to the United Nations' Security Council to determine what action is legitimate and what the next steps should be. Both states and the United Nations' Security Council are invited to be judge and jury in their own case. The article shows how international law is in an unstable position and needs, as Kant indicated, to be overhauled with the idea of federalism of states at its centre.[14] This arrangement would be a good deal more egalitarian than the present set up of the Security Council. It is likely that the kind of set up that would emerge from a Kantian league would approximate more closely to the decision-making procedures of the European Union than those of the UN. Arguably the UN Security Council, with its five permanent members – each with a veto – is too hierarchical to achieve the aim of uniting the states of the world in the pursuit of peace.

The contradictions of the inherited condition of international law are brought out strikingly in paragraph 54 of Kant's *Metaphysics of Morals*: 'The elements of the right of nations are these: 1) states, considered in external relation to one another, are (like lawless savages) by nature in a nonrightful condition. 2) This nonrightful condition is a condition of war (of the right of the stronger), even if it is not a condition of actual war and actual attack being made (hostilities). Although no state is wronged by another in this condition (in so far as neither wants anything better), this condition is in itself still wrong in the highest degree, and states neighbouring upon one another are under obligation to leave it' (6: 344/482).

The first two elements of international law depict then what Kant regards as implicitly non-legal circumstances. In the international state of nature we have powers that are judges in their own cause. States are depicted with heavy irony as 'lawless savages' that pay no heed to reason in their mutual relations. The tension of this natural condition is unrelenting. Although upholding law in relation to their own citizens states' leaders appear to pay little heed to maintaining it in relation to their fellow states' leaders. The hypocrisy of their position only adds to the stresses and strains of international politics. The law and freedom that exists within established civil societies stands in stark contrast to the lack of law and endangerment of freedom that occurs within world society. International law in so far as it sanctions this uncertain situation and permits war as a means of defending the state's interest itself can be taken as a threat to law in general.

And it is in this context that Kant speaks in paragraph 56 of the 'right' of states to go to war. This is the section of the Doctrine of Right is most often referred to by commentators who attempt to present Kant as a defender of the traditional view of just war. In a sense it is absolutely true that Kant includes within his Doctrine of Right the received justifications for going to war. But what has to be stressed is that he is not presenting these justifications as representative of his own views. He is simply repeating what the textbooks say. But for him this recognition of just war thinking is heavily conditioned by its framing which he states explicitly as 'in the state of nature among states' (6: 346/484). Thus it is absolutely clear that the right to go to war surfaces only in the tense and unstable condition of an absence of the full recognition of law amongst states. The right to go to war is not a legal or just entitlement: it is simply a right in the absence of right. Thus it is an entitlement that is built on sand.

Kant sees it as difficult to absorb traditional international law into law proper in so far as it entrenches the right of states to persist in this non-legal condition. It is only in the next two elements that we begin to enter the territory of law properly, since they attempt to compensate for the inadequate foundation for international legal order provided by the doctrines of Grotius, Pufendorf and Vattel. These next two elements as spelled out in the same paragraph 54 are:

3) 'A union of nations in accordance with the idea of an original social contract is necessary, not in order to meddle in one another's internal dissensions but to protect against attacks from without.'

4) 'This alliance must, however, involve no sovereign authority (as in a civil constitution), but only an association (federation); it must be an alliance that can be renounced at any time and so must be renewed from time to time. This is a right in *subsidum* of another and original right, to avoid getting involved in a state of actual war among the other members (*foedus Amphictyonum*)' (6: 345/482–3).

If the discussion on war by commentators on the *Metaphysics of Morals* were to focus heavily on these two stipulations in the doctrine of right, then the divergence between the treatments of the topic in *Perpetual Peace* and *Metaphysics of Morals* would not seem so great. Here as in the earlier book the focus is getting beyond the condition of war and not upon the conditions that might make it valid. In many respects Kant is as critical of the Westphalian international order in *Metaphysics of Morals* as he is in *Perpetual Peace*.

An important example of how Kant sustains the radical objection towards the Westphalian international order in the doctrine of right occurs at the end of the book, where he expresses his ideas about the overseas expansion of the European powers. *Perpetual Peace* provides a passionate critique of the impact of European colonialism in the section on the third definitive article, cosmopolitan right. There Kant condemns the ruthless exploitation of the Negro population in the sugar plantations of the West Indies or the 'sugar islands' 'that place of the cruellest and most calculated slavery' (8: 359/330). He also thoroughly commends China and Japan for preventing the Europeans from settling their interior and confining them to enclaves where they cannot enjoy 'community with the natives' (8: 359/330). If anything, however, the objection to any new acquisitions by European states is even more powerful in the doctrine of right as is his condemnation of the damaging effects of settlements gained at the native populations' expense. After noting how the sea brings trading nations together and provides access to remoter regions, Kant remarks in the doctrine of right that 'visiting these coasts, and still more settling there to connect them with the mother country, provides the occasion for troubles and acts of violence in one place to be felt all over it' (6: 353/489). Kant acknowledges as in *Perpetual Peace* that there has to be a right 'to visit all regions of the earth', but this cannot be transposed into 'a right to make a settlement on the land of another nation; for this a specific contract is required' (6: 353/489). Kant unequivocally denies any such right of possession of land already in use by other people. There has to been an agreement to accept immigrants and this agreement has to be entirely an honourable one. The contract granting such rights of settlement must 'not take advantage of the ignorance of those inhabitants with respect to ceding their lands'. Capturing those lands by force is a deplorable stratagem. 'This is true despite the fact that sufficient specious reasons to justify the use of force are available: that it is to the world's advantage, partly because these crude peoples will become civilized,' 'and partly because one's own country will be cleaned of corrupt men, and they or their descendants will, it is hoped, become better in another part of the world (such as New Holland).' The supposed beneficial consequences of evil acts do not excuse these evil acts for Kant, and in particular they do not justify their deployment now or in the future. Such 'supposedly good intentions cannot wash away the stain of injustice in the means use for them' (6: 353/490). Kant cannot justify the use of force in establishing colonies in the territories of pastoral and nomadic peoples in the same way as he cannot justify the use of revolutionary force within states to remove bad constitutions. Even if such steps are seen as once and for all moves to bring about a lawful condition 'the stain of injustice' remains upon them and deeply undermines any supposed just condition the illegal violence was meant to bring about.

The people of the European states have to reflect carefully on their own history and conduct in internal and international politics. They have to recognise the past injustices they have perpetrated and avoid repeating them in the future. The doctrine of right reflects the same contriteness and humility towards the European heritage in the national and international arena as the passages on cosmopolitan right in *Perpetual Peace*. Kant is just as much aware in the doctrine of right as he is in *Perpetual Peace* that the European powers 'make much ado of their piety and, while they drink wrongfulness like water, want to be known as the elect in orthodoxy' (8: 359/330).

Thus, whether or not one finds persistent contradictions between the doctrine of right and *Perpetual Peace* depends greatly on the reading strategy one follows. It is possible through selective reading (as we believe to have already shown) to demonstrate that the two works are very much at odds with one another. In particular it is possible to demonstrate that the doctrine of right is a good deal more susceptible to a just war interpretation than *Perpetual Peace*. However it is possible to adopt a reading strategy which takes the doctrine of right as a whole and provides a synthesis which is very much in harmony with the main precepts of *Perpetual Peace*. A reading that is favoured here is one that presents the argument of the doctrine of right in a cumulative manner where earlier avenues explored and evaluated are seen as contributing to one combined thesis, which reaches its high point in the final section of the doctrine of right where Kant outlines his theory of cosmopolitan or world-citizens' right. Without doubt the conclusion that Kant draws in the final section of public right at the end of the doctrine of right is every bit as radical as any presented in *Perpetual Peace*.

The case for continuity between *Perpetual Peace* and the *Metaphysics of Morals* is strongly re-enforced by the passage at the very end of the Doctrine of Right dealing with cosmopolitan right (paragraph 62). After movingly declaring that, as we have seen in chapter 1, 'moral-practical reason' expresses 'in us its irresistible veto: there shall be no war' Kant claims that 'it can be said that establishing general and lasting peace constitutes not merely a part of the doctrine of right but rather the final end of the doctrine of right within the limits of mere reason' (6:354–5/491). This is one of the very firmest objections to war that we find in the whole of Kant's writings. The core aim of international law is clearly then to establish permanent peace amongst states arguably following precisely the path set out in the essay *Perpetual Peace*. This path obliges the leaders of states to pursue policies that do not rely on the unilateral use of violent methods for their success. These leaders are not to listen to the siren voices of those who find ethical and legal justifications of such use of force under certain circumstances. It is not part of the task of international law so conceived to delineate circumstances where a war conforms with right. The proper task of international law is to delineate the international legal structure which will help bring all war to an end.

Kant does not accept the possibility of failure in the attempt to create lasting peace as grounds for political leaders giving up the ideal. As he notes in the conclusion to the doctrine of right: 'if someone cannot prove a thing is, he can try to prove that it is not. If (as often happens) he cannot succeed in either, he can still ask whether he has any interest in assuming one or the other (as an hypothesis), either from a theoretical or a practical point of view ... what is incumbent upon us as a duty is rather to act in conformity with the idea of that end, even if there is not the slightest theoretical likelihood that it can be realized, so long as its impossibility cannot be demonstrated either' (6: 354/490).

Perpetual Peace as the final end of the doctrine of right?

Contrariwise, it would be wrong also to suggest that *Perpetual Peace* ignores the possibility of war and the need for measures of self-defence on the part of states. Preliminary Article 3 does indeed suggest that 'standing armies' be gradually abolished, but Kant does not recommend that states do without defences altogether for 'it is quite different with military exercises undertaken periodically and voluntarily by the citizens of a state in order to secure themselves and their own country from attacks from without' (8: 345/318). He emphasises in the treatise that under current international law states do have the right to declare war upon one another. In the historical section of the book dealing with 'the guarantee of a perpetual peace' where he attempts to show that despite the often evident ill-will of political leaders the natural course of events will move towards peace, he accepts that 'the idea of the right of nations presupposes the separate existence of many independent adjoining states;' and 'such a state of affairs is essentially a state of war' (8: 367/336). Thus Kant is not blind to the inherited condition of international order. He is fully aware that the law of nations exists side by side with the right to go to war. In many respects, it is precisely this problem that the book tries to address. How can this contradiction in justice which permits states to use arbitrary and unjust means to settle their disputes exist and how can it be resolved? As he puts it, 'right cannot be decided by war and its favourable outcome victory; and by a peace pact a current war can be brought to an end but not a condition of war, of always finding pretexts for new war' (8: 355/327). This seeking pretexts for new wars cannot itself be declared wrong either, since there is nothing in the present condition that prevents each individual state from being a 'judge in its own case' (8: 355/327).

Thus it would be wrong to see the conflict in Kant's argument as deriving solely from two different versions of his international theory presented in two different texts. This is not simply a contrast between the doctrine of right in the *Metaphysics of Morals* and the supposed political invective of *Perpetual Peace*: it is a contrast to be found within both books themselves. Possibly the disparity is greater within the *Metaphysics of Morals* than it is in the book on peace, since Kant gives a fuller hearing to traditional international law as one would expect in the former – but the disparity is to be found within both. The paradoxical conclusion that we may have to draw is that Kant is both a highly limited advocate of war as a final, desperate step of self-defence and yet one of its sharpest critics. This would chime in with his being a fierce critic of the international law of his day, but not at all wanting to dismiss it. The respect for law that the just war theorists often demonstrate has to be admired and respected, however the manner in which they seek to deploy law morally to sanction war has thoroughly to be deplored. Kant in his *Metaphysics of Morals* engages in a radical overhaul of the theory of law and politics of the modern period, the theory of international law is included in this broad reforming sweep. He wants to preserve in existing international law what accords with the idea of our innate right, but at the same time he wants to reject its deficient aspects.

5
Bringing the Argument Together

Background: the rights of state in the state of nature

Thus even though there are discrepancies between the *Rechtslehre* account and the *Perpetual Peace* view, they are far from being wholly incompatible with one another – and if Kant's thinking is (legitimately) seen in a developmental perspective the former account can defensibly be seen as an initial attempt at attaining the point of view expressed in *Perpetual Peace*. Whilst recognising that as things now stand in statute and customary international law, war is in certain limited circumstances a permissible strategy to adopt; Kant does not endorse just war theory in its usual (traditional) sense. Kant does not want to present the possibility of political leaders opting for war and being legally and morally at ease with themselves in doing so. For him war is always a suboptimal moral choice and he wants to see it become an illegal choice in the publicly recognized law of nations. He wants to get away from the *Realpolitik* idea that anyone who is serious about being a state's leader must be prepared to dirty their hands by engaging in war. The problem with war being so regarded as an inescapable necessity of politics amongst states is that accepting the assumption itself heightens the possibility of war occurring.

It may be possible to explain Kant's apparently more permissive attitude towards war in the *Rechtslehre* by looking more closely at the function of the work in his system and comparing it with the role played by *Perpetual Peace*. It might be argued that *Perpetual Peace* is in its nature a more polemical piece than the *Rechtslehre* since Kant's purposes in the shorter book are not solely didactic. The book on peace was intended to capture the attention of the public at large and political leaders in particular in order to persuade them of the feasibility of a stable international order.¹ In comparison, *Rechtslehre* can be regarded as primarily a piece of advanced research that also could be deployed as a teaching manual. I am not suggesting that *Perpetual Peace* is less scholarly than the *Rechtslehre*, merely that the objectives of the latter are almost wholly scholarly and didactic whilst the former might legitimately be seen as a piece of applied ethics. The full title of the second, 'The Metaphysical starting-points (first principles) of the doctrine of right' (*Metaphysische Anfangsgruende der Rechtslehre*) indicates, in my view, that Kant was intending to show what the application of his critical philosophy led to in the field of legal and political philosophy and was not aspiring to a fully comprehensive account of the topic but rather an instructive overview. The subject of natural law or right was already an established field of study, and in teaching the subject it seems that Kant followed the standard texts of his day such as Gottfried Achenwall's *Elementa Iuris Naturae*. (8: 301–2; 6:286n). The German translation of Achenwall uses almost the same phrase, *Anfangsgruende der Naturrecht*, as Kant's book to translate the title.² Arguably Kant's *Rechtslehre* is a survey of issues that occurred in such books – but of course adapted to the critical perspective. If this is the case, it is only to be expected that Kant would include a section on international law where it would be deemed necessary to deal with the standard topics in the field.

It is worth pausing to reflect upon the influence that the Gottingen philosopher Gottfried Achenwall (1719–1772) may have had upon the development and presentation of Kant's philosophy of right, and so Kant's approach to the law of nations and war. Achenwall's objectives in philosophy were a good deal less intellectually ambitious than Kant's. Achenwall's objectives were primarily didactic. He wanted to introduce students and the public to the problems of natural law and its history.³ One of the earliest professors of statistics appointed to a German university, Achenwall's interests led in a good deal more applied direction than Kant's. As well as his book on natural law, one of Achenwall's better known works was an introduction to comparative politics, introduced from a statistical perspective. This book, *Staatsverfassung der vornehmsten europaischen Reiche und Voelker*, is written in an engaging way and places a great deal of emphasis on empirical and historical material. He has sections on all the leading powers of the day from Great Britain to Russia and the United Provinces of the Netherlands. Like Achenwall's book on natural law it is above all a teaching book which provides the reader with a valuable insight into the subject matter. In this sense it is right to connect Achenwall to the movement in popular philosophy which influenced public life in the mid- and late eighteenth century and also provided the intellectual climate within which Kant developed and expounded his critical philosophy. This climate was, of course, that of the Enlightenment.

In the *Biographical Encyclopedia of German philosophers* Bruno Jahn refers to Achenwall as a major influence on the teaching of natural law in German universities at the time of Kant's active career.[4] Jahn speaks of the *Iuris Naturae* as the most used compendium on natural law in the period 1765–90. According to Jahn, Kant's philosophy of right was written in constant disputation with Achenwall's work, as the philosopher continually used it as the basis for his lectures. The importance of Achenwall's teaching text on natural law is also affirmed by Sharon Byrd and Joachim Hruschka, who note that 'Kant was strongly influenced by Achenwall and often uses Achenwall's terminology'.[5] Kant is very complimentary towards Achenwall in the second section 'against Hobbes' in the essay on *Theory and Practice*, speaking of him as one of number of 'men worthy of respect' who presents his natural right in a 'very careful, definite and modest way' (8: 301). And surely Kant presents him with the greatest compliment in using the book on natural law as the principal text for his lectures on the subject. As is to be expected, Kant does not absorb Achenwall's ideas in an uncritical way. Even when complimenting him on the skill with which he presents the philosophy of right, Kant's main objective is to point out the mistake that Achenwall makes, along with other jurists, of according to citizens in the modern state a right of resistance. In quoting Achenwall's grounds for accepting such a right of resistance he makes some good deal less positive remarks on Achenwall's contribution to the philosophy of right. He includes Achenwall with those 'honest' or 'brave' (*wackeren*) men who using 'the most subtle reasoning' (*vernuenfteln*) have unanimously argued for such a right (8: 301). Kant is sure that if Achenwall, along with his peers, were in fact faced with the possibility of such a violent convulsion in their society they would hardly be likely to give the advice they do. Thus, in general, it might be said that whilst Kant regards Achenwall as a reliable source in the study of natural law, in some instances he regards him a little too open to utilitarian and prudential calculations of the moment, and as having a too literal understanding of the social contract.[6]

Achenwall's thinking on natural law does not then determine Kant's approach to the subject and so his approach to international law, but there is no doubt that it influences it. My argument here is that it particularly influences the subject matter that Kant deals with: the topics to which he pays attention and the concepts that he deals with. The main issues of international law as presented in such compendia are ones that

Kant most likely believed he too would have to touch on in his summary of international law. One other such textbook which was almost as successful as Achenwall's was Johann Georg Heinrich Feder's *Lehrbuch des praktischen Philosophie*.[7] There is no direct evidence that Kant may have referred to Feder's text in preparing his work on the philosophy of right, although Kant certainly knew of Feder's existence and his approach to philosophy in general. Feder is best known amongst Kantian scholars for the controversial review of Kant's *Critique of Pure Reason* which he authored with another popular philosopher Christian Garve.[8] Kant certainly knew of Feder in this context and also would have known of Feder's several later books, which took a standpoint different from his own, including one devoted to an examination of Kant's theory of space and time.[9] There appears to be a close similarity between the way in which Achenwall sets out his *Ius Naturae* and the way in which Feder's *Lehrbuch* is set out. Both speak of the natural right of war – looking at reasons for hostility on an individual basis. This is returned to then later when looking at the laws of war at an international level. Arguably this represents the influence of Grotius who begins his *De Jure Belli* with the discussion of the naturalness and acceptability of war. Both also seem to allow a right of necessity in international law; in circumstances of dire need it may be permitted to disregard some aspects of law. Feder divides his *Lehrbuch* into four main sections: Practical Philosophy in general; The Right of Nature; Morality; and the Doctrine of Prudence. With Achenwall in contrast there are two books: Natural law in general, dealing with right in the extra social condition; and Natural law *pars posterior* – family, public and international law. In the Preface to his *Lehrbuch* Feder speaks clearly of his indebtedness to Achenwall. Feder disdains novelty on his own account claiming to follow 'the excellent text of Achenwall.'[10] In particular he says he owes his own insight into this aspect of philosophy to Achenwall, for which he thanks him. In the beginning he had found it difficult to limit right, as Achenwall had recommended solely to what concerns external coercive right – but he gradually got used to it.

Feder's account of international law is of particular significance to our discussion because he uses the term 'unjust enemy' or '*ungerechtes Feind*' in dealing with the rights of states in war. This term is, as we shall see below, hotly disputed in interpretations of Kant's theory of war. Like Achenwall, Feder has little difficulty in according states the right to wage war when they suffer an injury to what is theirs. In discussing the 'right of nature with regard to nations' Feder connects the operation of international law immediately with the functioning of right at an individual level and indeed property right at an individual level. According to Feder, if the principle of right is to permit to everyone what is their own, and this is the essence of justice (*Gerechtigkeit*), then this equally applies to nations. From this point of view international law can be seen as natural law applied to peoples. Nations are like individuals in the state of nature and 'can be regarded as individual persons.'[11] Feder strongly emphasizes the reciprocally binding quality of natural right, so that if one side determines that they are not going to observe right then others are not required to do so as well. For Feder this brings the right of necessity into international law, whereby nations can take whatever actions they deem essential to bring about their security. Feder admits it is difficult to decide when this rule, or rather this absence of rules, comes into operation.[12] There is an unavoidable indeterminacy about the operation of international law.

It is the rule of reciprocity amongst states that leads to the possibility of war. Feder derives the right of war from the fact that all nations are equal and therefore if the one nation suffers an injustice at the hand of another it is entitled to seek redress. Feder divides war into three kinds: first, defensive war, secondly, offensive war, and thirdly what he describes as a 'war of decision' (*Entscheidungskrieg*).[13] The second kinds of wars of offence or attack should scrupulously be avoided.[14] With offensive war the opponent is treated as an unequal or aggressively. Defensive wars are acceptable because they respond to an unjustified attack by another power. The third category of wars arises because of the complexity of relations amongst states, and their lack of patience of some states in seeking a mediated solution. In this third instance because states are equal they are in a position individually to decide when their patience is at an end and put their case through war. In this third instance the outcome of the war decides the justice of the cause. All three categories of war advanced by Feder are problematic. It is not always easy to distinguish an act of aggression from an act of justifiable self-defence, and it would seem almost impossible to decide when a dispute between states had reached the point where it was so complex and embroiled that they could seek a decision through war. Feder, like Achenwall, brings a further complexity into his reasoning when he discusses the effects of the balance of power on possible decisions to go to war.[15] When such a change of balance occurs, Feder admits it may be possible for states to feel entitled to engage in defensive wars.

The idea of the unjust enemy arises in the context of this discussion of the grounds for war. A power that engages in an offensive or aggressive war immediately casts itself as an unjust enemy. In the same way as a burglar who enters a house at night to steal renders himself outside the law, similarly those who prosecute wars are unjust enemies who needed to be treated with the usual courtesy demanded by international law. However, a further possibility of becoming an unjust enemy arises (which limits the nature of the response that can be adopted even to unjust enemies), where an aggressive foe is defeated and excess trickery and violence is deployed in achieving the aim of security. Under these circumstances the victor also can become an unjust enemy and opens itself to the possibility of legitimate defensive war being declared on it by the vanquished. Thus the equilibrium point of reciprocal and equal relations amongst states is, for Feder, the point around which the idea of an unjust enemy turns. States that act or react in an aggressive manner are in danger of being put in this category. It is important in armed conflict always to maintain the status of the 'just enemy'.

Kant of course outlines the theory of international law in a novel, revolutionary way but fits it into it the main aspects of international law as it stood. This may explain the apparent prominence of the right to go to war in the final section of the Doctrine of Right. Kant responds to the way in which treatises on natural law, such as those of Achenwall and Feder, are set up. Most treatises on international law would devote space to the question so Kant is obliged to as well. The title of Kant's work with the highlighting of the notion of 'first principles' or 'starting points' indicates that the author's intention was to sketch what his critical ideas might mean for this traditional topic. Kant believes there are limits to what a critical metaphysical doctrine can achieve in outlining the theory of right. Although the concept of right is 'a pure concept' it 'still looks to practice (application to the cases that come up in experience)'. There is an empirical aspect to the application of right that makes completeness in its theoretical presentation impossible. As there is no end to the empirical variety of cases we have to expect only an approximation to a system in the application of right (6: 205/365). Thus, it would be wrong to expect in the discussion of the 'right to go to war' that Kant would be able or want to cover every eventuality.

Another feature of the presentation in the *Rechtslehre* that would distinguish it from *Perpetual Peace* is that Kant expressly wants to avoid the kind of controversy that a topical political book of the day (like *Perpetual Peace*) might arouse. The section on the right to go to war occurs towards the end of the book, where Kant acknowledges: 'I have worked less thoroughly over certain sections than might be expected in comparison with the earlier ones, partly because it seems to me that they can be easily inferred from the earlier ones and partly, too, because the later sections (dealing with public right) are currently subject to so much discussion, and still so important, that they can well justify postponing a decisive judgement for some time' (6: 209/368). Thus, Kant's intention in the *Rechtslehre* is possibly to suspend judgement on some of the more vexed issues or at least to deflect attention away from controversies that might stand in the way of the fundamental principles of the work being grasped.

Here then are several philosophical and academic grounds why we might expect differences between the two books and why Kant might have gone further in expressing his own beliefs about war in *Perpetual Peace*. *Perpetual Peace* is conceived as the intervention of a philosopher in the events of the day and as an attempt to influence them. *Rechtlehre* is in comparison a strictly academic work which of course has implications for current politics, but those implications are not developed. Kant is being sincere in both works, but the policy issues he touches on in the strictly academic work are narrowly circumscribed. There is no way of telling whether Kant saw *Perpetual Peace* as the occasion where he would deal in further detail with the subjects in public right that 'are currently subject to so much public discussion, and still so important' or whether he saw himself as having touched on them earlier in *Perpetual Peace* and no longer wishing to pronounce on these matters. It is possible to entertain the hypothesis that *Perpetual Peace* was composed later than *Metaphysics of Morals* (or at least some sections of the work), but I know of no firm proof. In the absence of evidence all that we can rely on is the supposition that the book on peace goes a good deal further than the *Metaphysics of Morals* in spelling out the implications of Kant's critical position for politics than the more conjectural and abstract work on right. The shorter book delves into impure ethics of war in a more radical way than the treatise on right.

Thus Paragraph 56 in the *Rechtslehre* (where Kant seems most tolerant towards the just war view) might be seen as providing the textbook grounds for why hostilities might be permitted under the law of nations as it prevailed in Kant's day. The phrases Kant is using appear to indicate that he is referring to what current circumstances allow and not what he personally thinks advisable or right. In 56 Kant is clear that he is talking about a 'state of nature amongst states' (6: 346/484). When he acknowledges the legitimacy of an attack by a lesser power upon a state that has gone through a 'menacing increase' in its power, he stresses that this is so in a 'state of nature'. His acceptance of the right to a balance of power falls within this constraint as well. Arguably it is a mistake to see this paragraph in isolation from the complete development of the idea of international law that Kant attempts to advance in the work. In paragraph 54, as we have seen, Kant sets out this idea in four stages that are wholly interconnected. The first two stages deal with the present nonrightful condition of international relations and the next two stages deal with the steps that have to be taken to remedy this condition. Thus the present permission to pursue right by force accepted in the first two stages has to be seen as a provisional condition that states leaders should seek to overcome. For an integral part of Kant's idea of international law is the creation of a union of peoples in accordance 'with the idea of an original social contract' (6: 344/ 482), which would not seek to interfere with the internal dissensions of the peoples making up the union, but would rather seek to defend the union 'against attacks from without'. Thus the permission granted to states to defend themselves militarily, if necessary, has to be weighed always against their obligation to seek to construct, and to be an effective part, of such a peaceful union of peoples. Thus, even in the *Rechtslehre* the prosecution of a war is hedged in by an equally important proviso to sustain such a union. If we are to conceive of international law at all, we must conceive of the alleged right of war in self-defence as part of our role in an emerging federation of peaceful states. Kant acknowledges there are extreme difficulties in the realisation of his idea of international law since not even the emerging federation will have the power to coerce its members into obeying the law. He thinks sovereign authority has to remain with the individual states themselves. But those who lead the states have to bind themselves voluntarily to refrain from war in settling disputes amongst themselves.

States cannot enjoy an unconditional right to go to war if international law is to be thought of at all. This 'liberty' that states enjoy has always to be seen through the lenses of a gradual movement towards a universally peaceful condition. This is Kant's outlook on the traditional *jus in bello*: 'The greatest difficulty in the right of nations has to do precisely with right during war; it is difficult even to form a concept of this or to think of law in this lawless state without contradicting oneself (*inter arma silent leges*). Right during a war would, then, have to be the waging of war in accordance with principles that always leave open the possibility of leaving the state of nature among states (in external relation to one another) and entering a rightful condition' (6: 347/485).

Potentia Tremenda *or the threat to the balance of power*

Perhaps the most glaring example of an apparent conflict between the interpretation of war in the *Metaphysics of Morals* and its understanding in *Perpetual Peace* is in the treatment of the question of a threat to peace posed by a dominant power that is continuing to enlarge its territories and its military capacity (*potentia tremenda*). In the *Metaphysics of Morals* Kant speaks of this increase in power as being 'a wrong to the lesser power merely by the condition of the superior power, before any deed on its part, and in the state of nature an attack by the lesser power is indeed legitimate' (6: 346/484). Thus Kant appears to grant the lesser power that feels threatened permission to undertake a pre-emptive or anticipatory attack on the hostile, more powerful neighbour. However in *Perpetual Peace* when discussing the role of the moral politician, and how in the leadership of such a politician, right and prudence can be combined by adhering to the idea of publicity he expressly rules out planning such an attack on a dominant and threatening power. Here he rules out as incoherent a policy of anticipatory attack he seems to condone in *Metaphysics of Morals*:

> "If a neighbouring power that has grown to a formidable size (*potentia tremenda*) arouses anxiety, may one assume that because it can oppress it is also going to will to do so, and does this give the less powerful a right to (united) attack upon it, even without having first being injured by it?" A state that was willing to make it known its affirmative maxim about this would only bring on the trouble still more certainly and quickly. For the greater power would anticipate the smaller ones, and as for their uniting, that is only a feeble reed against someone who know how to make use of *divide et impera*. This maxim of political prudence, declared publicly, thus necessarily thwarts its own purpose and is therefore unjust. (8: 384/349)

What Kant includes under the head of the law of nations and right as it is juridically understood in the *Metaphysics of Morals* he condemns as mere political prudence (*Staatsklugheit*) in *Perpetual Peace*. The discussion in *Perpetual Peace* of publicity where Kant takes this standpoint is admittedly forward-looking and concerns the political advice that can be given to leaders from the perspective of his critical philosophy rather than what is acceptable under international law (arguably more the focus of the doctrine of right in the *Metaphysics of Morals*), but even then there is no disguising the contrast between the two treatments of the *potentia tremenda*. Smaller states uniting to affect a pre-emptive attack on a larger, threatening power is excused in the one book and ruled to be incoherent in the other.[16]

I have suggested that the most appropriate way to deal with this conflict is to regard Kant's views in *Perpetual Peace* as the more authoritative account of his theory of international right. I have argued that *Metaphysics of Morals* can be seen as Kant's attempt to come to terms with the existing tradition of international law, to bring out both its strengths and weaknesses. In *Metaphysics of Morals* Kant provides no detailed justification of why lesser powers might be entitled to engage in war with a stronger, threatening power. He does refer to the prevailing balance of power doctrine deployed by political leaders but he gives no indication at that point (or to my knowledge in any of his other writings) that he approves of the doctrine (6: 346/484). In my view, this is consistent with a critical presentation of the weaknesses of current international law rather than an attempt wholly to support its recommendations. We have to bear in mind that the entire section in *Metaphysics of Morals* where he deals with the *potentia tremenda* has to do with the right of states in a state of nature. Thus here we are not in the realms of international right as it should be understood from the perspective of Kant's critical philosophy. The leaders of civil, republican, states will want to step out of this condition of war condoned by traditional international law to a developing association of peaceably inclined polities, where uniting to attack a powerful, threatening state would be contrary to the association's objectives.

One other possible way of resolving the conflict between the two passages in Kant's writings is to suggest that the two rules apply for Kant to two different conditions. The rule which is presented in *Perpetual Peace* as part of the 'transcendental formula of public right' (8: 381/347) applies, it is argued, to the relationships that exist between states that have already emerged from the state of nature amongst themselves (who form part of a federation of free states) and so can be accepted to abide by commonly agreed reciprocal rules – and the rule that is presented in *Metaphysics of Morals* applies to states in their more normal condition of unregulated independence.[17] However, if this were the case (i.e. Kant believed that it was right in the international state of nature to unite to attack a threatening, powerful neighbour) then the criticism of the policy he makes in *Perpetual Peace* would still be relevant. The less powerful states would undermine their position if they openly declared their intention to attack, and even if the preparations were undertaken secretly such would be the difficulties posed by such a policy (how does one hide the increased diplomatic contacts amongst the proposed allies; their increased military preparedness; the disquiet amongst their subjects about the prospects of war?) it is very difficult to envisage that it would be a success. In other words, I believe that attempting to resolve the apparent conflict by showing that both positions are sincerely and consistently held by Kant leads only to a demonstration that the defence of an anticipatory attack on the *potentia tremenda* in *Metaphysics of Morals* is a mistake.

We can never of course know with full certainty what Kant's objective in the *Rechtlehre* is in outlining when war might be legitimate under the law of nations, but I think an interpretation which suggests that his main purpose is to bring out the contradictory nature of that law is highly plausible. Those who suggest that Kant is outlining a view which he fully supports tend in the direction of implying that Kant in *Perpetual Peace* contradicts himself in opposing the just war theorists. Although clearly this is not out of the question[18] the view that I have put forward, namely that in the *Rechtslehre* Kant is presenting a pointed, paradoxical account of international law is both a more generous and more satisfying view. How else are we to understand Kant's conclusion that because of the state of nature in the international condition which the law of nations condones all 'rights of nations , anything external that is mine or yours which states can acquire or retain by war, are merely provisional'? (6: 349/487). It harmonises with his – in general – highly negative view of war and his overwhelmingly reformist intentions in relation to world politics. Surely it would be remarkable that a writer, who misses no opportunity to condemn war as the worst of all evils, would lend support to the just war doctrine that seeks to stipulate the circumstances under which war is legal?

At best Kant gives only a weak and passing endorsement of the right of less powerful states in the international state of nature to seek preventively to disarm a *potentia tremenda* in the *Rechtslehre*. In contrast his rejection of the maxim in *Perpetual Peace* is explicit and unequivocal. In *Perpetual Peace* he is as a philosopher offering advice to rulers. In the *Metaphysics of Morals* he is developing his views of international law for an academic audience solely. In my view the explicit rejection of a right to attack a threatening and overwhelmingly powerful neighbour trumps the equivocal and begrudging acknowledgment given in the *Metaphysics of Morals* to this traditional right recognised by some international lawyers.[19]

Unjust enemy

One further concept that Kant somewhat sceptically deploys to indicate conditions where war might be permissible in the state of nature which exists amongst states is that of the unjust enemy (*ein ungerechtes Feind*). The idea of an unjust enemy is of an opponent or an antagonistic state which refuses to recognize any binding rules upon the conduct of states. The idea appears in the writings of Gottfried Achenwall and J.G.H. Feder on the law of nations, and as Kant used Achenwall's text on natural law in his lectures it is highly likely that he was familiar with it and the apparent endorsement which Achenwall gives it.[20] An unjust enemy is an antagonist for whom then neither the laws of war nor the notions of legitimate cause have any meaning. Such an antagonist is bound only by its own notions of where its obligations and limits lie. This is an antagonist that believes that it is entirely free to pursue its own interests in its own way.[21] And this is not a view that the state's leaders secretly hold but it is one they are prepared openly to express: 'it is an enemy whose publicly expressed will (whether by words or deed) reveals a maxim by which if it were made a universal rule, any condition of peace among nations would be impossible and, instead, a state of nature would be perpetuated'. Where this is the case all other states are entitled to unite against the unjust enemy and subdue it. However, this would not give the united states the right to conquer and divide amongst themselves the territory of the offending state but rather they would be entitled to give the defeated 'ungerechtes Feind' a new constitution 'that by its nature will be unfavourable to the inclination of war' (6: 349/487).

Kant of course thinks that the only kind of constitution that by its nature is unfavourable to war is a republican one; thus we can assume that the constitution he believes should be adopted in these circumstances has to be of this kind. Kant argues that it would not only be permissible for all other states to unite against an unjust enemy, but also it would in fact be an obligation. Evidence of the unjustness of the enemy would be 'a violation of public contracts'. And 'since this can be assumed to be a matter of concern to all nations whose freedom is threatened by it, they are called upon to unite against such misconduct in order to deprive the state of its power to do it' (6: 349/487). So this appears to be a very strong just cause in the 'state of nature amongst states' for a state to go to war with another. However Kant invokes the idea sceptically because to 'speak of an unjust enemy in a state of nature' is pleonastic. A pleonasm occurs where more words are being used than is necessary to make sense. Examples of the pleonastic use of terms that occurs in everyday language are 'tuna fish' or 'safe haven'. Strictly speaking the use of 'fish' in the first instance is redundant – since it is should already be clear that tuna is a fish, and the use of 'safe' in the second instance is similarly redundant since a haven is by definition safe. The pleonasm occurs for Kant in the idea of an unjust enemy because 'a state of nature is itself a condition of injustice'. Invoking the idea of an unjust enemy threatens to identify all states as hypocrites. By reserving the right to be judges in their own case (under international law as it currently stands) all publicly agreed rules are placed under threat. Thus having invoked the concept of an unjust enemy in this passage of the Doctrine of Right as though it might give us a rule with which to determine and specify a just war in a condition of nature (injustice), Kant completes his analysis in a highly inconclusive way by remarking that the contrary concept of a 'just enemy' (*justus hostis*) fails to make a great deal of sense. The shakiness of the concept of a 'just enemy' would seem to imply that the concept of an 'unjust enemy' is equally open to doubt. Kant is not at all attracted to the idea of chivalry in warfare where there can be well fought wars amongst noble enemies. 'A just enemy would be one that I would be doing wrong by resisting; but then he would not also be my enemy' (6: 350). Here Kant simply leaves us with a paradox, hinting that there may be some states in the international state of nature that merit, by their aggressive behaviour, having all other states as their enemy. However the only way in which the other states could permissibly unite to vanquish the opponent would be by agreeing to enter into a stable legal relationship with each other.

Kant's discussion of the unjust enemy seems to emphasize the parlous condition of an international law that is based upon the complete freedom of every state to decide for itself what constitutes a just action. With his reference to the pleonasm upon which the notion of an unjust enemy rests, he casts doubt on the whole concept of such an exceptional enemy. A two-word description that contains within it one word too many is hardly one to be recommended for universal adoption. The demand that all states unite against such an exceptional enemy presupposes that all states have decided to leave the international state of nature so that war loses all its legitimacy under international law and international law has founded itself on a truly reliable basis. There is no *just war* under a reformed Kantian international law.

Carl Schmitt's complaint[22] that Kant makes the international order even more unstable by deploying the concept of an unjust enemy seems therefore to be overstated. He accepts that Kant's argument is a complex one, dealing with the 'old doctrine of *justus hostis* (just enemy)' in a 'thoroughly perplexing manner',[23] but Schmitt draws the strange conclusion that Kant wholeheartedly supports the concept of an 'unjust enemy'. From this Schmitt infers that Kant prepares the way for wars that are of discriminatory kind opposing and defeating enemies of humanity. Schmitt seems not to have grasped the irony that is part and parcel of Kant's treatment of the 'unjust enemy'. It is not at all clear that Kant brings up the concept as a prelude to identifying such possible unjust enemies; indeed I think it is more likely that Kant deploys the concept with the view to showing its difficulties and inapplicability to international politics as it is constituted in its Westphalian, sovereign state form. Kant is interrogating the concept of *justis hostis* as he finds it in the international law of his day and juxtaposes it with the 'unjust enemy' with a view to bringing out the paradoxes and limitations of that law.

Arguably international law as Kant found it before him in the relations amongst states of his day was a fractured and shaky structure whose foundations in the sovereign independence and equality of states made it almost unworkable. It is only because states are largely in a condition of nature in relation to one another (and so in a continuous condition of potential hostility) that the odd idea of an unjust enemy can possibly gain purchase. In the day to day working of the international system the leaders of states accept that certain circumstances (especially when it comes to the loss of property and self-defence) make the declaration of war just. The possibility of an unjust enemy arises where one or more state(s) or their leaders refuse to recognise the normal minimal restraints on the declaration of war. The unjust enemy is prepared to go beyond the usual latitude permitted to states in the use of force.

Here I read Kant as regarding both the normal enmity sanctioned by international law and the unjust enmity that arises outside its framework as wrong. In this respect I take a different view of this section of *Metaphysics of Morals* from that of the excellent Kant scholar Susan Shell. She draws the intriguing conclusion that Kant gives the impression in the *Metaphysics of Morals* that 'international "public" right is fundamentally "ambiguous".'[24] But then she makes the less persuasive comments about the unjust war passage (paragraph 60): 'Kant's thinking on international right opens up a space, on which recent US administrations have seized, allowing for a (new) distinction between those states and those states that do not count as fully-fledged members of the community of nations.'[25] In my view these comments fail to see the irony that permeates Kant's discussion of the notion of the 'unjust enemy'. My sense of the discussion in paragraph 60 is that Kant believes that no general distinctions can be drawn from the use of the term. All states are equally culpable for remaining in the international state of nature. The likelihood of an unjust enemy arises only because the system permits the existence of a 'just enemy'. Today's rogue or outlaw states are different only in degree and not in kind from the average, supposedly conforming or law-respecting states. Kant's doubts about the applicability of the concept of an 'unjust enemy' lie at the heart of his objection to just war theory. Here the continuity between *Perpetual Peace* and the Doctrine of Right could not be more evident.

Balthazar Ayala provides one of the best-known sources of the notions of just and unjust enemies in early modern international law. In his *On the Law of War* (1581) he says 'what we have laid down about keeping faith with an enemy must be scrupulously observed whenever we are dealing with a just and lawful enemy; but if anyone happens to be compelled, by one who is not a "just" enemy, to pass his word about paying a ransom-price or such like, we hold that he is under no obligation to keep his word.'[26] The law of war quite clearly applies only to just enemies – we have to act in good faith towards them even when we are engaged in hostilities. Being recognised formally in international law as an enemy brings with it duties and obligations. 'Since then those alone who are "just" enemies can invoke to their profit the law of war, those who are not reckoned as "hostes" and therefore have no part in the law of war, are not qualified to bargain about matters that only inure to the benefit of "just" enemies, nor are they justified in effecting such bargains by coercion.'[27] For Carl Schmitt Ayala is an important figure because he develops the 'non-discriminatory concept of war based on parity – the *Bellum utrimque justum* [just war on both sides]'.[28] Ayala's emphasis seems to be that what primarily is required to wage a just war is proper authority. For Schmitt that proper authority is conferred by sovereign status. For him Ayala also then establishes that 'only armed struggle between state sovereigns was war in the sense of international law, and only this type of struggle fulfilled the requirements of *Justus hostis*'.[29] Kant's treatment of the concept of an 'unjust enemy' shows up the paradox involved in Ayala's doctrine. The unjust enemy is somehow supposed to have stepped beyond the very permissive rules that govern the declaration and prosecution of wars. However if the parties to the dispute could abide by rules then there would be no dispute, and certainly they would not be enemies.

Both Carl Schmitt and Kant then are critical of just war theory as it derives from medieval international law (Aquinas) and is evidenced in modern international law, but they are critics from opposed perspectives. Schmitt objects to the theory, and especially its humanistic development towards the idea of an unjust enemy, because it detracts in his view from the understanding of the friend–enemy relationship he sees at the root of politics and the soundly based European system of international law that developed in the eighteenth and nineteenth centuries (*jus publicum Europaeum*). According to this view the occurrence of an enmity in the international sphere is only to be expected, and so war was not an exceptional experience, but rather an ever present possibility. For Schmitt it is an existential datum that nations face each other as potential enemies.[30] Such antagonistic relationships are inherent in human life and to seek to remove them, risks, in his view, civilization itself. In this dire outlook international relations and the risk of war are inseparable twins. Kant in contrast opposes the notion of a just war from a diametrically opposed perspective. Kant wants to de-naturalize the antagonisms of international relations and remove the assumption of the inevitability of war. From a Kantian critical perspective our limited capacity to know prevents us from making any final pronouncements about the nature of human existence, and from a moral/practical perspective the assumption of the naturalness of inevitability of war undermines our objective of progress. Just as Kant thinks we should not assume that we are condemned forever to act in an evil way, so equally he thinks we should not assume that we were are irreversibly bound to the condition of war. As the worst of all evils we should always strive to overcome war. Giving in to it by coining the notions of just and unjust enemies is to succumb to intellectual dishonesty.

As we can see in the final sentences of paragraph 60 of the *Metaphysics of Morals* Kant opposes both the notions of a just and unjust enemy. In referring to the notion of an 'unjust enemy' he demonstrates how hollow he thinks both notions are. For him the notion of an enemy that is unjust is as redundant as saying that 'he is a beginner who has just started'. Schmitt's assumption of the naturalness of the 'friend-enemy' relationship is alien to him. The notion of an unjust enemy represents one word too much: for Kant the idea of unjust is implicit in the idea of enemy in the first place. For if an individual or a state to be cast as an enemy is to demonstrate that things have already gone too far. The moral balance in the relationship between the parties is already askew. This is why Kant cannot embrace the concept that Schmitt is most willing to embrace: the 'just enemy'. For Kant there is no morally acceptable way of casting the relationship of enmity. Where hostilities exist between enemies there are better or worse ways in which the conflict can be conducted but there are no wholly good ways. Laying out rules for wrong conduct does not make it just; it simply brings it nearer to justice. The robber who decides not to deploy deadly force is not for that reason acting justly, he simply acts less unjustly. Thus Kant of course does not applaud anyone who is depicted as an unjust enemy according to conventional norms, but he regards them only as worse in degree rather than kind for the way in which they conduct themselves in international relations. The generally accepted rules of international law are insufficient even when they are upheld; those who do not uphold them go only one step further in that they betray not the usual partial cynicism of the strategically minded politician but a complete cynicism. Defeating the 'unjust' enemy would not restore world politics from a dangerous unstable condition to a more stable normal condition – it would simply reduce extreme instability to a 'normal' insecurity and instability. For Kant the usual insecurity and instability of international relations has to be overcome just as much as the extreme malfunction. Defeating the 'unjust enemy' only paves the way for a more comprehensive programme of peace and can, on Kant's understanding, only be achieved by committing to the more distant long-term goal required by that programme.

Declaring war

For Kant the occurrence of war is an unavoidable anthropological starting-point for international law theory, but it should not be accepted as an unchangeable fact. He is prepared to begin from the assumption that under present unreformed international law, states are not prevented from pursuing right by engaging in war. As a corollary he accepts a number of conditions under which a state leader might legitimately contemplate declaring war. But this will neither bring justice nor can the ensuing war be regarded as just. At best the ensuing peace may bring us closer to justice, at worst the chaos and disorder brought about by the war may present an insuperable obstacle to bringing about justice for generations to come. For Kant there are no circumstances under which war should be depicted as being the comfortable moral option for the political leader to adopt.

It is striking that when we come to the declaration of war we find Kant at his most democratic. In his political philosophy Kant only cautiously adopts the modern democratic theory of citizenship, strongly mediating it with the notions of a limited franchise and representative authority.[31] He is an opponent of direct democracy when it comes to legislation, believing that the people as a whole cannot draw up the laws for themselves. They need to elect representatives to do it on their behalf. However, when it comes to the decision to go to war, Kant appears to indicate the citizens as a whole have to be asked for their consent. Albeit that this consent is obtained through their elected representatives. Citizens of a state 'must always be regarded as co-legislating members of a state (not merely as a means, but also as ends in themselves), and must therefore give their free assent, through their representatives, not only to waging war in general but also to each particular declaration of war. Only under this limiting condition can a state direct them to serve in a way full of danger to them' (6: 346/484). The right to declare war cannot simply be given to one individual or even one group of individuals. Since fighting a war involves the citizens putting themselves at risk, it is something they should collectively decide for themselves. A people have the right to defend itself from an attack in the international state of nature, but this is a right it disposes over collectively and cannot delegate to a representative. In the context of impending war Kant's embraces the notion of popular sovereignty in a thoroughgoing way: 'We shall therefore have to derive this right from the duty of the sovereign to the people (not the reverse); and for this to be the case the people will have to be regarded as having given its vote to go to war. In this capacity it is, although passive (letting itself be disposed of), also active and represents the sovereign itself' (6: 346/484). For Kant human beings are not like things or animals to be disposed of as though they were the personal property of the ruler. In respect of the decision to go to war the ruler should be viewed as at the disposal of the people and not the people at the ruler's disposal. The sovereign has no right 'to lead them in to war as he would take them on a hunt, and into battles as on a pleasure trip'(6: 345/483). Here Kant shows himself to be remarkably at odds with Vattel, who claims in *The Law of Nations* that the 'sovereign is the real author of war, which is made in his name and at his command. The troops, both officers and soldiers, and in general all those persons by whom the sovereign carries out war, are only instruments in his hands. They execute his will and not their own.'[32]

Thus although Kant has little to say that is unequivocal about two of the traditional three headings of just war theory – just cause and right intention – he does have a very firm recommendation on what constitutes the competent authority. The solely competent authority is the people itself. The original concern of just war theorists that a war should be declared on proper authority was to ensure that the decision was that of the legitimate sovereign and not of one of its subordinates or an independent private force.[33] Within feudal states there were always rivals to the monarch's authority. Without the condition of competent authority being observed there was always the danger of states sliding into civil war. Kant shares this concern. He too wants to be assured that the decision is only that of the legitimate sovereign. But his concern is neither primarily that the wrong person or group of persons representing the sovereign should be effecting to take the decision nor that a private group of individuals are attempting to usurp the sovereign's authority. His concern is to establish how the legitimate sovereign's authority in the matter of declaring war should be understood. For him proper authority must come from the consent of the citizens – from those who have the main stake in any fighting that has to be done and whose lives, liberty and property might be threatened by the ensuing violence. On all issues other than the declaration of war, Kant is a firm representative democrat, but when it comes to this life and death matter only direct democracy will do. In maintaining law and order within the state Kant is clear that direct democracy will not work. He is convinced the people cannot rule themselves. The result of an attempt at direct democracy with domestic government will inevitably be the rule of one faction at the expense of the majority. Not everyone will be sufficiently capable, interested and effective to do the job, and unavoidably as individuals will be judges in their own case –thus law will be undermined. But the decision to go to war should not be seen as an act of executive authority to be undertaken on the people's behalf – it is rather a situation where it is right that individuals should be a judge in their own case. The declaration of war is one that will suspend even the pretence of an international civil condition, so the decision is not the same as that which occurs under everyday civil government. The competent authority that declares the war should regard itself not as exercising its right on behalf of the people but rather as carrying out a duty on their behalf. Legality under normal circumstances requires for Kant that the sovereign is the people's master, in declaring war the people is the sovereign's master.

Prosecuting a war should never be seen like the just punishment that occurs to criminals within a state. In providing the scope for the internal legal system to work effectively and in carrying out the judgements of the courts political leaders (who sit in the Executive) can be morally at ease with themselves. 'Strict right rests' for Kant 'on the principle of its being possible to use external constraint that can coexist with the freedom of everyone in accordance with general (universal) laws' (6: 232/389). Mistakes may occasionally be made by the authorities and judges, but overall justice requires that the law should be carried out and offenders be punished. The monopoly the state has over the legitimate use of violence is properly put to use here. However, in the international sphere because of the absence of a legitimate and unifying sovereign, strict right cannot be adhered to or achieved. Thus there is no legal right to use violence in relation to other states in order to punish then, but rather there is a prohibition on its use for this purpose. There is a disanalogy between the position of the convicted criminal in relation to the sovereign and the position of the state's supposed external enemies. Kant cannot agree with Aquinas's supposition in outlining the 'conditions of a Just War' that 'just as in the punishment of criminals' 'responsibility for public affairs is entrusted to the rulers' as 'they rightly defend the state against all internal disturbance with the civil arm', 'so also they have the duty of defending the state, with the weapons of war against external enemies'.[34] In this respect Kant also differs markedly from Michael Walzer, who endorses the 'conception of just war as an act of punishment'. And following the domestic analogy that Kant here rejects Walzer claims that 'the domestic maxim is, punish crime to prevent violence; its international analogue is, punish aggression to prevent war'.[35]

Thus in the inherited system of international law the use of force is a legal no man's land. Engaging in war represents a step in the dark. The consequences can never be wholly anticipated. Parcelling out sovereignty to every state means that each can be potentially judge in its own case and so no wholly reliable use of force can be envisaged. This is what leads Kant to recommend a complete transformation in the basis of international law. The requirements of the Second Definitive article that 'the law of nations be based on a federation of free states' (8: 354) arise from the contradictions within the traditional law of nations itself. For Kant international law only works as a concept when it is regarded as based on an extension of the social contract on to the international sphere. Kant's social contract not only establishes a legal sovereign at home but it also endorses a voluntary co-sovereign of sovereigns at an international level. International law will only function properly when it is seen as emanating from an authority of this kind. It is based upon the united will of the 'united general wills' of all the peoples in the world.

Thus there has to come into existence a union of free states that is non-exclusive – which all states can and ought to join. It is a moot point whether as this non-exclusive union establishes itself how it can relate to non-member societies. Kant's writings may sometimes be taken to imply that there might be the possibility of a justifiable war between this ever-expanding union and recalcitrant countries, since Kant mentions in the *Metaphysics of Morals* (paragraph 55) one use that might be made of the 'original right that free states in a state of nature have to go to war with one another' is maybe 'to establish a condition more closely approaching a rightful condition' (6: 344/483). But this arguably would have to be a war of defence only: not one that was intended to force non-members into the fold of the union, but rather a self-protective war that sought to counter threats to the existence of the peoples of the union or one of its member states. As Kant puts it in *Perpetual Peace* 'this league does not look to acquiring any power of a state but only to preserving and securing the freedom of a state for itself and at the same time of other states in league with it' (8: 356/327). The examples he cites in the *Metaphysics of Morals* are the amphictyonic league of Ancient Greece (§54) and the assembly of the States General at The Hague of the early eighteenth century. In the latter example 'the ministers of the courts of Europe and even of the smallest republics lodged with it their complaints about attacks being made on one of them by another. In this way they thought of the whole of Europe as a single confederated state which they accepted as arbiter, so to speak, in their public disputes' (6: 350/488). In the first example the states of Greece would form an alliance to defend a place of common religious importance as for instance when the Delphic Amphictyony was established 'to protect the temple of Apollo at Delphi and to direct the Pythian Games'.[36] In both examples the federations were formed without direct aggressive intent. They were aimed at safeguarding a common interest. Their object was clearly to avoid war rather than encourage it. And it cannot be their so-called success that led Kant to cite them (since both finally broke down under the weight of external and internal pressures) but rather the principles of cooperation, abjuring war and solidarity that they embodied. As in the nature of things each of these leagues had external boundaries and so potential antagonists; they cannot be regarded as perfectly analogous with the union Kant has in mind. What Kant seems to want to stress is the way in which the alliances would seek to maintain the peace amongst member states and ward against attacks from non-members. Direct interference in the affairs of member states should be avoided and there should be no crusade to enrol non-members. Until the world wide civil federation is in fact established, the declaration of war will always fall into a legal grey area where political leaders should necessarily be in doubt about the wisdom and justice of their actions.

Conclusion

We have found in this chapter that there are successful ways of bringing together the apparently divergent accounts of just war to be found in *Perpetual Peace* and the *Metaphysics of Morals*. The idea of just war belongs to an international system that is unjust overall. So the idea is thoroughly compromised by the context to which it belongs. The only way that is open to take advantage of the often humanitarian concern that motivates those who propound the doctrine is to argue for a system of world politics that takes us beyond the natural antagonism amongst peoples. The key theme of Kant's presentation of international law in both works is the idea of perpetual peace (*ewigen Frieden*) itself. In the *Metaphysics of Morals* he follows the circuitous route through the confusions and ambiguities of prevailing international law, yet ultimately the goal of perpetual peace is not lost sight of. As in the former work, in the *Metaphysics of Morals* republican government represents the path to peaceful external relations which should be cemented through a federation of free states. We are led in both works to cosmopolitan right or law which sets each individual human being at the centre of a peaceful, legal global order. As he puts it at the beginning of the concluding section of the doctrine of right: 'The rational idea of a peaceful, even if not friendly, thoroughgoing community of all nations on the earth that can come into relations affecting one another is not a philanthropic (ethical) principle but a principle having to do with rights (*rechtlichen Prinzip*). (6: 352/489).

6
Kantian Perspectives on Foreign Intervention

Introduction: a responsibility to protect?

A thorny issue that has been raised by recent just war theory is the question of armed intervention in the internal affairs of another state.[1] This issue is highlighted in the International Commission on Intervention and State Sovereignty report sponsored by the Canadian government and published in 2001. The report was brought together by a group of scholars and diplomats (led by Gareth Evans, a former Australian Foreign Minister) and was published under the title *The Responsibility to Protect*. The broad theme of the Commission's enquiry was: when is it right to interfere in the internal affairs of a sovereign state in order to prevent great harm to the state's subjects and the widespread general deterioration of international order which might follow if the apparent abuse of human rights continues?[2] It is clear from the structure of the final report and the accompanying research published in a supplementary volume that the team which produced the report turned to traditional just war theory as a means of determining when and in what way it might be right to intervene militarily. The supplementary volume notes that 'questions of the legitimacy of the use of military force are part of an older debate' and the discussion entered into focuses on the 'western just war tradition'.[3] Within the just war tradition the authors argue there is a considerable dispute about appropriate criteria and their deployment they think 'nevertheless, it is possible to identify core elements'. They suggest three of these core elements are already present in the writings of one of the main sources of traditional just war theory, Thomas Aquinas', 'namely, right authority, just cause and right intentions'. They wish to deploy three further elements they believe have emerged in the literature: 'last resort, proportionality and reasonable hope'.[4] These six elements of an appropriate basis for intervention are mirrored in the final report.[5] The supplementary volume and the report give a great deal of credibility to the just war theory tradition apparently removing entirely from the category of thinking that might be attributed to mere 'sorry comforters. As the authors of the supplementary volume put it, 'although it is seldom acknowledged, many of the ethical questions that need to be considered before using deadly force to protect civilians can be found within this tradition. Indeed, much of the contemporary debate seems to call for a carefully circumscribed approach to humanitarian intervention that in fact amounts to a modified just war doctrine'.[6]

Although it arguably adopts too uncritically the just war standpoint in setting out the problem of humanitarian intervention, the Commission's report shows considerable balance. The Commission's members were acutely aware of the conflict that is presented by the advocacy of intervention in a world political system that relied upon sovereign independence of states as one of the main principles of order. 'In a dangerous world marked by overwhelming inequalities of power and resources, sovereignty is for many states their best – and sometimes their only – line of defence. But sovereignty is more than just a functional principle of international relations. For many states and peoples, it is also recognition of their equal worth and dignity, a protection of their unique identities and their national freedom, and an affirmation of their right to shape and determine their own destiny.'[7] Albeit that this is a somewhat dramatic recognition of the role of states in maintaining domestic justice and making possible patriotic citizenship, it does bring out the commission's aversion to undermining the positive role that sovereignty can play. However, 'the defence of state sovereignty, by even its strongest supporters, does not include the claim of unlimited power of a state to do what it wants to its own people'. The Commission worked on the basis that 'sovereignty implies a dual responsibility: externally – to respect the sovereignty of other states, and internally, to respect the dignity and basic rights of all the people within the state.'[8] The Commission wanted the inherited world political system to work more effectively and in so doing 'sought to reconcile two objectives: to strengthen, not weaken, the sovereignty of states, and to improve the capacity of the international community to react decisively when states are either unable or unwilling to protect their own people'. The objectives of the commission and its report appear to be most laudable: who could object to the view that the international community has a responsibility to protect the weakest and most vulnerable human beings on the planet? However does not the report take too much for granted about the inherited international order and fail properly to come to terms with the disputed status of international law?

Arguably the Commission's report presupposes what it sets out to achieve. The Commission's objective is to bring about a more harmonious international order where breaches of human rights – wherever they may occur – are taken seriously. We need to be concerned about vulnerable human beings wherever they might be, and we must respond to their needs more urgently and effectively. This would bring us nearer to the goal of a world community. However, the paradox of the report is that it presupposes interventionist action would be undertaken by the present international community (which according to the report itself falls short of the ideal). The report moves too easily from a general sense that we as inhabitants of the one globe have 'a responsibility to react' to invoking a need for intervention. 'The responsibility to protect implies above all else a responsibility to react to situations of compelling need for human protection. When preventive measures fail to resolve or contain the situation and when a state is unwilling to redress the situation, then interventionary measures by other members of the broader community of states may be required.'[9] We have to be careful how the 'we' is established in these instances and what responsibilities are assumed by it.

Although motivated by clear ethical intentions I want to demonstrate here that Kant's authority cannot be invoked for any programme of humanitarian intervention based upon just war theory. Kant's opposition to just war theory means that attempts to improve the political, social and economic conditions of the subjects of other states by other states and international organisations should always stop short of the use of military violence.

Spreading the democratic peace?

Not surprisingly Kantian moral and political theory is a resource to which commentators have turned in attempting to deal with the question of intervention in the internal affairs of other states. In particular Kant's thinking has been invoked in relation to humanitarian intervention.[10] My view is that – as with the theory of just war and Kant's mooted contribution to it – Kantians should approach the topic of humanitarianism and forcible intervention with great caution. Not everything that is embraced under the idea of humanitarian intervention is necessarily compatible with a Kantian perspective. Indeed we shall find that Kant's writings can be invoked only with a minimal authority to justify direct interventions of any kind. But this has not put off those who seek to invoke Kant's name for the sake for a heavily oriented western liberal notion of progress. As Jeremy Moses notes, Kant's democratic peace theory has been deployed to argue 'implicitly or explicitly that "we" (always referring to Western liberal –democracies) should do all in our power to convert those states that do not subscribe to this political system, either by persuasion or, if necessary, by force, in order to bring about the promise of perpetual peace for generations to come'.[11]

Some recent commentators on Kant have suggested that Kant's republican peace theory implies that under certain circumstances it is right to intervene in the internal affairs of another state. Roger Scruton has argued this in the case of Iraq, and Fernando Teson has presented a more general case for intervention to safeguard human rights in unstable conditions. Scruton is a well known British right wing commentator and a philosopher of some distinction who is familiar with Kant's works.[12] According to Scruton, 'Kant indeed believed that war can be legitimately embarked on only as a defensive measure, and that pre-emptive attack is not defence. However, circumstances have changed, and I can see good Kantian reasons for the view that the civilised world, faced with the dangers that now confront it, should take pre-emptive measures when dealing with rogue states like Saddam's Iraq.'[13] Scruton accepts that a reading of *Perpetual Peace* would lead one towards the conclusion that Kant would be opposed to all foreign intervention of a coercive kind. But Scruton distinguishes between the tone of *Perpetual Peace* and the tone of Kant's discussion of the right to war in the *Metaphysics of Morals*.[14]

Here Scruton in my view turns Kant's argument against the doctrine of just wars on its head. Kant believed that just war doctrine was incompatible with the existence of a properly functioning international law, which must depend on the peaceful resolution of disputes amongst states. Whereas for Kant an account of international law which is based on the right to go to war is untenable, Scruton argues that Kant's doctrine of international law implies that the resort to war is from time to time unavoidable. For Kant, as Scruton sees it: 'the recourse to international law, he believed, presupposes that members of the League of Nations are republics. If they are not republics, but regard themselves as in a state of nature vis-à-vis other states, then it may be necessary to confront them with violence, in order to prevent them from imposing their will. Of course, the violence must be proportional to the threat, and its aim must be to bring about a lasting peace. But war conducted for the sake of peace was, for Kant as for his predecessors in the "just war" tradition, a paradigm of legitimate belligerence'.[15] Here the rhetoric far outreaches what Kant has to say. Nations that are in a state of nature vis-à-vis other nations should not 'confront them with violence' but rather confront them with the idea of a peaceful federation of states and under no circumstances does Kant envisage deploying violence 'to bring about lasting peace'. The hostile and coercive means can never be justified by the laudable end. Peace is the end and the only justifiable means are peaceful. Kant rules out just war notions because no state leader is in a position to judge what ultimately is right. For the federation of states he envisages, Kant confines himself to advocating peaceful measures alone as the means of bringing about world community. The federation is a pact of mutual defence, not a pact of mutual offence. Kant prefers the power of example to the example of power.

The nub of Scruton's argument is that a state like Iraq is not, according to his interpretation of Kant, immune to intervention by a republican state whose aim is not to annex Iraq and its people but to help them create the conditions for a rightful and ultimately republican state. Scruton's reasoning is seductive but false: 'Suppose, then, the following case. We are confronted with a state that is manifestly despotic, which is neither a republic nor a law abiding member of the League of Nations, in which people are denied elementary rights and in which crimes are regularly committed by the ruling power. It is a manifest threat to peace, has invaded neighbouring states without cause, has committed genocide against its own minorities, and seems determined to advance its own interests, whatever the costs to others. The state nevertheless claims a voice in the League, endeavouring to influence policy and international law in order to perpetuate and enhance its power. Suppose also that there is a larger power, which is a republic anxious to spread republican government around the world, motivated perhaps by some version of the Ideal of Reason that Kant puts before us in *Perpetual Peace*.' Scruton continues in the same subjunctive but optimistic mood: 'Suppose that this larger power is confident that it can destroy the despotic state with only minimum harm to its people – less harm than they would suffer were the despotism to remain in place.'

Here of course the larger power is the United States and the 'despotic state' Iraq, which merits being overthrown. 'Suppose that, by doing this, there is hope of planting the seeds of republican government in an area of the globe where until now only despotism or empire have held sway.' The larger power is entirely cleared of the possibility of having any ulterior motives: 'suppose that the republic goes to war intending not to possess the territory or resources of the despotic state, but with the intention of creating the conditions in which its people can decide for themselves on their form of government. Suppose that its intention in doing so is to create the conditions of lasting peace in a region of the world where peace is constantly being jeopardised by tyrants and fanatics.' Having made all these heroic suppositions we are then finally to: 'ask Immanuel Kant the question: would it be right for my hypothetical republic to go to war against my hypothetical despotism? He would be compelled by his own principles to say "yes".'[16]

This approach shows a missionary zeal not shared by Kant. Kant tries to avoid dividing the states of the world into 'goodies' and 'baddies' or 'cops and robbers' – and so perpetuating the whole warlike condition of states. Just as with internal politics where Kant wanted to avoid paternalistic government which made the state the custodian of individual welfare, so too in the international realm he wanted to avoid turning some states into guardians of the well being of all states. The major error of Scruton's overenthusiastic approach is that it fails to pay respect to the structures of international law that are already in place in the twenty first century. That international law has in our day a somewhat limited and imperfect application (less so than perhaps in Kant's day but he was familiar with the problem) does not imply that we can ignore or overlook its requirements when we are anxious to do good in the world. For Kant the pursuit of the good has always to be subordinate to the need to observe external law. Laws may be in need of amendment or changing altogether but this provides no justification for breaking them. Scruton's fanciful and idealistic scenario contains at each stage a disregard for law. In the first lines of his story he fails to identify who the 'we' implementing the will of the international community might be. Under current international law this could only be the United Nations, but there is no suggestion from Scruton that he accepts this. He then goes on to assume that a 'larger power' is in a position to embody the will of the international community (usurping the United Nations?) in order to create a republican form of government in a despotic state and that it is legitimate to use military means to bring this about. Scruton is advocating no less than a revolution in the international legal order whereby one system of emerging law is to be overthrown and replaced by one more to his enthusiastic pro-Western republican liking. It is a recipe for chaos similar to the path advocated and followed by the Jacobins in France in executing the King and so deplored by Kant (6: 322/464). Scruton's casual reflections are in danger of putting violence before right and so repeating the wrongs of which

Saddam Hussein is accused. The Kantian expectation is that republican states lead by example and not through force. There is an obligation to work with the existing institutions of international law, however imperfect they might be, rather than against them.

Fernando Teson and hyper-interventionism

Many of today's cosmopolitan writers may express dismay with Kant's restrictive view of the role of intervention in world politics.[17] Understandably in view of the world's acute social and political problems, made more alarming now with the ecological crisis, they would like to see a more activist approach that aims at prevention rather than amelioration or an emergency response. However concern for the world's poor and oppressed does not of itself make any policy motivated by such concern right or effective. I would argue that a Kantian approach has to be more measured and based on Kant's reformist outlook on domestic and international politics. The Westphalian system of international politics which prevailed in Kant's day was arguably best described by Hobbes's political philosophy. At the centre of Hobbes's view of politics was the powerful domestic sovereign that held its subjects in awe and its external enemies at bay. Kant was clearly a critic of this system but his aim was not wholly to destroy the Hobbesian model of politics but rather to transform it into an arrangement that kept not only the domestic peace but also the international one. In his political philosophy Kant retains the idea of the social contract, admittedly interpreted more in a Rousseauian way than a Hobbesian one, and the notion of a powerful sovereign that commands the obedience of its subjects. He also accepts the idea of the equality of each sovereign state and so the idea of the inviolability of the borders of each state in relation to each other. With his idea of a federation of free states that would form the proper basis of a reformed international law, Kant is seeking to complement the domestic order brought about by the civil commonwealth of Hobbes's *Leviathan* with a system of cooperation amongst sovereign peoples. Kant does admittedly have the far-off goal of a world republic, but this should never simply displace existing sovereign states: it can always only be an outgrowth of their power. Kant never underrates the value of keeping the Hobbesian world order going; after all the focus of Hobbes's order is not the creation of empires but the maintenance of domestic peace. Hobbes places as much emphasis on getting on with other sovereign states (albeit it in a competitive environment) as getting the better of them in any potential war. The natural laws that Hobbes sees as operating amongst the various sovereign states does bring to the fore rules of mutual accommodation which might be seen as precursors to the picture of a reformed international law which Kant advocates in *Perpetual Peace*.

Humanitarian intervention or human rights intervention would not seem to make a lot of sense from a Hobbesian perspective. Since the primary objective of sovereign power is to maintain internal peace and so provide liberty for its subjects, it would seem that the responsibility for safeguarding the rights of individuals falls primarily on the domestic state itself. Where that fails there appears to be no direct obligation upon either neighbouring states or their subjects to help out. As Hobbes's ethics centres on considerations for self-preservation, it seems unlikely that he would be drawn to an idea of a worldwide human rights community. Grounds for intervention might only arise where the peace and order of other states was threatened and so our own self-preservation was called into question. As it is an obligation for sovereigns to look after the safety of their people, they are empowered to take the actions they see fit to ensure it, and might well intervene to remove any threat. But this could not be contemplated with impunity because sovereigns have always to have an eye to the power of other states and so would have to measure their intervention so as not to cause other unsustainable conflicts.

Kant's ethics generates far greater expectations since it is based on freedom and not merely self-preservation. Like Hobbes, Kant begins from the equality of each human individual but is not prepared to sacrifice autonomy to order. Kant looks for a social and political system that combines both autonomy and order. He is also a universalist. He presents an ethical outlook that can apply to each human individual on the planet. His inclusive outlook highlights in his view that we should seek as virtuous human beings to become part of a 'kingdom (or realm) of ends' seems to imply that he would support the ambitious aims for the world community in implementing human rights.[18] In one respect this is entirely true. From a Kantian perspective the enforcement of human rights in one part of the world should be greeted with enthusiasm in all parts of the world. It seems an easy step from this enthusiasm for the advance of human rights to an advocacy of an activist approach in dealing with abuses wherever they arise. We can see that Fernando Teson adopts this approach. However, this is not necessarily a coherent Kantian approach. Here I will suggest that an adequate Kantian approach is far nearer to the Hobbesian perspective than might be expected.

Fernando Teson's work merits close consideration since he regards himself as an advocate of a Kantian internationalist position. He has developed a strongly interventionist line of argument based on the idea of the defence of human rights.[19] He correctly argues that a Kantian standpoint would require acceptance and respect for the idea of rights inhering in each person in virtue of their humanity, but he extends this idea contentiously to the suggestion that states collectively have the obligation to deal with abuses of human rights wherever they may occur. As Teson understands the Kantian position the obligation to defend human right trumps the right of states to have their sovereignty respected. A duty of 'democratic government is to uphold and promote human rights and democracy globally'. 'The first reason is simply that human rights are universal' and 'accrue to every human being, regardless of history, culture, or geographical circumstance' (p. 56).

'This human rights approach helps us analyze many kinds of international acts. Take the case of insurgency or counterinsurgency.' For Teson 'the Kantian thesis includes a theory of just war; it is the war waged in defence of human rights' (p. 57). Teson extends the Kantian argument for an unequivocal respect for the rights of humanity into a virtual crusade. 'In most wars, international or civil, there is a side that is morally right. That side may be waging a war to defend itself from an aggressor, or to overthrow a tyrannical government (at home or abroad), or justly secede from a parent state.' In his moral enthusiasm Teson throws circumspection to one side and suggests that 'insurgency operations by a democratic state designed to assist just revolutionaries are justified, provided that the help is welcome by the revolutionaries themselves'. Anticipating his own later writings Teson (in 1997) claims that 'for example, a response to a request for assistance by Iraqi revolutionaries aimed at overthrowing Saddam Hussein would be morally justified' (p. 56). These remarks reflect none of Kant's painstaking care to avoid any accusations of illegitimacy in the concern shown by the interested international public in the effects of the revolution in France. He wanted strictly to rule out any suggestion of interference in the internal affairs of the French people even by individuals who approved of the creation of republican institutions. The notion that other people's reforms towards a fully civil constitution could be helped along by the intervention of other states is entirely alien to his approach. For Teson's hyper-interventionism to be identified with Kantian thinking would be a great shame. Both on grounds of prudence and morality Kant's expressed views are in conflict with Teson's position.

Teson follows a line that is fairly similar to the International Commission on the Responsibility to Protect. He argues that state sovereignty does not represent an absolute boundary to potential intervention. He does not see sovereignty solely in the positivist sense of a government being able to command the obedience of the subjects under it. Teson would not recognise as legitimate a Hobbes style of state authority based primarily on awe towards the currently effective power. A legitimate government has to command the assent of its people as expressed by representatives and through representative institutions and 'offices to which political power is attached.' 'These offices are occupied by persons who are democratically chosen by the citizens of the state.' (57) Sovereignty for Teson has both an external and internal dimension of legitimacy. 'Sovereignty is the outward face of legitimacy. A government is legitimate when it genuinely represents the people and generally respects human rights. Such a government must be respected by foreigners, in particular foreign governments' (p. 58). International recognition is the proper counterpart to internal good order. However, 'the illegitimate government' is not similarly 'morally protected'. Where there are continuous abuses of human rights and the government is not properly accountable to the people this moral protection no longer holds. For Teson it is important that illegitimate governments are not accorded the support of international law and the world community at large.

Teson's doctrine of legitimate sovereignty produces a *carte blanche* for intervention for states that enjoy legitimacy. Of course this is only a liberty to intervene in states that do not enjoy a similar legitimate rule. The only legitimate 'aim of the intervenor is the protection of human rights'. In advancing this claim Teson produces an entirely new view of the just war. Just wars are not fought primarily defensively to maintain sovereign integrity or the lives and property of domestic citizens; rather 'the overriding aim of a just war is the protection of human rights' (p. 59). This leads to a similarly idiosyncratic understanding of humanitarian intervention; 'a government's war to defend the citizens of a target state from human rights violations by their own government is called humanitarian intervention' (p. 59). It is good to hear from Teson that dictators do not enjoy this right to intervention because they cannot be assumed to command the loyalty and assent of their own subjects; thus they are neither in a position to judge how acceptable the institutions and practices of the 'target state' might be, nor in a position to order their own subjects to risk their lives in any military hostilities that occur.

Just as in Kant's time we are still now dealing with a world where political power on the global scale is decentralized, in the hands of a variety of sovereign states – some more powerful than others and so extraordinarily difficult to coordinate. Arguably since Kant's time the world political system has moved a little nearer to a kind of centralized coordination, especially with the emergence of the United Nations since the Second World War, and various regional forms of coordination such as the European Union and the Organisation of African States, but the essential feature of an international law made and enforced only by the consent of independent sovereign states remains the same. The fact that the leaders of sovereign states both frame and are the sole legitimate enforcers within their own territories of international law creates considerable difficulties. Kant's response to this difficulty was to retain the feature of sovereign independence whilst calling on free states voluntarily to enter an alliance with each other to maintain peace and further the voluntary enforcement of international law. Teson's suggestion is a good deal more radical. He wants international law to be enforced not only by states themselves within their own territories but also by a self-chosen group of them and, if necessary, by individual states themselves *on a worldwide basis*. Not surprisingly given his radical interventionism, Teson has to call into question the good sense of Kant's fifth Preliminary Article in *Perpetual Peace*, which prohibits forcible interference in the constitutional affairs of other states when it comes to the foreign policies of liberal democratic states. The constitutions of such states should of course not be open to restructuring by others, but they should in certain circumstances be entitled to modify coercively the constitutions of non-liberal states.[20] Kant's alliance is a mutually supportive one where like-minded peoples agree to maintain the adherence to law that exists amongst them and are prepared to help one another if one or more of them is attacked. The alliance has no programme for subduing or coercively changing any other states that do not belong to the alliance. The alliance always remains open to new membership, so stands as an example to all other states, but each non-member is free to join at its own pace and would not be physically compelled to do so. With Teson's model one group of states (or even the one state) is elevated above other states in the international system and given license to judge whether or not states on a worldwide basis are complying with a standard of legitimacy set by the group (or itself). This is a doctrine fraught with difficulties, apparent in the applications that Teson has sought to give to his principles in developing a model of humanitarian intervention,[21] and one which is a good deal different from anything advanced by Kant in his legal and political writings.

Habermas and the dilemma of Kosovo

We shall also consider here arguments that Jürgen Habermas presented for intervention by NATO in the internal Serbia conflict over the province of Kosovo. Habermas in his later writings presents himself as a defender of a Kantian project for international peace[22] so an examination of his arguments on Kosovo will also help highlight this difficult problem. I have argued for a minimal and parsimonious permissibility for intervention based on a close reading of Kant's writings, and I suggest that attempts to broaden Kant's doctrine into a widespread argument for human rights interventionism and the overlooking of the significance of state boundaries cannot be legitimized on the basis of his published views.

In sharp contrast to Fernando Teson the German philosopher Jürgen Habermas is an unenthusiastic advocate of interference in the internal affairs of other states to bring about change. Habermas's reluctance fits in well with his own background in the Frankfurt school and his recent avowal of a Kantian view of world politics. Unlike Teson, Habermas has thoroughly distanced himself from the 2003 invasion of Iraq and has published several highly polemical essays condemning the Bush administration, both for straying away from the best traditions of United States foreign policy and for riding roughshod over the rights of the Iraqi people. However Habermas departed from his general veto on supporting armed intervention in the internal constitutional affairs of other states when he gave qualified support to the NATO bombing campaign against Serbia as a means of resolving the problems brought about by the mass expulsion by Milosevic's regime of the ethnic Albanians from Kosovo. What led Habermas to this conclusion, and how does he seek to make it compatible with the wider Kantian outlook on world politics he holds? Is the path he recommends a sensible one that all Kantians should embrace?

Habermas dealt with the Kosovo question in a very moving essay which first appeared in *Die Zeit* 29 April, 1999. It was translated into English with the title 'Bestiality and Humanity: A War on the Border between Legality and Morality'. In the essay it is clear he is not advocating armed intervention in Kosovo as his own policy; nor is he putting forward a general case for an activist pursuit of human rights in this manner globally. His support for intervention on behalf of the ethnic

Albanians goes no further than a qualified endorsement of an aspect of the foreign policy put forward by the Red–Green coalition German government of the day. He describes this aspect as legal pacifism which 'wants to fence in the spectre of war between sovereign states, but also strives to supersede it by means of a thoroughly legalized cosmopolitan order'.[23] As Habermas sees it, Foreign Minister Fischer and Defence Minister Scharping are seeking the Kantian ideal of 'domesticating the existing state of nature between countries by means of human rights'. This is a very ambitious aim since it would involve 'the transformation of international law into a law of global citizens'.[24] But in language reminiscent of Teson, Habermas describes this new system of law as one that is 'able to penetrate the sovereignty of states' and takes as a primary example of its effect 'the personal liability of functionaries for crimes committed by them as part of their political and military service'.[25] Here Habermas has in mind examples such as the attempted prosecution of Pinochet in British courts for crimes of torture and murder committed whilst he was the leader of the Chilean military junta in the 1970s and 1980s. The loss of immunity under international law for even de facto bearers of sovereign power when committing crimes against humanity is a symptom, for Habermas, of the gradual embedding of a cosmopolitan justice. Thus, the Kosovo enterprise gains Habermas's guarded support as part of an attempt to establish a global civil society. He recognises the contingency of the situation and its risky and presumptive dimensions. The member states of NATO were acting in an audacious way: 'When they authorize themselves to act militarily, even nineteen indisputably democratic states remain partisan. They are making use of interpretative and decision-making powers to which only independent institutions would be entitled only if things were properly in order today; to that extent their actions are paternalistic.'[26] Habermas accepts that his stance implicates him in the contradictions of power politics and is intensely aware that the perspective of legal pacifism is not shared by all the states who are members of NATO. Whereas 'most of the EU governments see the politics of human rights as a project committed to the systematic legalization of international relations', one which is 'already altering the parameters of power politics 'the USA conceives the global enforcement of human rights as the national mission of a world power which pursues this goal according to the premises of power politics.'[27]

Given the multiplicity of factors involved in the Kosovo intervention, and the divergent motivations of the various states leaders and diplomats involved, it is perhaps surprising that Habermas felt it necessary to take sides. An astute commentator on Habermas's thinking has sought to show that it is difficult to find an endorsement for Habermas's interventionist approach in Kant's writings.[28] In her study of the Kosovo war within the context of Kant's *Perpetual Peace*, Sabine Jaberg argues persuasively that for Kant peace can only be brought about through observation and respect for law.[29] And even though law in some circumstances only takes on a 'rudimentary' form, Jaberg thinks it is part of the Kantian outlook that one even then has to respect and observe it. As Jaberg sees it, this applies at both the internal and external state levels. So if a country is going through a process of upheaval, or it is still in the process of creating an effective system of law, where there is evidence of stabilization towards the rule of law then we are bound to respect the authorities in charge. It is not clear from Kant's writings what might be conclusive evidence of a process of stabilization towards the rule of law, but it appears from Kant's views on resistance (which is ruled out even where the subjects are badly abused) that the threshold is not set very high. At an international level Kant never suggests that the problems about the enforceability of law amongst states provide a justification for not observing it. No matter how primitive the system of international law may appear, Kant wants to work with it and enhance its applicability and acceptability. For Jaberg a close reading of Kant's texts would indicate an extremely circumspect approach to the Kosovo crisis. There are many things to be said in support for Jaberg's view. At the international level the case for overlooking the requirement to gain United Nations Security Council support to which signatories of the United Nations' Charter were legally bound was extraordinarily thin, and at the internal Yugoslav level the case of total breakdown and the emergence of anarchy was yet to be fully established. As Habermas acknowledges there was a strong element of presumption and anticipation in the whole NATO enterprise.[30] It was presuming that NATO could replace the United Nations as the proper international authority and it was anticipating the worldwide civil society that many of the participants in the NATO countries were hoping to bring into being. Jaberg's stark conclusion appears particularly apt. 'Kant's thinking on freedom on the whole shows itself to be extremely unwieldy vis-à-vis attempts to legitimize intervention of all kinds. This applies also in relation to the NATO Kosovo War. Under today's stipulations of international law a consistent application of the essay on peace would indeed have called for non-intervention.'[31] Jaberg feels that those who do not see this, and seek a Kantian authority to intervene, are engaging not in a plausible interpretation of Kant's essay on peace but rather an eclectic acquaintanceship with the work 'contrary to the intention of the author'. Jaberg's conclusion on Habermas is that he is attempting a 'fundamental reformulation' of the Kantian notion of cosmopolitan law. In her view Habermas' reformulation is so far from the original that it could be accurately described as a 'new creation'.[32]

This is perhaps too harsh a conclusion since Habermas is only too well aware of the riskiness of the Kosovo enterprise and that it draws those of a Kantian disposition into the contradictions of power politics. But Jaberg's essay does draw attention to what precisely is at stake. Any appreciation of Kant's attitude to intervention has to take into account the cornerstones of Kant's international outlook. Habermas shows tolerance towards NATO intervention in Kosovo on the grounds that he is drawn to a notion of cosmopolitan right which seeks to transcend the sovereign state. But as Jaberg points out, Kant does not regard cosmopolitan right as trumping law amongst nations. Cosmopolitan law for Kant builds on international law. Thus Kant has no ambition thoroughly to break the barriers established by traditional international law; rather his project is one of transforming international law whilst maintaining it. Jaberg fears that Habermas tends towards the 'upgrading of cosmopolitan law' at the same time 'marginalizing international law'. As a result she believes Habermas neglects the Kantian 'analogy between the state and a moral person' which should be the bedrock of responsible international relations. As Jaberg sees it, the spirit of Kant's essay on peace runs wholly contrary to the idea of an 'interventionism promoted by military means'.[33] Rightly she is not quite sure whether Habermas' line on Kosovo amounts to the 'tolerance' or 'legitimization' of such means, but she does come to the telling conclusion that if generalized such a tolerance would disregard the 'idea of the original contract as the final source of legitimate rule'[34] that is a hallmark of Kant's political philosophy as a whole. Kant sees international cooperation as moving out from the domestic social contract which contains within it a worldwide dimension. A presumption of the social contract that establishes the republican ideal domestically is that all such legally founded states will seek to participate in a gradually expanding peaceful federation without which the domestic contract is never finally secure. Domestic popular sovereignty of a republican form is a key staging post in the gradual creation of a worldwide civil society brought together through a pacific federation. Where it exists, internal political sovereignty cannot be simply cast aside at the behest of another state or an alliance of other states, however well-meaning. The legitimacy of the pacific federation depends on safeguarding and forwarding republican popular sovereignty within states, so at no point can internal sovereignty be treated lightly. Arguably Habermas is fully aware of this, but does not sufficiently guard against being interpreted differently.

Kant shows, for example, little enthusiasm for the idea of 'puncturing' state sovereignty in the manner canvassed by Teson and Habermas. At best Kant's approach favours a policy of pooling state sovereignty through federation on an entirely (and always reversible) basis, and most generally Kant is drawn very strongly to the benefits of popular sovereignty within states. So he would regard external interference as undermining the key representative status of modern states. Where there is an opening for intervention in Kant's doctrine – and here this might apply to Kosovo – is where (as noted in Preliminary Article 5) internal sovereignty breaks down under the strain of civil war. Where that condition of anarchy is reached then, as Kant understands it, states are doing no wrong in intervening to bring a return to order. For Habermas the Kosovo emergency represented 'the terrorist misappropriation of state power' which transformed a 'classical civil war into mass murder'. He finds that strict adherence to the classical doctrine of the inviolability of state sovereignty would force 'us to accept the maxim that victims are to be left at the mercy of thugs'.[35]

This raises the factual problem of how far down the road of civil war had the former Yugoslavia gone when the Kosovo crisis occurred? Habermas clearly thought the situation in 1999 was dire. Not all commentators would agree and Habermas himself acknowledges that not all European states were of the view that intervention was necessary: in particular 'in heavily armed nuclear Russia, the solidarity of wide circles of the population with their "fellow Slav comrades" [*Brüdervolk*] is putting pressure on the government'.[36] Thus whether or not the armed intervention of NATO was compatible with the requirements of Preliminary Article 5 of *Perpetual Peace* – that effective sovereign power had disappeared and civil war reigned – is open to dispute. Arguably within the province of Kosovo civil war, anarchy had erupted, but the ex-Yugoslavia authorities would argue that in the ex-Yugoslavia as a whole civil war was far from occurring.

Habermas is fully aware of the ethical hornet's nest he is stirring and is by no means sure that any general lessons can be drawn from the Kosovo case. As he acknowledges 'the war in Kosovo touches on a fundamental question widely disputed in both political science and philosophy. The constitutional state has realized the enormous civilizational achievement of taming political power by legal means on the basis of recognizing the sovereignty of the subjects of international law'. Thus, Habermas by no means undervalues the contribution of the

Westphalian system – delineated by Hobbes and targeted for reform by Kant – however, Habermas is drawn to the arguments which would lead to its immediate supersession by a transnational political order with perhaps the United Nations as its head.[37] He accepts therefore that pressing in this way for 'a cosmopolitan political legal order places the independence of the nation-state in question'. Here there is 'a realist thorn in the flesh of the politics of human rights' and he asks rhetorically 'does the universalism of the Enlightenment collide here with the obstinacy of political power ineradicably inscribed in the drive for the collective self-assertion of a particular community?'[38] Clearly the attempt to bring the objectives of achieving national self-determination and an effective world-wide legal order into harmony with one another presents us with an intractable problem. Kant wanted to resolve the problem upwards into the international plane from the representative legislative union of different peoples under a social contract; however in his discussion of the Kosovo crisis, Habermas is by his own admission, driven to a top down solution brought about through a coalition of democratic states. It is not surprising that his conclusion is highly ambivalent: 'It is one thing if the USA – however remarkable the political tradition at the root of its action may be – plays the role of hegemon guaranteeing the instrumentation of human rights. It is something else if we try to understand the precarious transition from classical power politics to a global civil society as a learning process with which all of us together are going to have to come to terms, across the trenches [*Graeben*][39] of an ongoing conflict in which weapons are being used. This broadening of perspectives also admonishes us to take greater caution. NATO's self-authorization should not be allowed to become the general rule.'[40] This conclusion suggests he is neither fully convinced of the appropriateness of the intervention in Kosovo at the time nor is he at all convinced that it should represent a precedent for world community as a whole. This is abundantly clear in Habermas's highly critical approach to the second 2003 war in Iraq; unlike Scruton, Habermas finds no Kantian arguments for intervention, and instead regards the American led invasion as one of its gravest foreign policy mistakes. Instead of seeing virtue in the Americans taking a risk by seeking to eliminate a rogue regime in Iraq, Habermas insists that 'an illegal war remains a violation of international law, even if it leads to normatively desired outcomes'.[41] Habermas's assessment of the Kosovo War represents an important exception then to his generally sceptical attitude towards military intervention.[42] I conclude that this general scepticism is the better position to adopt, and that although the risk taken in intervening in Kosovo may possibly have paid off in the particular instance, the wider risk taken in blurring the boundaries of justifiable intervention seems to me to have had undesirable consequences.

A defensible Kantian view: a non-activist, supportive 'interventionism'

The position that would gain the greatest support from Kant's writings would, I believe, neither be hyper-interventionist nor indifferent towards the fate of citizens of other states. Given Kant's universalist moral outlook, he takes the view that the life of one individual on the planet is equal in ethical value to the life of any other individual on the planet. Clearly Kant's political philosophy provides support for a doctrine of universal human rights. But it does not provide support for the enforcement of these rights by an unspecified international community. Governments within states should do it for their subjects. If they fail to do so, subjects should in the first instance lodge complaints with their own governments. These complaints may or may not be heard and may or may not be acted upon. But this is the primary line of action, where a central authority of some kind remains in place. Of course, we should not knowingly sacrifice the well-being of others to enhance our own. This would be to treat others simply as means and not also as ends. But this concern for the fate of others, our equal right to liberty and our moral equality does not mean that the citizens of one state have a legal liability to redress wrongs that the members of other states might suffer at the hands of their governments. We indeed have a moral responsibility to be concerned about how citizens in other states are treated by their governments, but this responsibility should neither disable our freedom nor should it necessarily lead to the active involvement of our government in attempting to redress or punish wrongs in other states. Kant sees the state on the home territory as the main vehicle for redressing such wrongs, and if it fails to do so the main responsibility for correcting the situation lies with the government of that state and its subjects. Of course encouragement can be given by other governments and the citizens of other states in helping this process occur, but this should not involve active interference in the constitution of the offending state. So long as there is a sovereign power within that state and some constitutional procedures for dealing with violations of human rights, improvements should be sought exclusively in that way.

Just as individual citizens within states should be given a sphere of freedom in which to exercise their choices unhindered by others, independent states should be allowed to follow their own choices, make mistakes and correct them in their own ways. As Kant puts it in *Perpetual Peace*, a state 'is a society of human beings that no one other than itself can command or dispose of.' Like the trunk of a tree it has 'its own roots' (8: 344/318) and cannot be manipulated externally as though it were a belonging or piece of property open to anyone's use. What can justify interference even though things might be going badly wrong within a state? 'Perhaps the scandal that one state gives to the subjects of another state?' We might naturally be offended by the radical changes and abuses that are occurring in another state. We might for example find offensive large and apparently unfair redistributions of property within another state. However, so long as the situation is not critical Kant thinks we should tolerate such change and upheaval. Each state has a legitimate right to undergo such experiences free from interference. If wrongs occur this can 'much rather serve as a warning' to the subjects of other states 'by the example of the great troubles a people has brought upon itself by its lawlessness; and, in general, the bad example that one free person gives another (as *scandalum acceptum*) is no wrong to it' (8: 346/319). The scandal that occurs through the wrongs perpetrated in other states is passive and it may also be exaggerated through the ignorance and misinterpretation of others. In general we should take the same approach to such errors as we would do towards the bad behaviour of our fellow subjects: so long as it is not harming us we should permit them to experiment freely.

But this tolerance should not be interpreted as indifference. Just as at the individual level we should wish others success in their personal endeavours (or at least wish they do not lose from their experiences), so we should wish that the inhabitants of other states enjoy happiness in what the path they choose to follow. Equally it is important to bear in mind that Kant rules out active interference in the constitutions of other countries only so long as sovereign power is maintained and constitutional structures remain in place. As he put it in *Perpetual Peace*: 'It would be a different matter if a state, through internal discord, should be split into two parts, each putting itself forward as a separate state and laying claim to the whole; in that case a foreign power could not be charged with interfering in the constitution of another state if it gave assistance to one of them (for this is anarchy)' (9: 346/319). Thus where legal order entirely breaks down and there is no longer scope for internal constitutional change outside powers are permitted to intervene, but never to conquer or acquire that state but only to hasten its return to legal order. In all other circumstances 'interference of foreign powers would be a violation of the right of a people dependent upon no other and only struggling with its internal illness; thus it would itself be a scandal given and would make the autonomy of all states insecure' (8: 346/320). In contrast to the *passive* scandal caused by the sickness being endured by an independent state in going through a period of social and political turmoil, the coercive interference of other states in the constitution of an independent state would be an *active* scandal, and so much more greatly to be deplored and regretted.

The most powerful evidence that Kant cares greatly about the fates of individuals elsewhere in the world, and more particularly individuals in less fortunate states, is to be found in the Third Definitive Article of *Perpetual Peace*, which presents his complex principle of hospitality. Here Kant claims that 'originally no one had more right than another to be on a place on earth' and the 'right to present oneself for society belongs to all human beings by virtue of the right of possession in common of the earth's surface on which, as a sphere, they cannot disperse infinitely but must finally put up with one another' (8: 358/329). In visiting other territories we should expect no more than that we should not be treated with hostility. All other inhabitants of the earth are our equals and we should not expect any exceptional treatment when we visit them. There are no superiors and inferiors when it comes to the human inhabitation of the planet: exploitation, colonialism and imperialism are wholly ruled out. Indeed 'the (narrower or wider) community of nations of the earth has now gone so far that a violation of right on one place of the earth is felt in all'. However, that a violation of right in one place is registered amongst people throughout the world does not mean that there is a legal obligation upon the citizens of other states to intervene (with force, if necessary) to correct the violation. What is required or what is to be applauded is that the citizens of other states demonstrate a sympathetic concern for the fate of the people involved. This is what Kant found so laudatory in the response of outside observers of France's revolution in his time. This 'spectator' mind-set, 'which reveals itself publicly in the face of this show of large-scale transformations and which makes known such a universal and yet unselfish sympathy with the players on the one side against that on the other, even at the risk that this partiality could become detrimental to them'(7: 85/Kl 155). A virtuous response to the troubles of another people is one that looks for and encourages progress in its ability to govern itself properly. From the standpoint of right it is the duty of the subjects of other states to see 'that a people must not be hindered by other powers in giving itself a civil constitution that it regards as good' (7: 85/Kleingeld 155).

This duty not to intervene when a state is trying to progress should not though be transformed into a positive duty to intervene where a state fails to progress – or there is a clear setback to the development of republican institutions. The balance of judgment should always fall in favour of a state sorting out its own difficulties and not in favour of outside powers acting on the state's behalf. Tragedies may occur, but it is better that these tragedies should be self-inflicted rather than being the consequence of misplaced (however well-intentioned) outside interference.

If we look at the example in Preliminary Article 5 of *Perpetual Peace* where Kant thinks intervention is permissible ('where a state is split into two parts through internal discord'(8: 346/319)) we can say this:

First, the breakdown of order has to have reached such a point where there is a condition of civil war and there is no clear sovereign power. Until the conflict has reached this decisive point no intervention is permitted.

Secondly, intervention has to be at the behest of one of the warring parties. There can be no complaint if a foreign power lends its support to one of the parties at the party's request.

Thirdly, the support offered by the outside power should be in accord with the development of international right. The authorisation that Kant gives to intervene has to be seen in the context of his theory of right as a whole. The authorization is not given to all powers to get themselves involved in any way they see fit. To take one historical example: Kant's interventionist principle could not be deployed to underwrite the support offered to Franco by Fascist Italy and Germany in the 1930s. From Kant's second definitive article in *Perpetual Peace* we can see it is an obligation on all countries to join a peaceful federation of states whose aim is not to acquire 'any power of state' but only to preserve and secure 'the freedom of a state itself and other states in league with it' (8: 356/327). A state that is a member of this federation could not support a party to the civil war that was likely to have aggressive intentions towards other states and was not prepared to accord its own subjects freedom. Thus any intervening state would have an obligation to support only the party that would bring the disputed territory into the peaceful federation. Interference whose objective was to add to the influence and power of the intervening power by making the aided party dependent upon it would be contrary to the idea of the peaceful federation. Such an intervening state would not be seeking the freedom of the disputed territory but its subordination.

Fourthly, to act in accord with right the intervening state should have regard not just for its own interests but also for the interests of the peaceful federation of which it is part. In the *Metaphysics of Morals* where Kant speaks of the make-up of this federation he describes it as a 'permanent congress of states' 'which each neighbouring state is at liberty to join' (6: 350/488). He takes as a loose example of this kind of federation 'the assembly of the States General at the Hague' of the early eighteenth century. A feature of this arrangement of which Kant approved was that states involved in disputes 'lodged their complaints with the States General' and that members saw 'the whole of Europe as a single confederated state which they accepted as arbiter' (6: 350/488). Although the arrangement later broke up, it is none the less evident that it established for Kant the correct principle that any proposed intervention in the affairs of another state had to be seen from the perspective of all other member states of the federation. No state could unilaterally judge the legitimacy of its own cause. In intervening in a troubled state with no central sovereign power a state should act in accord with the interests of the peaceful federation it should always seek to maintain. Thus another clear principle for permitted intervention must be the agreement of the law abiding peaceful international community.

If we sum up there is one clear negative condition and two positive conditions permitting intervention. The one clear negative condition is the decisive emergence of a civil war situation. The first positive condition is authorisation from the peaceful federation of states; and the second positive condition is that the intervention should take place in conformity with right, putting the freedom of the disputed state at its forefront. This second positive condition implies that subjects of the state in disarray have requested such support. Roger Scruton's case for intervention in Iraq is ruled out on all three grounds: he sees no need to wait for the emergence of civil war; he believes that one powerful state can act on the behalf of others; and he believes the intervention can take place contrary to existing international law. Teson's argument for intervention where the state clearly fails to uphold the human rights of its subjects is equally flawed where it does not see the need to establish unequivocally in the first place that a state is divided by civil war and no sovereign power exists. Secondly it is flawed because he believes individual states that are legitimate (and so democratic) can intervene without seeking the support of the wider world. Thirdly, it is flawed because although Teson bases his case for intervention on a theory of human rights and a quasi-Kantian theory of international law, there is overwhelming evidence he does not accept a view of international law that reaches out from state sovereignty. Teson's theory intends to subvert the historically inherited system of state sovereignty rather than work with it to transform it. Finally Habermas's account – though it recognises the need for all three of Kant's tests to be met: a clear breakdown of sovereign authority; support of the peaceful international federation; and that the actions should accord with right – falls down because it seeks to anticipate too hastily arriving at this condition of right. Habermas sanctioned the NATO intervention in Kosovo as an anticipation of a future worldwide civil society where international and cosmopolitan law would be upheld in a peremptory way. Thus although he treats the Kosovo intervention as an exceptional case, wishes to uphold peaceful international federation and expresses support for Kantian international right, he is too impatient in wanting to transcend national sovereignty and international law as they stand. As Sabine Jaberg shows, a more authentically Kantian approach requires more patience with the 'collective self-assertion of a particular community'.[43] 'The realist thorn in the flesh of the politics of human rights' is not that easily removed. As the historical guarantors of the actual rights that individuals have to this point enjoyed, nation states can only gradually be required to pool their power and resources to preserve the peace and maintain rights everywhere. The extent and efficacy of the enforcement of human rights universally cannot be achieved at the expense of undermining the nation-state; it can only be achieved through the voluntary cooperation of such states.

Thus, a Kantian attitude to intervention, and in particular military intervention, has to be an extremely cautious one. Even if the above three conditions are fulfilled there is no indication that states are obligated by law to intervene. Whether states want to risk the lives of their own citizens to help bring a settled order to troubled territories is a matter that the representatives and citizens of other states have to resolve for themselves.

The drawback with yielding too readily to the path of humanitarian military intervention from a Kantian perspective is that it opens up the possibility of unrestricted war on the part of self-appointed guardians of the international community against a recalcitrant minority of delinquent or purportedly delinquent states.[44] Humanitarian military intervention of this kind is contrary to the Kantian critique of just war theory advanced here in that it deploys war ('the greatest of all evils') to rid the world of conditions that are often (admittedly) underlying causes of war. There is too much missionary zeal about the cosmopolitan interventionist positions represented by Scruton and Teson. Any discussion of military intervention from a Kantian perspective has to acknowledge that war is always wrong, and at the very best it might be necessary to establish the conditions for the emergence of law, but it is never right in itself.[45] Cosmopolitan military intervention, as espoused by Teson, Scruton and to a lesser extent by Habermas, cannot seriously be on the agenda from the perspective that we are developing here because it is based on the premises that war can directly be an agent for improvement in the world. Minimization and the eventual eradication of war, and not the regretful endorsement of it, are what are needed.

Conclusion

In looking at humanitarian intervention in this chapter, and especially the issue of military humanitarian intervention, I have come to the conclusion that it is not convincing from a Kantian perspective to try to link just war theory with its ethics and practice. The disquiet Kant displays in providing grounds for war in the context of international law in general is shown to be entirely vindicated in looking at the attempted deployment of just war theory in the area of humanitarian intervention. A more appropriate framework for determining a Kantian approach to humanitarian intervention can be found in the distinction Kant draws between legal and moral obligation and the fuller development of an applied account of cosmopolitan law. The distinction between moral law and juridical law allows us to decide whether or not there are, on the one hand, enforceable duties of humanitarian intervention or, on the other hand, whether or not there are imperfect duties of this kind which allow latitude in determining how, when and where they might be carried out.

The duties of cosmopolitan law are ones we must peremptorily carry out. These are duties for individual persons and for the moral person of the state. It is their legal obligation not to treat foreign nationals with hostility when they are visitors in our territory. Equally when we are visitors elsewhere, we accept that the hospitality we are shown there should be confined to our not being treated as enemies or wrongdoers (until we have committed some wrong). We are not legally entitled to a more generous right to be treated as guests, and clearly we are not in a position to demand that the state we are visiting undertake changes in its legal and political arrangements. At best we are entitled freely to voice our opinion about such arrangements: to seek to reform them ourselves would take us well beyond the scope of a visitor's right. Thus there is no direct legal duty for states or their citizens to offer special help when subjects of other states run into severe difficulties with their own rulers. This legal disinterestedness towards the subjects of other states is an element of outward freedom. Allowing a free hand for intervention would threaten the independence of other states and their subjects. The subjects and the government of one state are not in a position to command how their counterparts in other states should organise their common lives. Both international and cosmopolitan law assume that peoples create their own laws which their representatives execute on their behalf. No people can forcibly legislate for another. International law deals with the relations amongst states as they necessarily impinge on one another and are regulated by treaties and customs amongst independently legislating peoples.

Alongside our legal obligations there are of course personal, moral obligations that are experienced and should be accepted by all individuals to show concern towards our fellow human beings wherever they might be. From a Kantian perspective we have a duty towards mankind in general to seek its happiness (6: 393/524). Ignoring the sufferings of others in neighbouring or distant lands would be contrary to this duty. But as seeking the happiness of others is an imperfect duty we can seek to discharge it in ways we individually (or collectively as a people) determine. At an individual level we can make representations to our government that it should seek to offer aid to victims. We can also try to persuade our fellow citizens and government that in certain extreme circumstances military aid might be necessary. But our government and fellow citizens are not under a direct legal obligation to provide this aid. Other citizens and members of the government have to deliberate for themselves and be convinced by our arguments before voluntarily accepting an obligation to act.

Thus humanitarian intervention cannot be commanded of other individuals and our state (or of other states and their citizens). Humanitarian intervention has always to be a matter of persuasion and not compulsion. The problem with the deployment of just war theory by humanitarian interventionists is that it attempts to transform voluntarily undertaken obligations into hard and fast rules of international law, and so to legal obligations for all states. To be sure, governments have an obligation to protect the subjects of their own states, but they only have an indirect obligation to protect the subjects of other states. Put quite simply, this means they should do nothing that deliberately seeks to harm the subjects of other states. Once we establish the obligation that one actively is not to cause harm, it becomes clear the appropriate partner for a theory of humanitarian intervention is a theory of just peace. The proper question to pose: is how can we help those suffering in other countries from human rights abuses in a way that advances world peace? Where our own freedoms and rights are not endangered the duties of humanitarian intervention are ethical only and not legal. 'Ethical duties involve a constraint for which only internal law giving is possible, whereas duties of right involve a constraint for which external law giving is also possible' (6: 394/595). Seeking to bring humanitarian intervention under just war theory – and so a Grotian version of international law – is wrong and may undermine international law altogether.

The duty to assist others outside our state whose human rights are being denied by their governments is an imperfect duty. This does not mean that such infractions of human rights can be treated lightly. 'A wide duty is not to be taken as permission to make exceptions to the maxim of actions but only as permission to limit one maxim of duty by another (e.g. love of one's neighbour in general by love of one's parent)' (6:390/521). Thus we have always to abide by the maxim of helping others in distress (including those suffering abuses in other states) but we may legitimately constrain the help we offer in order to carry out similar obligations in relation to our own fellow citizens. It is important to bear in mind that the fulfilment of an 'imperfect duty is a merit or +a' (as Kant puts it mathematically), 'but failure to fulfil them is not in itself culpability = –a' but 'rather mere deficiency in moral worth = 0' (6: 390/521). So to be doing wrong by failing to carry out an imperfect duty you would have to have adopted it as a maxim not to comply with imperfect duties in general. Thus the people of Russia would have done nothing wrong had they refused to aid the persecuted Albanian majority of Kosovo in the late 1990s (since there is evidence that they have helped others around the globe): they would simply have shown a deficiency of moral worth.

Carla Bagnoli takes a contrary view. She thinks that from the Kantian perspective that humanitarian intervention is a perfect duty. In her view where abuses of human rights take place 'there is a duty to intervene independently of considerations of proximity, friendship, capability, expertise or effectiveness'.[46] She claims she is making 'a moral case for the duty of armed intervention to protect fundamental human rights' and 'this should not be confused with a legal case'.[47] None the less her line of argument has legal implications. Because she identifies perfect duties with external enforceable duties, she speaks of humanitarian intervention as a juridical duty. Where she equivocates is in determining on whose shoulders the duty falls. Although the duty arises in reflecting upon the obligations of each individual human being she is not convinced that it is up to the individual to seek to enforce it. She also has grave doubts about states enforcing the duty. 'Because the perfect duty falls on the moral community as such, and not on specific states, an international agency would best represent such community.'[48] Thus Bagnoli's understanding of the perfect duty of humanitarian intervention leads to recommendations for institutional changes in the international order to bring about a supranational authority that can carry out the duty. I would argue that this is not wholly the direction in which Kant's views take us. I suggest that Kant's understanding of the harm caused by the abuse of human rights wherever they occur leads him not to abandon states' responsibility to rectify the wrong, and where the state fails to defend human rights the first course should always to be to encourage them to improve so that matters do not deteriorate.

Bagnoli correctly suggests that we are from a Kantian perspective morally required to be concerned about abuses of human rights in all parts of the globe, but it is not correct to assume that this concern has always to transform into a duty to act. Where the abuses occur within the land of which we are subjects, the offences should immediately be brought to an end and those responsible should be punished. Each subject has a duty to support the action and to provide help to the authorities in implementing law. Equally we should all voice concern about a violation of human rights as soon as we are aware of it – this we should similarly do with violations that occur in other states and territories. But in the second instance neither can we nor our government be expected directly to do anything to halt the offences and punish the offenders. We have a perfect duty not to hinder the implementation of law throughout the world, but it does not follow from this that we and our fellow citizens always have to play a part in carrying it out. The nature of republican law enforcement is that others have generally to carry it out on our behalf. Dealing with abuses of human rights is first and foremost the responsibility of the state government concerned. Of course the calls for humanitarian intervention generally arise where state authorities have failed to implement their legal duties and often are themselves implicated in abuses. Faced with a corrupt government of this kind, placing primary responsibility on state authorities to enforce human rights appears an empty gesture. But this is where the perfect duty to act lies, and not with the international community. Releasing the corrupt government from its 'strict moral duty to intervene'[49] implies that the government has lost all capacity to act as a sovereign under international law. It may indeed be true that this situation has already been reached. However, faced with the complete collapse of a state the question of intervention no longer arises.

It is doubtful however that Kant would draw the conclusion that Bagnoli indicates that 'there is no obligation to respect the integrity of a state that fails as a state' and that there is a moral 'obligation to obstruct the obstruction to freedom'.[50] First, the conclusion is too sweeping. At what point can one give up on a regime that is purporting to sustain a state? It is very rarely the case that regimes reach a point of no return. Secondly, in these dire circumstances is it true that all governments and subjects are legally or morally bound to participate in the reconstruction of a 'failed state'. Kant emphasizes that the actual implementation of rights is contingent upon the founding of a civil society[51] and as there is as yet no worldwide civil society, we have to look to individual civil societies to maintain legal order and they have first to look to themselves. The priority for an existing civil society is, in a Hobbesian manner, to maintain law and order within its own boundaries. This it cannot do on its own even if it is very large. So there has to be an assumption that there are further civil societies that allow the one society to persist. But this mutual cooperation cannot be enforced from above. It has to be brought about by agreement amongst states. They agree to rely on each other to maintain order within their respective borders. They cannot at the same time agree to accept intervention if their internal order breaks down. At the present stage of development each society has to be given the freedom to mend its own deficiencies. Moving to a perfect duty of humanitarian intervention skips a great number of stages in the development of a global order, and might indeed not be the best way of bringing about the goal of republican, legal and peaceful world that is sought.

This is how Kant puts it:

> *Nun ist hierwider kein anderes Mittel, als ein auf öffentliche mit Macht begleitete Gesetze, denen sich jeder Staat unterwerfen müßte, gegründetes Völkerrecht (nach der Analogie eines bürgerlichen oder Staatsrechts einzelner Menschen) möglich; - denn ein daurender allgemeiner Friede durch die so genannte Balance der Mächte in Europa ist, wie Swifts haus, welches von einem Baumeister so vollkommen nach allen Gesetzen des Gleichgewichts erbauet war, daß, als sich ein Sperling drauf setzte, es sofort einfiel, ein bloßes Hirngespinst.*
>
> (8: 313)

7
The Hegelian Premises of Contemporary Just War Theory and Their Kantian Critique

Introduction

In this chapter we shall take a close look at the implications of Kant's novel, critical approach to war for contemporary just war theory. We have already had many occasions to refer to this just war literature in indicating the controversies and disputes brought about by Kant's philosophy of peace and its interpretation in recent decades. Now we have an opportunity to assess not simply where Kant's ideas lie in relation to today's just war theory, but how Kant – and more broadly how a Kantian – might respond to the dilemmas posed by the growing genre of just war theory. Clearly in a chapter of this kind the treatment of just war theory cannot be comprehensive. We shall aim at analysing a small number of contributors to the genre who are, we believe, representative of the genre as a whole.

According to one specialist in the field, interest in the subject of just war theory amongst academics has undergone a revival in the last forty years or so.[1] This increased interest has been especially apparent since the end of the Cold War and has of course been most evident in the responses to the first and second Gulf Wars. Much of the debate about the justice of intervention by western powers in Iraq in 2003 has centred on the theory. As we have seen, Immanuel Kant has been brought into this debate. Another trend that has been noted by Cian O'Driscoll is towards a widening of the application of the theory, particularly in its *jus ad bellum* aspects – which are the rules that apply to the appropriate declaration of war. Previously, he suggests the theory was couched as a restraint upon war; however, it has increasingly been deployed in the opposite direction – to engage in wars that might otherwise not have been contemplated. 'The end of the cold war brought about by the collapse of the Soviet Union, signalled a sea change in the conduct of world politics. One of the more significant changes to take place was the "loosening" of the just war tradition, which has occurred in the wake of the Soviet Union's disintegration. This loosening amounts to a more favourable disposition toward interventionist politics and represents a reversal of the narrowing and tightening of the *jus ad bellum* that took place over the previous two hundred years.'[2] Such generalizations are of course somewhat hazardous – since O'Driscoll's contention might be countered by the assertion that in practice states seemed not to have found difficulty in discovering grounds for declaring war in the twentieth century, regardless of the apparent tightening of the just war criteria. However there is no doubting that the idea of just war has been cited more regularly by politicians and scholars in the last two decades, and there has been a degree of widening of the ambit of the debate.[3]

I may have taken great liberties in describing contemporary just war theory as Hegelian, since it is not entirely clear from Hegel's writings on international law that he himself embraces just war theory. Hegel is a liberal-conservative figure in the history of political philosophy who defended the European state and its structures as it was found in Europe in his day (1770–1831). He favoured a reforming constitutional monarchy, but he counselled that subjects try to discover the rationality of whatever political system they found themselves in.[4] Indeed he has very little that is positive to say about the tradition of international law from Grotius onwards that help bring the theory into existence. But I think I can justify and explain this paradox. Hegel's brief account of international law in the *Philosophy of Right* suggests that he finds war an acceptable aspect of the international political system of his day but he does not seem to indicate that in any such conflict one side necessarily has a stronger ethical case than any other. As Hegel puts it 'there is no praetor to adjudicate between states, but at most arbitrators and mediators, and even the presence of these will be contingent, i.e. determined by particular wills.'[5] (333/ p. 368) Indeed, it is only after a war that the philosophical analyst can determine in what sense justice was implicated. This arises of course from Hegel's dynamic view of history which involves the gradual unfolding of spirit or *Geist* in a way that the mere human spectator cannot wholly predict what the genuinely progressive outcome may be. However, after the event the role of the philosopher is to discover what is actual in the present situation and so show what is rational: 'it is not just the *power* of spirit which passes judgement in world history – i.e. it is not the abstract and irrational necessity of blind fate. On the contrary, since spirit in and for itself is *reason*, and since the being-for-itself of reason in spirit is knowledge, world history is the necessary development, from the *concept* of freedom of spirit alone, of the *moments* of reason and hence of spirit self-consciousness and freedom. It is the exposition and the *actualization of the universal spirit*.' (342/ p. 372)

Arguably this philosophical history and legal-political analysis does not amount to a fully-fledged just war theory, but important elements are evident in Hegel's account which are shared and often developed by today's just war theorists. One of the most apparent elements is the assumption of the legitimacy of war as a means of resolving disputes in the current international framework. Hegel's presumption that the outbreak of war is not always something evil, and good can come of it, is also implicit in the work of contemporary just war theorists. These theorists may not all say with Hegel that 'the higher significance of war is that through it' the 'ethical health of nations is preserved' (324/ p. 361) but they do indicate that war has its part to play in the normality of international relations. Another feature in the understanding of the international system that is shared by Hegel and just war theorists is the recognition and acceptance of the state as the prime focus for the political loyalty of individuals. Today's just war theorists, like Hegel, are strongly nation-state orientated. As with Hegel, the focus of political community is the nation-state. Hegel sees nation-states as subject to international law, but also as its authors he accepts their 'right' to determine themselves how the law might apply: 'International law applies to the relations between independent states. What it contains in and for itself therefore assumes the form of an obligation, because its actuality depends on distinct and sovereign wills' (330/ p. 366). Hegel accepts that it is a principle of international law that 'treaties' should 'be observed.' But everything ultimately must come down to the will of the individual state. We are who we are and what we are as members of a state: 'the nation state (*das Volk als Staat*) is the spirit in its substantial rationality and immediate actuality, and is therefore the absolute power on earth; each state is consequently a sovereign and independent entity in relation to others' (331/ p. 366). What is noteworthy from the perspective of today's just war thinking is the ethical precedence this gives to the nation state above all other points of focus.

My aim here is to engage in a Kantian critique of contemporary just war theorists, particularly to the extent that those theorists share the same framework as Hegel. For Kant war has to be assessed from a moral perspective but that moral perspective is not the just war one. The appropriate moral perspective from which to deliberate about the occurrence of war is that of the metaphysics of right. The perspective of the metaphysics of right takes in not only the assessment of international right or law – the philosophical context where the problems of war arise – but also the establishment of individual right, constitutional right and cosmopolitan right. Kant therefore does not take the issue of the justice of war in isolation as a matter for international law solely, but rather it is encompassed within the whole sphere of moral and political responsibility. Kant brings a complete moral and political theory to bear on the problem of war rather than resorting to moral and political theory in order to deal with the exigency of war. With Kant there is no search for moral resources to face up to war, but rather war appears as one amongst many challenges to the development and presentation of a cogent practical philosophy.

The most notable of the theorists of just war is the American academic and political journalist Michael Walzer. He commits himself in *Just and Unjust Wars* to a partial and incomplete view of practical philosophy from the beginning. He says 'I am not going to expound morality from the ground up. Were I to begin with the foundations, I would probably never get beyond them, in any case, I am by no means sure what the foundations are. The substructure of the ethical world is a matter of deep and apparently unending controversy. Meanwhile we are living in the superstructure.' Instead of basing his discussion on a complete view of morality, Walzer presents himself as a person who is writing 'a book of practical morality.' Walzer sees himself as an engaged and concrete thinker. 'The study of judgments and justifications in the real world moves us closer, perhaps to the most profound questions of moral philosophy, but it does not require a direct engagement with those questions.' For Walzer there is a need for academics to remove themselves from the ivory tower and to concern themselves with the world as it is actually experienced. Those philosophers who focus on the larger questions of the foundations of moral philosophy will 'often miss the immediacies of political and moral controversy and provide little help to men and women faced with hard choices.'[6] In the name of concreteness (a line of reasoning Hegel might well share) Walzer puts forward the very briefest of sketches of his own general moral position (rights first, utility second) and devotes most of his reasoning to the direct experience and discourse of war as engaged in by political leaders, soldiers and civilians.

There are others who belong to this trend of concreteness and I shall deal with some of their ideas also below. In one respect however none of these 'neo-Hegelians' carry the Hegelian project to its fruition. They subscribe to the patriotism and communitarianism of the Hegelian project, but they do not seemingly subscribe to its philosophical indeterminism. For Hegel modern states are entitled to engage in war, and to advance their interests by its means – but there is no certainty that justice in a full spiritual sense is on the side of one or other of the protagonists. As we have seen the justice of any war unfolds only subsequently in the forward development of world spirit. In contrast contemporary just war theorists are looking for the full justification of the military actions of the specific protagonist in any conflict. In contemporary (Hegelian) just war theory, the one cause engaged in a military conflict has to be vindicated over any another. Indeed the object of contemporary just war theory is to build an account of just war that allows political leaders to judge in advance whether or not they ought to deploy force in any particular circumstance. Whereas from Hegel's perspective all states are set on an equal footing in the judgment to declare war – each sovereign power has to weigh up the justice and good sense of its own cause – contemporary just war theory seeks to create a vantage point beyond that of any particular state in order to recommend what is the just course of action from the perspective of world politics as a whole. With contemporary just war theory the possibility emerges of one power (or a group of powers) setting itself up as the judge of the rightness of the resort to war in any one instance and then of seeking to impose that judgement on all other states. This just war theorizing is followed through with alarming consequences in the contemporary discussion of 'the duty to protect', which draws on the just war tradition where the international community is asked to make judgements about where and when it is necessary for humanitarian intervention to occur.[7] For Hegel this is not a judgment the theorist/philosopher can make in the present. The rules of international law entitle states to declare war on one another – to that extent their actions are not unjust. However whether their actions will serve justice in the longer term and whether one cause has greater legitimacy than another can only be determined in retrospect.

Just war doctrine – Michael Walzer

By a Kantian critique of just war theory I mean one which focuses on the unspoken acceptance of the inherited Westphalian international system and so fails to question the permissibility of war in the current environment of interstate relations. The Westphalian international system is, as we have noted, the one that came into existence after the religious and inter-dynastic European wars (The Thirty Years War) of the seventeenth century. The Treaty of Westphalia (1648) helped stabilize the European international order by establishing rules of interstate conduct and the treatment of religious dissent. By many scholars this Westphalian arrangement is regarded as the basis for international legal relations today. The great merit of Kant's approach to politics and international politics is, in my view, the manner in which he highlights the state-centred nature of conventional attitudes to politics and law epitomized in the Westphalian system. Kant does not look for lasting human security (of life and property) from the legal and political arrangements of one state in isolation, but rather argues that it is only through the proper peaceful arrangements of all states with all others that such perpetual security can be brought about. This is of course the main gist of *Perpetual Peace*, which appeared in the last decade of Kant's life; however he expresses similar sentiments in the 1784 article 'Idea for a Universal history from a Cosmopolitan Perspective'. In the seventh proposition of the article he argues that 'the problem of establishing a perfect civil constitution is dependent upon the problem of a law-governed external relation between states and cannot be solved without having first solved the latter. What good does it do to work on establishing a law-governed civil constitution among individuals, that is, to organise a commonwealth? The same unsociability that had compelled human beings to pursue this commonwealth also is the reason that every commonwealth in its external relations, that is, as a state among states, exists in unrestricted freedom and consequently that states must expect the same ills from other states that threatened individuals and compelled them to enter into a law-governed civil condition' (8: 24/9–10). Here Kant expresses the view that appears consistently in his mature writings that establishing one state within one distinct civil society represents only a stepping stone to the ultimate condition of security where there is the one worldwide civil society. Until states have established a stable international society based in the first instance on a federation of free states, they can be regarded as existing in a similar condition to that of individuals in the state of nature. For Kant 'states' have to make 'precisely the same decision (however difficult this may be for them) that the savage individual, just as reluctantly, was forced to make: to give up his brutish freedom and to seek peace and security in a law-governed constitution' (8: 24). Contemporary just war theory does not embrace this critical view of interstate relations by taking for granted the past, present and future antagonism of states, and implicitly condoning the recourse to violence in the final instance to maintain the vital interests of individual states. The Kantian view is that the mutuality and interdependence of states should be set at the heart of any explanatory and normative theory of war. Almost without exception contemporary just war theorists put the lack of mutuality of states and their sovereign independence at the heart of their theories.[8] This view they share with Hegel.

Just war theory represents something of an orthodoxy within current international relations theory. Some years ago I asked a senior colleague who had taught international relations for a quarter of a century or more to make list of those books that had most influenced him in the discipline. In that shortlist Michael Walzer's book *Just and Unjust Wars* figured prominently. My colleague had included it because it was one of several books that had made him 'think again' about the subject. It is understandable why Walzer's book is such a popular one with teachers and students of international relations. The book demonstrates great philosophical depth in tackling effectively major ethical issues, but it is also a book that draws extensively on actual historical events and practices. A great deal of the book is taken up with a lively and close analysis of key examples of what has occurred under wartime conditions. The subtitle of the book brings out this bias towards the concrete. Walzer presents his work as 'a moral argument with historical illustrations'. Each of the chapters contains a historical illustration ranging from the battle of Agincourt to General Sherman and the burning of Atlanta and the Second World War British decision to bomb German and occupied cities. Walzer seeks to make his argument rooted in the reality of war. 'The proper method of practical morality is casuistic in character. Since I am concerned with actual judgments and justifications, I shall turn regularly to historical cases. My argument moves through the case, and I have often foregone a systematic presentation for the sake of the nuances and details of historical reality.'[9] This represents an excellent didactic technique which allows the introduction of complex moral and political issues to an audience of learners. Quite clearly ethical questions come alive when they are set in a controversial and historically well known context. Undoubtedly Walzer's text is installed as a staple for undergraduates in international relations and often forms the core of courses on the ethics of war taught in British and North American Universities.

Relations amongst states in the contemporary world are for Walzer based upon an analogy with the relations amongst individuals in settled domestic societies. He believes that states enjoy rights and bear responsibilities in a manner similar to that of individuals in a law-governed state. Crime is possible at the international level and it takes on the form of aggression. 'The wrong the aggressor commits is to force men and women to risk their lives for the sake of their rights.' For Walzer there is a 'strange poverty' of language in current international law. 'The equivalents of domestic assault, armed robbery, extortion, assault with intent to kill, murder in all its degrees, have but one name. Every violation of the territorial integrity of political sovereignty of an independent state is called aggression' (pp. 51–52). Thus international society is similar to domestic society in that there is the possibility of crime – but it is different in that at the international level there is, as he sees it, only the one crime of aggression. This difference does not trouble Walzer in attributing moral and legal identity to the state. He does not question the state's existence as the primary focus of our political loyalty. There is no need for supra-national authority to take its place now or in the future. 'International society as it exists today is a radically imperfect structure. As we experience it, that society might be likened to a defective building, founded on rights; its superstructure raised like that of the state itself, through political conflict, cooperative activity and commercial exchange; the whole thing is shaky and unstable because it lacks the rivets of authority. It is like domestic society in that men and women live at peace within it (sometimes) determining the conditions of their own existence, negotiation and bargaining with their neighbours. It is unlike domestic society in that every conflict threatens the structure as a whole with collapse. Aggression challenges it directly and is much more dangerous than domestic crime, because there are no policemen. But that only means that "citizens" of international society must rely on themselves and one another. Police powers are distributed among all the members' (pp. 58–9). States thus for Walzer have police powers not only in relation to their subjects but also indirectly in relation to the subjects of other states if those act aggressively towards other members of the international society. Hegelian sovereign independence is affirmed and sovereigns are in a position to judge when to declare war. 'There is, as Walzer puts it, 'a presumption in favour of military resistance once aggression has begun' (p. 59).

Hegel puts the state at the centre of international relations. Each state is fully independent of others and can determine for itself where its well-being lies: 'the substantial welfare of the state is its welfare as a particular state in its specific interest and condition and in its equally distinctive external circumstances in conjunction with the particular treaties that govern them.' For him intervention in the internal affairs of another state is contrary to the logic of the international system. The state's 'end in relation to other states and its principle for justifying wars and treaties is not universal (philanthropic) thought, but its actually offended or threatened welfare in its specific particularity' (337/ p. 370). Hegel embraces the idea of anticipatory war in his notion of the state's external sovereignty. This is a topic much canvassed by contemporary just war theorists who see the legitimate remit of the state in declaring war, extending under specific circumstances to wars declared to deal with perceived future threats. Walzer's manner of couching the capacities of the state externally does not diverge markedly from Hegel's. For Walzer 'there exists an international society of independent states. States are members of this society, not private men and women. In the absence of a universal state, men and women are protected and their interests represented only by their own governments. Though states are founded for the sake of life and liberty, they cannot be challenged in the name of life and liberty by any other states. Hence the principle of non-intervention' (p. 61).

It is the object of this book on Kant and the end of war to challenge the taken-for-granted nature of the understanding of war in contemporary western culture. For all its merits, therefore, the installing of Walzer's work as the main text in ethics and international relations courses reinforces the view that the prosecution of war is a natural part of world politics. Walzer's line of argument, though presented as anti-realist, is that there is a morality of war to be discovered in our everyday use of language in dealing with these prominent historical examples. Walzer assumes in a manner that is similar to Kant in his moral philosophy that morality is present in our everyday consciousness – but unlike Kant, Walzer goes on to assume that a stable moral outlook can be constructed from this everyday consciousness. This he proceeds to do in *Just and Unjust Wars*. As Walzer puts it there, 'we really do act within a moral world; that particular decisions really are difficult, problematic, agonizing, and that this has to do with the structure of the world; that language reflects the moral world and gives us access to it; and finally though our understanding of the moral vocabulary is sufficiently common and stable so that shared judgements are possible' (p. 20) .The just war project as Walzer understands it is to sift out – from our ordinary moral vocabulary about war – a stable kind of grammar that will be suited to dealing with the political and moral occurrence of war in general. Thus with Walzer ordinary moral awareness is our source, but also our touchstone, in determining what is just. There appear to be strong Hegelian overtones to this line of argument. Hegel also preferred the unaffected morality of the ordinary individual to the mere opinion of many of his contemporary fellow philosophers.

As Brian Orend points out, this overlap between Walzer's and Hegel's approach to political philosophy is no coincidence. 'While Walzer only sparingly cites Hegel, he does share substantive motifs with the controversial and influential German philosopher. Like Hegel, Walzer views self-understanding , identity and recognition from others as key elements in political life, indeed in human existence more broadly conceived.'[10] Walzer neither expressly see himself as a Hegelian nor does he identify himself solely with the contemporary communitarian trend that derives from Hegel's philosophy; however he does not reject the lines of similarity between his views and those of Hegel and Hegelian scholars, and the communitarian school. 'Like Hegel, Walzer emphasizes the active, constitutive role that ideas and values play in life, and that one cannot meaningfully speak of things like justice, whether in distribution or war, outside the flow of history.' [11] Walzer favours a highly socialized view of the subject in political philosophy. For Orend 'the largest shared motif between Hegel and Walzer' is 'the understanding of social life in general, and of politics in particular, as being rooted in a particular state, in a concrete community at a particular place and time, thoroughly contextualized in the flow of historical events.'[12] This view is echoed by Toni Erskine in her article 'Qualifying Cosmopolitanism? Solidarity, Criticism and Michael Walzer's "View from the Cave".' In her view, in his major theoretical work in political theory, *Spheres of Justice*, 'Walzer presents a theory of social justice that relies upon the deciphering of 'shared understandings', or local meanings, that are given to goods to be distributed in society. In other words, he claims to forego any appeal to universal principles of justice.'[13] With Erskine it is important to acknowledge that it is difficult to categorize Walzer wholly as a communitarian because there are many respects in which he steps beyond its boundaries – including within the international sphere. However Walzer is very much at home with the local, the particular and the culturally embedded in determining his moral and political views.

Walzer separates the just war doctrine into *jus ad bellum* and *jus in bello*. These broadly can be categorised as justice leading up to war (a consideration of the grounds upon which war might be declared) and justice in war. I have suggested that part of the Westphalian outlook is the acceptance of the normality of war in the international system.

Alongside this assumption of its normality is an attempt to moderate its worst consequences. Walzer, like other contemporary just war theorists, is very much in favour of limiting the impact of war through the adoption of rules of its appropriate conduct. Here they are at one with Hegel who assures his audience that 'modern wars' are 'waged in a humane manner, and persons do not confront each other in hatred. At most, personal enmities will arise at military outposts, but in the army as such, hostility is something indeterminate which takes second place to the duty which each respects in the other'. For Hegel there is a code of conduct for combatants that very much resembles Walzer's 'war convention'. The purpose of this 'war convention' is to establish the duties of belligerent states, of army commanders, and of individual soldiers with reference to the conduct of hostilities.[14] Although wars inevitably mean the use of extreme force they should not lead to the complete abandonment of decency and morality. 'Belligerent armies' are 'subject to a set of restrictions that rest in part on the agreements of states but that also have an independent foundation in morality'.[15] Hegel says much the same: 'the fact that states reciprocally recognize each other as such remains even in war – as the condition of rightlessness, force and contingency – a bond whereby they retain their validity for each other being in and for themselves, so that even in wartime, the determination of war is that of something which ought to come to an end'. Civilized standards are therefore maintained in wartime. 'War ... entails the determination of international law that it should preserve the possibility of peace – so that, for example, ambassadors should be respected and war should on no account be waged either on internal institutions and the peace of private and family life, or on private individuals' (338/ p. 370).

Hegel shows a remarkable confidence in *jus in bello* and points to the European context in dictating this modification of the harshness of war that occurs over time: 'the European nations form a family with respect to the universal principle of their legislation, customs and culture, so that their conduct in terms of international law is modified accordingly in a situation which is otherwise dominated by the mutual infliction of evils' (339/ p. 371). In this respect Kant is a good deal less sanguine. For him the idea of right or justice in war appears to be inherently contradictory. Although the idea of *jus in bello* is one he cannot dismiss it is an idea that he struggles with.[16] As he sees it, 'the greatest difficulty in the right of nations has to do precisely with right during war; it is difficult even to form a concept of this or to think of law in this lawless state without contradicting oneself (*inter arma silent leges*)'

(6: 347/485). The Hegelian approach demonstrates the acceptance of an international condition that from time to time will bring about war. For Hegel it is 'inherently indeterminable' which 'injuries should be regarded as a specific breach of treaties or an injury to the recognition and honour of the state' and so lead to war (334/ p. 369). It is for the state leaders themselves to decide when they may wish to pursue their welfare through armed conflict. This arbitrariness in deciding when to go to war is mitigated by the mutual recognition amongst states of the human limits of war. In contrast Kant does not accept the legitimacy of the prior international condition that permits war and links the idea of right in war with the objective of replacing the state of nature amongst states with a condition of lasting peace. For Kant 'right during war would, then have to be the waging of war in accordance with principles that always leave open the possibility of leaving the state of nature amongst states (in external relation to one another) and entering a rightful condition' (6: 347). *Jus in bello* makes sense to Kant only so long as it is connected with the project of establishing perpetual peace. The laws of war should reflect the fact that war is an unacceptable way of resolving disputes amongst states and point to a condition where it is no longer permitted. For Kant war is a pathological and not a normal human activity. He recommends legislation for it with great reservation. He certainly shows very little faith in the supposed high standards attained by European nations. How far the European family of nations veered from those high principles to which Hegel thought it adhered can be gleaned from a close reading of Michael Walzer's book, where the details of some the worst excesses of the First and Second World Wars are carefully catalogued.

Jean Bethke Elshtain and James Turner Johnson

The contemporary just war theorist Jean Bethke Elshtain is more influenced by Augustine than Hegel; none the less, her thinking shares the same features as Hegel's theorizing about war. Like Hegel she holds that it is utopian to think about a condition of international relations where war will not occur. This does not mean that there is not a relative orderliness that can apply to relations amongst states, but 'this civic peace is not the kingdom promised by scriptures that awaits the end of time.' For Elshtain 'the vision of beating swords into plowshares and spears into pruning hooks' is 'connected with certain conditions that will always elude us.' She takes it for granted here that 'our condition of pluralism and religious diversity alone precludes the rule of one law.'[17] When she says our 'fallibility and imperfection precludes a world in which discontents will never erupt' she therefore means that states will always have to look to themselves to enforce law in the international sphere. There cannot be one international law that binds all states but rather always competing conceptions of political justice – where force ultimately has to decide which conception prevails.

The state is the prime source of people's security in a complex and often troubled world. As Elshtain sees it, 'the primary reason for the state's existence is to create those minimum conditions that prevent the worst from happening – meaning the worst that human beings can do to one another' (p. 49). The state seems always to have to act in a sovereign and independent manner in preventing people 'from devouring one another like fishes' (p. 49). Just war theory provides a framework within which sovereign states can decide to act. As with Hegel, Elshtain takes the view that war should not always be regarded as evil. 'Consider the terms: *justice* and *war*. The presupposition of just war thinking is that war can sometimes be the instrument of justice; that, indeed, war can help put right a massive injustice or restore a right, order where there is disorder, including those disorders that sometimes call themselves "peace"' (p. 49). 'So peace should not be universally lauded even as war is universally condemned' (p. 49). Contrary to Kant, she declares 'indeed there are worse things than war'. She follows this with the highly tendentious claim 'that the world would have been much better off if the violence of particular regimes had been confronted on the battlefield earlier; fewer lives would have been lost in the long run' (p. 51). What makes this tendentious is not simply the unverifiable claim that if some unpleasant regimes (presumably Nazi Germany) had been attacked sooner that lives would have been saved, but more particularly the suggestion the only way to confront the violence of 'particular regimes' is 'on the battlefield'. Elshtain is trying to convey the picture that the option of war has always to be kept open as a legitimate way of conducting foreign policy.

Clearly Elshtain shares many of Hegel's views about war and can be legitimately included as one of today's Hegelian just war theorists; there is little doubt that some Hegelians might want to reject the identification of Elshtain's vision with that of Hegel's idealist philosophy. Such Hegelians might wish to argue that Elshtain, rather than subscribing to Hegel's overall idealist outlook (of which politics and war is a part), takes a contrary view which is based on a realist understanding of world politics. In this respect her starting point in the political philosophy of Augustine apparently stamps her as such a realist. However there is room to believe that she does not subscribe uncritically to this realist view. A realist view of world politics that Elshtain would be familiar with is outlined in the letter posted on the internet by the Institute for American Values in February 2002 – an organization included in her book (as a co-signatory) *Just War Against Terror*. This describes realism as 'the belief that war is basically a matter of power, self-interest, necessity and survival, thereby rendering abstract moral analysis largely beyond the point'.[18] This school of thought is rejected by the signatories because 'they largely disagree with it'.[19] There is no way of telling from this how great Elshtain's disagreements with realism might be. But according to Elshtain and her co-signatories, the just war tradition on war represents a significant alternative. This brings us on to the ground that Elshtain is happier with, since for the signatories just war thinking represents a school of thought in its own right, which is based on the belief 'that universal moral reasoning, or what some would call natural moral law, can and should be applied to the activity of war'.[20] Thus it would appear that it is not realism that stands in the way of identifying Hegel's thinking with Elshtain, but rather it has to be the different normative standpoint Elshtain adopts, which eschews all talk of any world spirit playing a decisive role in determining past and future changes in world history.

Less militant than Elshtain but no less committed to the Hegelian view of the primacy of the state is James Turner Johnson. This Hegelian commitment to the primacy of the state is less evident in Johnson's writing because he presents himself as a critic of the Westphalian system. Johnson's thinking harks back to a much longer tradition of just war thinking than that of the early modern period. He is an advocate of just war thinking as it emerges in the writings of Augustine and is then systematized by Aquinas. He subscribes to the traditional canon of Aquinas's just war theory by advocating that for there to be a just war there has to be 'sovereign authority, just cause and right intention'. [21] Sovereign authority for Johnson lies in the political community, and like a good medievalist, Johnson believes that individual states are not always the sole and proper judge of what the political community requires. What the Westphalian system lacks is a final authority to determine what the will of the political community is. Not daunted by this deficiency, Johnson looks for such authority either in existing states or in appropriate combinations of them. As the discussion is presented from the perspective of the United States, the United States immediately offers itself as one such state or as an actor in the combination of states. Thus the questioning of the Westphalian system is superficial.

Johnson questions it only from the standpoint of its being unable to provide a lead in prosecuting the aims of the true political community, but it is triumphantly re-affirmed in its ability to provide a candidate to take on the role of the overarching medieval authority that Johnson appears to long for. Individual states can act on behalf of the sovereign authority morally defined.[22] It turns out that the Westphalian system is wrong only in according absolute sovereignty to some dubious states; it is not wrong in according absolute sovereignty to those states that deploy their sovereignty in the morally appropriate manner: 'In traditional just war terms, the state is inherently most capable of meeting the moral requirements of the idea of sovereign authority.' Although Johnson sees flaws in the Westphalian system, his thoughts do not run in the direction of improving it through the acceptance of an overarching international authority such as the United Nations or the North Atlantic Treaty Organisation: 'The United Nations lacks several important attributes of such authority: it is not in fact sovereign, taking its power from the agreement of its constituent states; it is not responsible or accountable to the people of the world, but only to these states; and it lacks command and control mechanisms, so that it cannot direct the use of force responsibly. Regional security alliances such as NATO have a level of authority, in just war terms, somewhere between that of sovereign states and the United Nations.' Indeed Johnson wants to distance himself from internationalists who want to act only through such international organisations. He fears that limiting the authority to declare war to such communities will weaken the prospect for international order and so peace. Johnson would prefer to accord authority in specific circumstances to 'properly governed and rightly motivated states' to act on behalf of the world political community. The 'internal politics' of the United Nations, particularly of the Security Council, often prevents it from acting in glaring cases where, in Johnson's view, international action is required. 'Recent examples,' for Johnson, 'include the cases of Rwanda and Kosovo, not to mention Iraq in 2002–3.' The authority of 'properly governed and rightly motivated states' in declaring war in Johnson's account of just war runs very wide. They can by-pass obstructive international organisations and they can also encourage and anticipate the actions of regional organisations:

As for uses of armed force by regional alliances, such as the NATO intervention over the conflict in Kosovo (undertaken in the absence of a Security Council mandate, though the Council's approval was given after the action), I think we should regard these essentially as the consensual joining together of individual states in support of a purpose widely recognized in international humanitarian law.' There is little limit that needs to be placed on the well intended actions of 'properly governed states', both individually and when they get together in prosecuting war against certain generally recognized threats. It is a good thing that as many as possible of the apposite states should agree that action is necessary; however the need for such a wide consensus should not stand in the way of action. 'The more robust the consensus the better; yet I would insist that the just war understanding of authority means that individual states may also act alone in cases of pressing need.'[23] Johnson's criticism of the Westphalian political system does not lead to the abandonment of its basic principle of the sovereign independence of states, but rather an *a la carte* deployment of it depending on when it is to the advantage of a very loosely defined 'political community'. Johnson's revival of just war theory leads to the kind of top-down authoritarian attempt to create world order that Kant sought especially to avoid. At best Kant believed that leading states could set an example by adopting republican constitutions and behaving amicably with neighbouring states and not even the' peaceful federation of free states' would have the authority to coerce other states into joining. Johnson also overlooks Hegel's dictum that 'there is no praetor to adjudicate between states' (333/ p. 368). For Hegel what the future world political community might be is not something that we can discern. No state can have higher authority in these matters; there is only the clash of competing wills. Both Johnson and Hegel have a metaphysical outlook on this issue, but Hegel does not share Johnson's theology which permits the latter to declaim: 'I suggest that within the Catholic context the proper frame for such argument is a normative understanding of good statecraft in the service of the goods that the political community exists to secure.'[24]

John Rawls and Just War Theory

International relations are very little emphasized in *A Theory of Justice*. Rawls deals with international issues primarily in the context of the possibility of civil disobedience and the question of conscription to fight a disputed war (understandable given the Vietnam War) loom large.[25] Here there is a fairly brief, but highly informative, discussion of just war theory and in connection with this a short reflection about the nature of relations amongst states at present. Rawls's starting point is that 'the national interest of a just state is defined by the principles of justice that have already been acknowledged'. So the view of what is legitimate in the international arena hangs upon how justice is seen in the domestic sphere. The distributive view of justice (uniquely developed by Rawls in *A Theory of Justice* – which gives a key role to the benefits enjoyed by the least well-off in society) conditions how relations with other states should be seen. The lexically ordered equal liberty principle and the difference principle have to be accommodated in the international sphere, and also colour the just society's view of another state. Consequently 'conscription is permissible only if it is demanded for the defence of liberty itself, including here not only the liberties of the citizens of the society in question but also of those in other societies as well'.[26] The leaders of a just state are entitled not only to use arms to oppose threats to liberty within the state but also if this occurs in other states, as long as the principles of justice are not violated in attaining this end. But Rawls is far from arrogating to the leaders of states an entirely free hand in determining whether or not liberty is threatened. 'Given the often predatory aims of state power, and the tendency of men to defer to their own governments' decision to wage war, a general willingness to resist the state's claims is all the more necessary'.[27] There has to be freedom of conscience within the just state and the open discussion of the wisdom of government's policies should be encouraged. Publicity is a key element in freedom. Thus the foreign policy of a state which subscribes to Rawls's view of justice is always subject to criticism. Engaging in war is a move of profound significance: it cannot be automatically sanctioned by an unthinking patriotism. Although Rawls is not a pacifist, he none the less favours a discriminating 'conscientious refusal to engage in war in certain circumstances'.[28] Thus the theory of justice can extend its reach beyond its own territory based only on the consent of the citizens that subscribe to the principles of justice in the original position.

In understanding Rawls's account of war and the international order we need to have a firm grasp of the way in which he sees the international realm being related to the domestic in his theory of justice. He regards his theory as justice as falling into the broad philosophical category of *practical reasoning*. Another way of putting this is to say that Rawls presents his view of justice as an aspect of ethical thinking. The theory of justice belongs to the sub-category that comes under 'the concept of right'. This concept of right can be seen as applying to 'social systems and institutions', 'individuals' and the 'law of nations'.[29] Rawls argues that there has to be a definite order of precedence in determining right in each of these three spheres. As he regards the social context as playing a critical role in the formation of the individual, he believes that the derivation of the just 'social systems and institutions' has to come first. Thus Rawls's concept of international justice is state-centric. As he puts it, 'the principles for the basic structure of society are to be agreed first, principles for individuals next, followed by those for the law of nations'.[30] Although these distinctions should not be seen as entirely hard and fast in Rawls's eyes, they do none the less represent guiding threads in his political theory. Rawls focuses first and foremost on the social institutions of the just domestic political order. Since we are social beings we have first to enquire how we can live together in one discrete society before moving on to the wider international stage. Thus the international sphere is originally presented as one which lies outside the properly determined just political order.

Non-ideal theory

In *A Theory of Justice* Rawls, as is well known, presents only the briefest sketch of how international justice might come into being. For a more detailed understanding of how he sees the problem of just war we have to turn to the *Law of Peoples* where he seeks to extend his novel theory of justice to the international realm. In the first part of that book he outlines how peoples should come together to establish a second original contract that would regulate relations amongst them. The contract would be determined in a similar way to the original contract at the individual level: the various representatives of people would remain behind a veil of ignorance with regard to their endowments in a military, social and economic sense. Rawls then sets out various principles that the representatives would agree in this position of ignorance. At the political level the greatest test for Rawls's *Law of Peoples* is when the theory is extended into the non-ideal situation where not all states are well ordered and maybe even not well disposed to the liberal nations that create the second contract. Clearly the law of peoples does not apply to non-liberal and non-decent states (as non-signatories) in the same way as it applies amongst its own liberal members. But this does not mean that the liberal core can abandon its principles in relation to these non-complying states. Rawls sees this as a test and acknowledges the 'highly non ideal conditions of our world'.[31] The question for the society of just peoples is not how to transform the situation immediately but rather 'non ideal theory asks how this long-term goal might be achieved or worked towards, usually in gradual steps'.[32] This provides the context within which the theory of just war is elaborated.

Just war theory has to be admitted since the specific conditions of the world at the present time include both 'well-ordered peoples' that are prepared to live in peace with all similarly 'well-ordered peoples' and less 'well-ordered' regimes which are not prepared to cooperate with the society of peoples. Thus liberal states have to guard against the dangerous effects of the existence of such outlaw states on their own security. Indeed not only liberal states may legitimately resort to war but also non-liberal states: 'Any society that is non-aggressive and that honors human rights has the right of self-defence'.[33] A benevolent absolutism may legitimately preserve its institutions when subjected to an unprovoked attack. However 'when a liberal society engages in war in self-defence, it does so to protect and preserve the basic freedoms of its citizens and its constitutionally democratic political institutions'.[34] As we might expect, in his account of war in *The Law of Peoples* Rawls remains true to the position he outlines earlier in *A Theory of Justice* that wars in self-defence are compatible with right.[35]

There are two sides to foreign policy for a liberal state in the non-ideal situation (that we are in now and are likely to remain in for the foreseeable future). There is of course the immediate goal of defence, but there is also the long-term or ultimate goal of bringing all peoples within the fold of 'well ordered societies'. This has to be reflected in the law of peoples. 'A reasonable law of peoples guides well-ordered societies in facing outlaw regimes by specifying the aim they are to have in mind and indicating the means they may use or must avoid using.'[36] In doing this, liberal states will want to support international organisations such as the United Nations or similar ones (possibly at a regional dimension) that accord with the goal of creating a just relation amongst peoples. 'Their long run aim is to bring all societies eventually to honor the Law of Peoples and to become full members in good standing of the society of well-ordered peoples.'[37] We would know that this had been achieved where we could with confidence speak of human rights being respected everywhere. The main actors that Rawls has in mind in achieving this goal are the leaders of the already 'well-ordered' states. We might add that it should also be possible for the citizens of such states to play a hand as well in encouraging their leaders to follow such paths and in connecting with the citizens of other such states to help the process advance.

Institutions, as I have suggested, can play a role in this. 'For well ordered peoples to achieve this long-term aim, they should establish new institutions and practices to serve as a kind of confederative center and public forum for their common opinion and policy toward non-well-ordered regimes.'[38] Here Rawls does seem to envisage bringing citizens into the picture as supporters of the confederative centre, but they seem largely to be doing this in his account through their representatives. This is something that might be thought through more fully. Rawls works seemingly with an idealized picture of the well-ordered states who do not apparently need each other's help in maintaining their valuable positions. Historically it might be argued that where such confederative centres have emerged (such as perhaps the European Union), member states have placed as much value on the mutual support the centre affords in maintaining their own liberal status as upon the united face it may present to a less than well-ordered world.

In some respects the fact that just war theory plays such a prominent part in Rawls's non ideal theory reflects timidity in his approach, but in other respects it also might be said to reflect a certain robustness. It reflects timidity or apprehensiveness, on the one hand, in the sense that its prominence suggests that he has little faith in the capacity of the union of well-ordered peoples to extend its boundaries, but it reflects robustness, on the other hand, in that his just war theory tries to reign in severely the use of violence. The reason why this is so, is that his just war theory provides a much needed limit to merely military–instrumental reasoning in the prosecution of war. 'Practical means-end reasoning must always have a restricted role in judging the appropriateness of an action or policy.'[39] To this Rawls gives the exception of the 'supreme emergency'. Here he follows Michael Walzer's reasoning in *Just and Unjust Wars* in arguing that in certain circumstances things are so desperate as to excuse normally unacceptable actions, such as the deliberate bombing of civilian targets.[40] However, generally speaking policy should be determined within the framework of political liberalism and the international goal that accords with it, the creation of a society of well ordered peoples.

Although in general Rawls's account of international relations conforms with the picture of Hegelian just war theory, I have attempted to show that there are respects in which he adds a non-Hegelian reforming and progressive touch. To do this Rawls introduces a healthy division between the role of the philosopher and the politician: 'it is the task of the student of philosophy to articulate and express the permanent conditions and the real interests of a well-ordered society. It is the task of the statesman, however, to discern these conditions and interests in practice.'[41] The politician who is also a statesmen pays heed to the 'society's fundamental interests'[42] which are expressed presumably by the student of philosophy. To observe the rules that the law of peoples requires, the guidance of the statesman is necessary for Rawls. He acknowledges that such an individual represents an ideal. None the less he thinks that there are examples to be drawn from history. The political leader who is also a statesman looks beyond the concerns of the moment to the wider concerns of the human race as a whole. The short turn policy is determined not only in the light of present interests but also in a long-term perspective. Abraham Lincoln and George Washington are depicted as statesmen by Rawls but not Bismarck. Lincoln is picked out in particular for his lack of vindictiveness in relation to his opponents, a crucial consideration in attempting to bring together all parties in ending successfully the American Civil War. 'Above all, statesmen are to hold fast to the aim of gaining a just peace, and they are to avoid the things that make achieving such a peace more difficult. In this regard they must assure that the proclamations made on behalf of their people make clear that once peace is securely re-established the enemy society is to be granted an autonomous well-ordered regime of its own.'[43] Thus Rawls breaks out of the Hegelian mould in granting there may be a better and more peaceful world society to come, but re-affirms it by tying the statesmen to the long-term interests of his own society.

I began by noting that Rawls's account of justice among people, though underpinned by a progressive liberal political philosophy, may inadvertently lend support to a less than desirable foreign policy. Though the discussion has shown that there is a great deal to support in Rawls's extension of his theory of justice into the international realm, there are still some respects in which the original suspicion of unconscious bias holds. There are four points to this untoward bias I should like to bring out.

In the first place the highly laudable distinction that Rawls makes between states and peoples in grounding his theory – although it has the distinct advantage that it affords an opportunity to criticise a great deal of traditional state-centred international theory – does also have the drawback that it creates the possibility of intervention by other states in the internal politics of sovereign countries in an almost open-ended way. I agree with Rawls that we cannot regard what goes on in our country as entirely our own affair, and we certainly cannot use it as an excuse or justification for abusing human rights. Yet I don't think that this entitles other sovereign peoples or their leaders to act as the final court of appeal as to what may or may not go on within the confines of a territory. If we are to move away from the notion of the sovereign independence of states then the conditions for this change have to be spelled out more fully than Rawls does. If the laws and human rights practices of other countries are to be judged (as well as our own), then I should like to see publics and their representatives play a more important role in this than is implied by Rawls's account.

Rawls differentiates in a persuasive way between peoples who are eligible for the peaceful international order that forms a 'realizable utopia' and those who belong to outlaw states that do not recognise the law of peoples. But maybe in making this distinction Rawls glosses over too quickly the problems that might be posed in identifying what constitutes an 'outlaw' state. The term is perhaps too hastily taken up from the vocabulary of the American 'Wild West', where it was evident who the 'bad guy' who lived outside the law was. On a day-to-day basis in international relations many states hover between 'outlaw' and legal status. Usually the difference between the behaviour of states is more one of degree than kind. Occasionally the most legally embedded state may engage in dubious behaviour and often the most legally insecure states can behave impeccably in relation to their neighbours and the world at large. Where states actually overstep the mark and violate the rights of the world community in a way that justifies their exclusion is difficult precisely to define. I would agree that in certain individual cases, such as that of Nazi Germany, Fascist Italy and the Iraqi invasion of Kuwait this is very clear to see. But the more usual case is a good deal more complex. Thus Rawls's term the 'outlaw' state does yield up a hostage to fortune that might well be capitalized on by overambitious world powers.

Thirdly, I believe that Rawls too readily grants the 'right' to war in self-defence. Whilst agreeing that some wars are perfectly excusable and that a leader would be unwise to rule out in advance war as an instrument of foreign policy, here I am defending the view of Kant that the notion of a right to war or 'just war' is a contradiction in terms. Once theorists introduce into international relations the possibility of war as legally justifiable, then this opens the doors to the depicting of all sorts of aggressive policies as necessary in self-defence. Of course, this is not at all what Rawls has in mind. For him the possibility of a just war being declared is extremely limited, and his aim is to narrow down the possibility to where it becomes in practical terms obsolete. But he none the less provides the political leader with the terminology of 'outlaw states' and the line of argument in 'self-defence' with which present, past and future wars might be seen in a positive light. Illuminating as Rawls's discussion of the statesman is – and I can only endorse his view that a statesman will think of the next generation whilst the politician thinks only of the next election – the idea that the statesman should not hamper himself with the

Christian view that innocents should always be spared, the consequences of war seems to me to be too stark an acceptance of the logic of war.⁴⁴ A genuine law of peoples would not give such prominence to the right of war and justice in wars. At least if we are to speak of justice in these contexts it should always be noted that we are speaking of justice in the absence of justice. Measures to ensure that there is justice in the absence of justice are indeed necessary, but they are not the essence of justice.

Fourthly, and this is perhaps only an extension of the last point, Rawls's depiction of international relations accepts too readily that wars will occur. For all its emphasis on the realistic utopia of a society of liberal peoples, war is none the less depicted as a legitimate form of political interaction – not of course with the liberal core but with the non-liberal periphery. Rawls does not go in for preserving the 'ethical health of peoples' in a Hegelian style within the society of peoples, but some scope is provided for maintaining the martial ethos in relation to those outside the liberal core. Instead of the denunciation of all war as immoral – as an activity unfit for human beings – we are given these wise but ultimately not reassuring words: 'Well ordered peoples, both liberal and decent, do not initiate war against one another, they go to war only when they sincerely and reasonably believe that their safety and security are sincerely endangered by the expansionist policies of another state'.⁴⁵ Although this was probably the furthest away from Rawls's thinking when he framed these lines, it is difficult to resist the chilling thought that this is precisely what President Bush and Prime Minister Blair believed about the policies of Iraq in 2003. For all Rawls's emphasis that war should only be declared as a last resort, I fear that his formulation is sufficiently loose to encompass the possibly well-meaning, but unjustifiable action taken against the Iraqi state in 2003. Although Rawls's theory is sufficiently flexible to provide us with grounds for criticising the United States and Britain for engaging in the war in the manner they did – arguably they were 'regimes' who thought, in Rawls's terms, that 'a sufficient reason to engage in war is that it advances , or might advance, the regimes rational (not reasonable) interests',⁴⁶ the most likely line that the western interpreter of Rawls is going to take is that Britain and the United States had a case for starting the war based on the principle of self-defence. Supporters of Rawls, who might respond by saying that the term 'self-defence' is being interpreted here in far too elastic a sense, are open to the objection that it is a term that Rawls himself chose. Rawls carefully chooses terms that will carry his Anglo-American audience with him. In many instances this has a laudable and civilizing effect. Here that effect is not sustained.

Conclusion

Kant's account of the moral standing of war is integrated into a comprehensive philosophical system of ideas. It draws in particular on his moral theory and his connected theory of politics and right. Although there is some argument as to how precisely Kant's general moral philosophy feeds into his theory of right and so his theory of international right, there is general acceptance that his view of war draws from his general moral position and the idea of duty he presents in his *Groundwork of the Metaphysics of Morals* in the categorical imperative. In contrast, contemporary theories of just war do not generally draw from an overarching philosophical system. Quite frequently writers in the tradition refer to the influence wider philosophical systems have had upon their thinking but this is usually in an incidental manner. Kant is very clearly a deontological thinker who focuses upon the principles that bind us in seeking to act ethically and in accordance with justice. This focus on *a priori* principles becomes evident in his treatment of war, and throughout helps structure it. The main point of philosophical reference for contemporary just war theorists is the tradition of just war thinking itself. Philosophically this tradition has diverse moral points of origin – varying from Augustine and Aquinas's complex metaphysical systems to nineteenth- and twentieth century utilitarianism and consequentialism. Insofar as it is possible to detect an underlying philosophical aura/theme to just war thinking, here again there is some accuracy in depicting it as Hegelian. Just war theorists can be depicted as Hegelian in the manner in which they draw upon concrete historical circumstances themselves to provide the grounds for the rules of conduct they recommend. Walzer is notably contextualist in presenting *Just and Unjust Wars* as a 'moral argument with historical illustrations' and Jean Bethke Elshtain and James Turner Johnson both draw attention to the need to pay attention to questions of the moment and the historical context.[47] In this respect Rawls represents an exception, since his account of war and international relations is embedded within a broader political philosophy. He also situates this political philosophy in relation to moral philosophy in general by adopting a Kantian constructivism. This constructivism is avowedly political and not metaphysical. so it does not address the broadest philosophical issues which engage Kant in the presentation of his practical philosophy. But with Rawls there is a line of reasoning to follow which takes us back from the moral case study of just war to general philosophical questions. Arguably those general philosophical questions are answered in a manner that is more reflective of Hegel than Kant, since Rawls strongly emphasizes the contextual nature of his political philosophy and that it begins from certain facts of political life in contemporary North America and Europe. Rawls treads a fine line between Kantianism and Hegelianism. Arguably with just war theory he steps over more into the Hegelian than the Kantian realm.

Thus diverse and sometimes unspecified moral theories enter the presentation of contemporary just war theory. In my view the best of this moral theory can be presented as of Hegelian kind. But given that contemporary just war theorists do not themselves draw such boundaries, it is not surprising that notable thinkers such as Walzer and Elshtain can draw different conclusions about appropriate policy with regard to the same circumstances. Walzer on the basis of his understanding of the just war tradition rejected as illegitimate the 2003 invasion of Iraq;[48] Elshtain in contrast thought that 'on balance, just war criteria were met'.[49]

Disagreement is of course possible in deploying a Kantian perspective in dealing with the possibility of war. However Kant is very hesitant about giving any advice on when engaging in armed conflict might be right, and his general disposition is to rule out war with other states which have a foundation in law. Thus the scope for disagreement within the Kantian perspective is very small, whereas the exponents of just war theory give individual interpreters considerable latitude in determining the possibility of a just cause. With Hegel just war theorists appear to be in the position that it is up to states themselves or the appropriate political community to determine the application of just war theory in any particular instance. Kantian theory recommends itself for me, therefore, because its tendency is towards the minimization, if not the elimination of war. Just war thinking in comparison may have a bias towards the minimization of war, but seems generally committed to the unavoidability of war as an instrument of foreign policy.[50]

8
Conclusion: The Kantian Critique of Just War Theory

> [...] unter denen allein ein allgemeiner Völkerbund möglich ist. Denn wenn gleich keine öffentliche Gerechtigkeit da ist, so sind doch Völker an das gebunden,wodurch sie allererst möglich ist.
>
> Kant: AA XIX, Erläuterungen zu
> G. Achenwalls Iuris..., Seite 598

Conclusion

In this book we have looked at Kant's theory of war in a number of steps, seeking to place it in the context of his philosophy as a whole and within the context of his two major publications on politics: *Perpetual Peace* and the *Metaphysics of Morals*. What I have tried to bring out is not merely Kant's predominant thinking about war and its justifiability but also a view that is internally consistent. Arguably no thinker is wholly consistent throughout the extent of their philosophical systems, and Kant is as fallible as most philosophers in this respect. Indeed it is possible to suggest that he is such a fecund and continually innovative thinker – never quite repeating the same precise sequence of argument – that it would be wrong to expect total consistency in his approach. This is certainly the case with his treatment of the acceptability of war where at times his views seem starkly to diverge. Nonetheless, I have attempted to bring together an account that explains the basic place of the idea of war in his system and then seeks to bring a harmony to the various diverging judgments. It is of course for the reader to judge my success in doing this. But it is my firm view that there is a coherent Kantian view on war that can be defended in the context of Kant's political, historical and legal philosophy.

We began our story with an overall assessment of the role of war in Kant's critical philosophy. We found that he alludes remarkably often to war, not just in his practical philosophy (in his writings on morality, politics, religion and history) but also in his theoretical philosophy. A clear attitude to war becomes evident in *The Critique of Pure Reason* that underpins his later treatment of it and also represents a key element in the argument of the First *Critique* itself. Systematically important accounts of war are to be found also in Kant's historical writings, underpinned by his theory of judgment, and of course also in his moral and political philosophy. War stands condemned as a moral course of action in all Kant's major writings in practical philosophy – and though it is presented as having a positive role to play in his philosophy of history and the *Critique of the Power of Judgment*, this positive role is contained and hemmed in by the overall powerful moral commitment to its eradication. Thus, although some divergences appear in Kant's treatment of war in the early work *Observations on the Feeling of the Sublime and Beautiful* (1764) – and also in the *Critique of the Power of Judgment* where Kant detects a positive side to the experience of war in the dynamic of the sublime which contrasts with his overall moral disapproval of the practice – these divergences are fitted into a coherent pattern in the later political and legal writings, where war is depicted as part of the pathology of human history and as the spur to improvement towards the highest political good of perpetual peace.

The three following chapters looked at the debate on war that occurs in *Perpetual Peace* and the *Metaphysics of Morals*. As the object in this book has been to bring out the critical dimension of Kant's treatment of war, chapter 2 focused first and foremost on the dismissal of just war theory and its protagonists in international law that takes place in *Perpetual Peace*. I have aimed to emphasize this dismissal as a core theme of the book. I have wanted to reassert the previously (and justifiably) predominant view that Kant has no just war theory. As a result I have sought to interpret whatever else Kant has had to say about the acceptability or advisability of war in the light of this core position. Chapter 2 set out the way in which the judgement on war in Kant's political and legal writings seems to be ambivalent. Allowing for the possibility that Kant's judgement changed over time, it considered the conjecture that there may not simply be one view on just war in Kant's philosophy but two.

Chapter 3 attempted to identify as clearly as possible the case that Kant makes against just war thinking in *Perpetual Peace*. I examined closely the terms that Kant uses in rejecting the approach of Grotian international law to the problem of law. I suggested that the Biblical allusion to the troubles of Job evoked by the term 'sorry comforters' is a significant one. Kant shows a close interest in the circumstances of Job's life and religious experiences in his philosophy of religion, and I argue that it is the apparent defeatism and cynicism of Job's interlocutors that he sees in the interpretation of war in the Grotian law of nations. Thus Kant's rejection of just war theory is closely connected to a wholesale reform he should like to see in international law itself. He wants international law transformed into a system of rights that upholds peace rather than maintains the possibility of war.

Having pressed the divergence in Kant's views on the justifiability of war in chapter 3, chapter 4 made the case for their continuity and ultimate unity. If chapter 3 followed an analytic method in separating out the apparently contrary views on the acceptability of war in Kant's political writings, chapter 4 followed a synthetic method in attempting to show their coherence and consistency. As I have indicated previously, the strategy followed was to subordinate the judgements on war in the *Metaphysics of Morals* (which seem to indicate a modified acceptance of just war doctrine) to those of *Perpetual Peace* which indicate no such reconciliation. In doing this I did not wish to suggest that I have discovered the 'true Kant' or the 'authentic Kant', but rather I believe I have outlined the most cogent account of war that can be drawn from Kant's philosophy.

Chapter 5 examined a topic which is closely allied to just war theory in contemporary twenty first century political and international debate – intervention, including armed intervention for purportedly humanitarian purposes in the affairs of other states. Building on Kant's criticism of just war theory, this chapter showed how complex the connection between Kant's legal and political theories and possible grounds for intervention is. Kant's international theory is not as disposed to supporting intervention as many cosmopolitans of today believe. The chapter looked closely at the way in which Kant interprets cosmopolitanism and the grounds for the divergence of his views from those of today's purportedly Kantian commentators such as Roger Scruton and Fernando Teson, who wish to derive from Kant great latitude for humanitarian intervention and armed intervention in general. In the final section of the chapter Jürgen Habermas's support for NATO intervention in Kosovo was closely examined in order to demonstrate that his argument can garner very little support from Kant's legal and political writings. I argued that Kant's writings on international law indicate that a far more cautious approach on the part of Western European states and the United States was called for.

The next chapter looked at the implications of Kant's approach to war for the contemporary genre of just war theory. Since the beginning of the twenty-first century, just war theory has been a prominent concern for political theorists and international relations thinkers. This chapter reviewed the ideas of a number of prominent thinkers in the field with the view to contrasting their approach with the one which arises from Kant's theory. The chapter concluded that there is a remarkable divergence between Kant's objective of bringing an end to war with the project advanced by thinkers such as Michael Walzer and Jean Bethke Elshtain to provide a regulated and agreed moral framework for engaging in war. In this respect these writers are more in agreement with Hegel's communitarian approach to political philosophy than Kant's cosmopolitan view.

Contemporary just war thinkers are, I argued, concerned to normalize war, whereas for Kant it is impossible ever to overlook its pathological aspect. Contemporary just war thinkers such as Walzer and Elshtain see the nation state as the main focus of our loyalties and the bedrock of the international system. They do not take the same step as Kant in seeking to found international law upon a federation of free states. They appear to share Hegel's scepticism about the functioning of such a federation. Distancing Kant from contemporary just war theory provides one of the main impetuses for writing this book, hence the dividing lines presented here are strongly emphasized. At the same time as accepting that Kant is not a pacifist, I none the less wish to stress that he is far from providing a legal or legitimate framework within which war can be waged by peoples and states. War is evidence for Kant that the international system has strayed away from legality and legitimacy. War may help rectify this condition, but it is always a regrettable lapse from civilisation and never to be presented as in itself just.

Is just war theory therefore only for 'sorry comforters' who are not serious about fundamentally altering the human (international) condition? Does it seek to establish a right to something that can never be right? Or is it better than not trying to justify international state violence altogether, falling short of what might be required of a convincing theory of international justice, but at least attempting to bring some moral coherence to an activity which the human race has yet to outgrow?[1] In trying to establish moral and legal conditions where it might be right to go to war, does not just war theory perform an important service in pointing to some situations where war may no longer be permitted to occur? The short answer to these four questions is: yes. But to what extent can we draw the conclusion that the positive answer to the last two questions goes some way towards mitigating the negative impact of the affirmative answers to the first two? Kant's judgement seems to be that the mitigating effect is insufficient to exonerate the just war theorists of his time. His conclusion is that an international justice that rests on the right to go to war is in need of radical revision, and whatever respect he shows to that tradition (and his recognition that its norms still prevail) is thoroughly outweighed by his adherence to a completely revised vision of international law. This revised vision is not one he holds to be utopian and so beyond the reach of current international relations, but one that is immanent within it. We cannot have international law and the right of states to go to war based solely on their sovereign interpretations of self-defence. We can only have international law on the assumption that sovereign states form part of an ever expanding union of peaceful (republican) states. There is of course an inevitable tension here between the actual behaviour of sovereign states and the rules to which they have to conform to realize law. This is a tension that should provide a continuous spur to improving our condition, and not one for which we should seek consolation in just war theory.[2]

In order to illustrate just how abhorrent Kant found war to be, let us consider his preparatory Notes to *Perpetual Peace* Kant draws attention to the plight of the Negroes enslaved by the European powers and traded throughout their colonies in Africa and South America. He deplores this as contrary to the principle of hospitality that provides the foundation for cosmopolitan law. However what is surprising is that Kant draws attention to slavery being even a worse dereliction of right on the part of the Europeans. He means this not only because they are principal perpetrators of the inhuman system of slavery, but also because of the consequences the institution of slavery has for the European powers and their mutual relations. He decries the slavery because it fuels the flames of war amongst the advanced states, which can in his view lead only to even greater destruction and the undermining of civilisation. What is remarkable is the way in which Kant presents war as an even greater evil than slavery (23: 174).

Engaging in war can never be a matter of unequivocal pride for the human race. Indeed if we are as a nation ever involved in war and emerge from it successfully, there can be no room for complacency or joy. Rather, it would be fitting to conclude in Kant's eloquent words: 'at the end of a war, when peace is concluded, it would not be unfitting for a nation to proclaim, after the festival of thanksgiving, a day of atonement, calling upon heaven, in the name of the state, to forgive the great sin of which the human race continues to remain guilty, that of being unwilling to acquiesce in any lawful constitution in relation to other nations but, proud of its independence, preferring instead to use the barbarous means of war (even though what is sought by war, namely the right of each state, is not decided by it). Festivals of thanksgiving during a war for a victory won, hymns that (in the style of the Israelites) are sung to the *Lord of Hosts*, stand in no less marked contrast with the moral idea of the father of human beings; for, beyond indifference to the way nations seek their mutual rights (which is regrettable enough), they bring in joy at having annihilated a great many human beings or their happiness'(8: 357/328).

Notes

Preface

1. First published in 3: AM Magazine: Friday, November 15th, 2013. Other reviews of *KEW* appeared by Alyssa Bernstein (which raises some of the same concerns) in *Ethics and International Affairs* 27, 3, 2013; by Christopher Finlay in *International Affairs* Issue 88, 3, 2012; by Sarah Holtman in *Kantian Review*, 18, 2, 2013.
2. *War and Self-Defence* Oxford: Oxford University Press, 2012
3. A contrary view is put by Heather Roff in her book *Global Justice, Kant and the Responsibility to Protect: A Provisional Duty* London: Routledge, 2013 which I address in *Kantian Review*, 20, 1, 2015

Introduction

1. Cf. Cavallar, Georg *Kant and the theory and practice of International Right* (Cardiff: University of Wales Press, 1999); Covell, Charles *Kant and the Law of Peace* (London: Macmillan, 1998); Easley, Eric *The War over Perpetual Peace* (New York: Palgrave, 2004); Fukuyama, Francis *The End of History and the Last Man* (London: Penguin, 1992); Orend, Brian *War and International Justice: A Kantian perspective* (Waterloo: Wilfrid Laurier University Press, 2000).
2. Doyle, Michael 'Kant, Liberal Legacies, and Foreign Affairs, Part 1 & 2', *Philosophy and Public Affairs* 12, 1983.
3. Fukuyama, Francis *The End of History and the Last Man* (London: Penguin, 1992).
4. Russett, Bruce *Grasping the Democratic Peace* (Princeton, N.J: Princeton University Press, c.1993).
5. Cf. Mark Evans, 'Moral Theory and the Idea of a Just War' in Evans, M. *Just War Theory: A Reappraisal* (Edinburgh: Edinburgh University Press, 2005): 'The fact that we need a just war theory arises from the assumption that, in our non-ideal world, war might at times be morally unavoidable. On such occasions it is justified in response to very great injustice' (p. 9).

1 The Motif of War in Kant's Critical Philosophy

1. References (volume and page number) to Kant's Collected Writings are made to the *Akademieausgabe* (Berlin: Prussian Academy Edition, 1902 onwards). Unless otherwise stated translations are taken from *Kant's Practical Philosophy* translated and edited by Mary Gregor (Cambridge: Cambridge University Press, 1996).
2. In *On the Citizen* (*De Cive*) Hobbes asserts that 'the majority of previous writers on public affairs either assume or seek to prove or simply assert that man is an animal born fit for society...this axiom, though very widely accepted, is nevertheless false; the error proceeds from a superficial view of human nature.' *On the Citizen* edited and translated by Richard Tuck and Michael Silverthorne, Cambridge: Cambridge University Press, 1998, pp. 21–22.

3. English references (second) to *Toward Perpetual Peace and other Writings on Politics, Peace and History*, translated by David L. Colclasure, edited by Pauline Kleingeld (New Haven: Yale, 2006).
4. English references are to (first) *The Critique of the Power of Judgment* translated by Paul Guyer and Eric Matthews (Cambridge University Press, 2000) and *Toward Perpetual Peace and other Writings on Politics, Peace and History*. The translation draws on James Creed Meredith's earlier translation *The Critique of Judgement* (Oxford University Press, 1969), p. 96.
5. For a discussion of these issues see Yovel, Y. *Kant and the Philosophy of History* (Princeton: Princeton University Press, 1980), pp. 158–180; Williams, H.L. *Kant's Political Philosophy* (Oxford, Blackwell, 1983), chapter 1; and Paul Guyer, 'Purpose in Nature: what is living and what is dead in Kant's Teleology', in P. Guyer *Kant's System of Nature and Freedom* (Oxford: Oxford University Press, 2005), pp. 342–72.
6. English translation (first) *Kant's Political Writings* (Cambridge: Cambridge University Press, 1991) translated by H. B. Nisbet edited by H. S. Reiss and *Toward Perpetual Peace and other Writings on Politics, Peace and History*.
7. Andrea Simari, *Pace e guerra nel pensiero di Kant : studi su un tema della filosofia critica* Pubblicazioni dell'Istituto di Filosofia del Diritto dell'Università di Roma; Ser. 3,32 Milano : Giuffrè, 1998.
8. *Geschichte und Naturbeschreibung der merkwürdigsten Vorfälle des Erdbebens, welches an dem Ende des 1755sten Jahres Einen großen Theil der Erde erschüttert hat.* 1: 461.
9. *Observations on the Feeling of the Beautiful and Sublime*, translated by John T. Goldthwait (Berkeley: University of California Press, 1960).
10. *Kant's Political Writings*.
11. *Religion within the Boundaries of Mere Reason*, translated and edited by Allen Wood and George di Giovanni, Cambridge: Cambridge University Press, 1998.
12. *Kant's Political Writings*.
13. *Religion within the Boundaries of Mere Reason*.
14. The article 'Verkuendigung des nahen Abschlusses eines ewigen Friedens' did not in fact appear until June 1797 (See AA 8, 515).
15. *Kant's Political Writings*.
16. For a highly instructive treatment of the problem see Georg Cavallar, *Kant and the theory and practice of International Right* (Cardiff: University of Wales Press, 1999), pp. 61–74. As Cavallar puts it, 'Kant tries to bridge the gap between the imperative of practical reason ('there shall be no war') on the one hand and the realities of war and bloodshed on the other. Kant employs the faculty of reflective judgement, which declares that wars serve an indispensable positive function in the development of humankind. Thus Kant arrives at two mutually exclusive perspectives on war, one based on practical reason, the other one on reflective judgement' (p. 62). As elsewhere, my interpretation of Kant varies somewhat from Cavallar. Here I would also note that the conflict between the imperative of practical reason and the 'realities of war' is also to be found within Kant's reflective judgement.
17. *Critique of the Power of Judgment* translated by Paul Guyer and Eric Matthews (Cambridge: Cambridge University Press, 2000).
18. Hegel expresses a strikingly similar view of war in his *The Elements of the Philosophy of Right*, paragraph 324: 'War is that condition in which the vanity of temporal things and temporal goods – which tends at other times to

be merely a pious phrase – takes on a serious significance.' *The Elements of the Philosophy of Right*, (Cambridge: Cambridge University Press, 1991) p. 361. Hegel of course does not follow Kant in regarding this as an aesthetic judgment. For Hegel it represents a final ethical judgment on war and he rejects Kant's views on perpetual peace as inappropriate to the individuality of states. See addition to p. 324, *The Elements of the Philosophy of Right*, p. 362.
19. Kant suggests that the moment of the 'dynamically sublime' has to be observed from a reflective present perspective where those reflecting are in a position of safety. The ground of the sublimity of the sacrifice is therefore paradoxically a position of present security where no such sacrifice is called upon.
20. This would provide us with a very interesting perspective on twentieth-century history. From a moral perspective it has been marred with the most horrific and destructive of wars; yet from an aesthetic perspective who can deny that it has not seen the most extraordinary creativity? Does great art always have to be paid for in this way by great suffering? This is not, of course, Kant's view but we can see how the Nietzschean standpoint possibly derives from such insights.
21. 'Now, however, although an intelligible world, in which everything would be actual merely because it is (as something good) possible, and even freedom, as its formal condition, is a transcendent concept for us, which is not serviceable for any constitutive principle for determining an object and its objective reality, still, in accordance with the constitution of our (partly sensible) nature, it can serve as a universal regulative principle for ourselves and every being standing in connection with the sensible world, so far as we can represent that in accordance with the constitution of our own reason and capacity, which does not determine the constitution of freedom as a form of causality, objectively, but rather makes the rules of actions in accordance with that idea into commands for everyone and indeed does so with no less validity than if it did determine freedom objectively' (*Critique of the Power of Judgment* 5: 404/274).
22. 'An avid reader of travel narratives concerning distant peoples and alien cultures, he reconceptualised the study of anthropology in popularly accessible lectures on the subject delivered over a period of twenty five years (this was Kant's most frequently given, and most widely attended, university lecture course)' Allen Wood, *Kant* (Blackwell, Oxford, 2005), p. 2.
23. This point is put well by John Rawls in his *Lectures on the History of Moral Philosophy* (Cambridge, Massachusetts: Harvard University Press, 2000) when he says 'it is not enough to affirm our freedom and to recognise the freedom of all persons in virtue of their powers of reason. For we can believe the realm of ends is possible in the world only if the order of nature and social necessities are not unfriendly to that ideal. For this to be so, it must contain forces and tendencies that in the longer run tend to bring out, or at least to support, such a realm and to educate mankind so as to further this end.' So 'we must believe, for example that the course of human history is progressively improving, and not becoming steadily worse, or that it does not fluctuate in perpetuity from bad to good. For in this case we will view the spectacle of human history as a farce that arouses loathing of our species. In our social unsociability that drives us to competition and rivalry,

and even to seemingly endless wars and conquests, we may not unreasonably hope to discern a plan of nature to force mankind, if it is to save itself from destruction, to form a confederation of constitutional democratic states, which will then ensure perpetual peace and encourage the free development of culture and the arts. By this long path we may reasonably believe a realm of ends will come about in the world' (pp. 319–20).

24. 'The universal true religious faith' 'contains no mystery' and 'is also by nature available to all human reason and is therefore to be met with in the religion of most civilized peoples' (6: 139–40; Wood & Giovanni, p. 142).

25. Maria Chiara Pievatolo describes Kant's pacifying philosophical procedure as 'The Tribunal of Reason'. The tribunal or reason is a metaphor Kant himself deploys. For Pievatolo its task is 'not the foundation of our frameworks of theoretical and practical knowledge, but their legitimation' (p. 311). And 'two contending parties appeal to a court or a tribunal when they set up conflicting claims, but agree to settle their quarrel in a legal manner, namely following particular proceedings and a particular syntax' (312). From 'The Tribunal of Reason: Kant on the Juridical Nature of Pure Reason', *Ratio Juris*. Vol. 12 No. 3 September 1999, pp. 311–27.

26. Onora O'Neill draws attention to this coalescence of theoretical and practical goals in Kant's philosophy in her essay 'Reason and Politics in the Kantian Enterprise'. where she makes the suggestion that 'the first *Critique* is a political work' (*Constructions of Reason: Explorations of Kant's Practical Philosophy*), p. 4.

27. As O'Neill puts it when speaking of the kind of authority that Kant wishes to invoke with his *Critique of Pure Reason* : 'it is not like the discipline imposed by dictators or conquerors who coerce obedience, but like the discipline of those who must interact without relying either on imposed or preestablished harmony' (*Constructions of Reason*, p. 15).

2 Kant and Just War Theory: The Problem Outlined

1. Comments on G. Achenwall's *Juris naturalis pars posterior complectens jus faliliae, jus publicum et jus gentium*. Another way of putting this is to say that with Kant for a genuine law of nations to take effect requires that nations should regard themselves as already part of a union of peoples.
2. *Religion within the Boundaries of Mere Reason*, 6: 37; 59.
3. Cf. Allen Wood 'Kant's Compatibilism', in A. Wood (ed.) *Self and Nature in Kant's Philosophy* (Ithaca: Cornell University Press, 1984).
4. *Erlaeuterung zu G. Achenwall's Juris naturalis pars posterior complectens jus faliliae, jus publicum et jus gentium. Editio qvinta emendatior*, Göttingen 1763. *Casus necessitates* is often translated as a 'right of necessity' and 'occasion of necessity' represents a more literal translation. Kant specifically rejects the idea of a right of necessity in the appendix to the introduction to the Doctrine of Right. 'The alleged right is supposed to be an authorization to take the life of another who is doing nothing to harm me, when I am in danger of losing my own life. It is evident that were there such a right the doctrine of right would be in contradiction with itself.' 'The deed of

saving one's life by violence is not to be judged inculpable (*inculpabile*) but only unpunishable (*impunible*), and by a strange confusion jurists take this subjective impunity to be an objective impunity (conformity with law). The motto of the right of necessity says: "Necessity has no law" (*necessitas non habet legem*). Yet there could be no necessity that would make what is wrong conform with law' (6: 235/391–2).
5. T. Aquinas, *Selected Political Writings* ed. A.P. D'Entreves, translated by J. G. Dawson, Oxford: Basil Blackwell, 1965, 159.
6. Robert L. Holmes: *On War and Morality* (Princeton: Princeton University Press, 1989), p. 153.
7. Michael Walzer *Just and Unjust Wars* (New York: Basic Books, 1977), p. 62.
8. 'There exists an international society of independent states. States are members of this society, not private men and women. In the absence of a universal state, men and women are protected and their interests represented only by their own governments', Walzer, *Just and Unjust Wars*, p. 61.
9. 'Taken as a whole, just war tradition has to do with defining the place of the resort to force in statecraft and with specifying the limits of justified uses of force. A body of historical wisdom, reflection and precedent attaches to each of the criteria that make up the classic *jus ad bellum* and *jus in bello*, defining their meaning with a great deal of clarity and precision. Yet just war tradition, like the field of law in the Anglo-Saxon legal tradition, is not fully defined at any time by these criteria understood as principles or by a static understanding of their meaning as developed in past wisdom, reflection and precedent'. James Turner Johnston, *Morality and Contemporary Warfare* (New Haven: Yale, 1999) 39–40 See also: Rengger, Nicholas (2002) 'On the just war tradition in the twenty-first century.' *International Affairs* 78 (2), pp. 353–363.
10. Hugo Grotius: *De iure belli et pacis* (1625); Samuel von Pufendorf: *De iure nature et gentium* (1672); Emmerich von Vattel: *Droit de Gens* (1758). On Grotius' and Vattel's views of international law and relations see the chapters 'Grotius, Law and Moral Scepticism' by Benedict Kingsbury and 'Vattel: Pluralism and its limits' by Andrew Hurrell in Iver Neumann and Ian Clark (eds) *Classical Theories of International Relations* (Houndsmill: Macmillan, 1996) pp. 42–71 & 233–56. For Pufendorf see David Boucher.
11. B. Orend *War and International Justice* (Waterloo: Wilfrid Laurier Press, 2000) see especially chapter 2 'Kant's Just War Theory' pp. 41–61; S. Shell 'Kant on Unjust War and "Unjust Enemies": reflections on a pleonasm', *Kantian Review* 10, pp .82–102.
12. Gottfried Achenwall: *Juris naturalis pars posterior complectens jus faliliae, jus publicum et jus gentium. Editio qvinta emendatior*, Göttingen 1763. Kant studied this text in depth. Volume 19 of *Kants Gesammelte Schriften* pp. 323–442 includes detailed extracts and a commentary.
13. Christian Wolff *Jus gentium methodo scientifica pertractatum* Halle, 1750. Although there are no detailed notes to this work in Kant's writings, Kant plays close attention to Wolff's philosophy in general so there is reason to believe that he was familiar with the treatment of natural law it contains.
14. 'John Locke and International Politics' in H. Williams *International Relations and the Limits of Political Theory* (Houndsmill: Macmillan, 1996) pp. 90–109, see especially p. 96.

15. T. Aquinas, *Selected Political Writings* p. 121: 'all laws, so far as they accord with right reason, derive from the eternal law.' Natural laws are discovered through the deployment of right reason. 'Natural law is nothing else than the participation of the eternal law in rational creatures' p. 115.
16. Hugo Grotius *Commentary on the Law of Prize and Booty*, translated by Gwladys L. Williams (Indianapolis: Liberty Fund, 2006), p. 16.
17. Hugo Grotius *Commentary on the Law of Prize and Booty*, p. 20.
18. Hugo Grotius *Commentary on the Law of Prize and Booty*, p. 21.
19. Hugo Grotius *Commentary on the Law of Prize and Booty*, p. 21.
20. *Commentary on the Law of Prize and Booty* was Grotius's first major publication which was commissioned by the Dutch East India Company to provide a defence for the seizure by Jacob van Heemskerck of the Portuguese merchantman Santa Catarina in the Strait of Singapore on February 25, 1603. At the time the northern Netherlands were in revolt against the Kingdom of Spain and Portugal from which they were only to attain their independence in 1648. Grotius' brief was to demonstrate that the seizure of the valuable ship and contents was part of the rightful fruits of similarly rightful war. See Martine Julia van Ittersum's Introduction pp. xiii–xiv.
21. Hugo Grotius *Commentary on the Law of Prize and Booty*, p. 67.
22. 'Grotius believed that war itself was neither inherently right nor wrong. Correctly used, it could be an instrument used by rational people to preserve society. International law, Grotius believed, provided a framework for evaluating when and how war could be legitimately used.' Alex Bellamy *Just Wars* (Cambridge: Polity, 2006), p. 71.
23. 'The Grotius Factor in International Law and Relations: A Functional Approach', *Hugo Grotius and International Relations* (Oxford: Oxford University Press, 1992), pp. 307–8. Schwarzenberger also gives an interesting summary of Grotius 'treatment of international law' which 'can be condensed into three propositions. First, primary natural law is immutable and would exist even if God did not. Second, secondary natural law, which is based on primary natural law, coexists with positive law but may be modified by the latter. Third, the principles of natural law and the rules deduced from these principles may manifest themselves at any time and in any walk of life. Thus they can be demonstrated by evidence from any kind and from any quarter – holy or otherwise' (pp. 305–6).
24. B. Kaposy & R. Whatmore Introduction to E. Vattel *The Law of Nations* Indianapolis: Liberty Fund, 2008.
25. Vattel says in the Preface to *The Law of Nations*: 'From Monsieur Wolff's treatise, therefore I have only borrowed whatever appeared most worthy of attention, especially the definitions and general principles; but I have been careful in selecting what I drew from that source, and have accommodated to my own plan the materials with which he furnished me. Those who have read Monsieur Wolff's treatises on the law of nature and the law of nations, will see what advantages I have made of them. Had I everywhere pointed out what I have borrowed, my pages would be crowded with quotations equally useless and disagreeable to the reader. It is better to acknowledge here, once and for all, the obligations I am under to that great master' p. xii/15.
26. *The Law of Nations*, pp. 301/483.
27. *The Law of Nations*, p. 302.

28. *The Law of Nations*, pp. 306/489.
29. *Law of Nations*, pp. 305–6.
30. Susan Shell 'Kant on Unjust War and "Unjust Enemies": reflections on a pleonasm', *Kantian Review* 10, 2005.
31. Brian Orend *War and International Justice: A Kantian Perspective* (Waterloo: Wilfrid Laurier University Press, 2000), p. 42.
32. Brian Orend *War and International Justice: A Kantian Perspective*, p. 43.
33. S. Shell 'Kant on Unjust War and "Unjust Enemies"', p. 100.
34. S. Shell 'Kant on Unjust War and "Unjust Enemies": reflections on a pleonasm', pp. 98–100.
35. What are the signs that the discipline of international law wants entirely to give up its role as 'sorry comforter'? These are the remarks of a progressive and reform-minded international lawyer: 'More than any other corpus of legal rules, international law directly and transparently reflects power relations. It only partially restrains States' behaviour. War marks the passage from relatively harmonious relations to armed contention. War is the area in which power politics reach their peak and law relinquishes its control over international dealings. In the daily wrangle between force and law, the latter, of necessity, loses ground: international legal rules hold Armaggedon only partially at bay. First, it refrains from imposing restraints on the most dangerous forms of armed violence. Second, all too often existing legal restraints are checkmated by sheer power. This state of affairs is only natural, given the mental disposition of most people and, what is even more important, the division of the world community into self-seeking nation-States, each of them claiming – as Suarez observed – to be *communitas perfecta* (a perfect community). Therefore, realistically one can simply require international law to *mitigate* at least some of the most frightful manifestations of the clash of arms. This is precisely what the rules on warfare do.' Antonio Cassese, *International Law* (Oxford: Oxford University Press, 2004), p. 325. Quite clearly Cassese sees many insuperable obstacles in human nature and the sovereign state system to the overcoming of war.
36. M. Gregor, 'Introduction to the metaphysics of morals' *Practical Philosophy*, (Cambridge: Cambridge University Press, 1996), p. 360.
37. M. Gregor, 'Translator's note on the text of the metaphysics of morals' *Practical Philosophy*, p. 355.
38. The translation has been modified here.
39. Sharon Byrd and Joachim Hruschka, *Kant's Doctrine of Right: A commentary* (Cambridge: Cambridge University Press, 2010, p. 13.
40. S. Byrd and J. Hruschka, *Kant's Doctrine of Right*, p. 13.
41. S. Byrd and J. Hruschka, *Kant's Doctrine of Right*, p. 15.
42. S. Byrd and J. Hruschka, *Kant's Doctrine of Right*, p. 15. See also p. 195.
43. *Kant: Practical Philosophy*, p. 313.

3 *Perpetual Peace* and the Case against Just War Theory

1. B. Orend *War and International Justice*, p. 48.
2. For an alternative reading of the differences between the individual state of nature and the international state of nature see Susan Shell 'Kant on Unjust

War and "Unjust Enemies.": 'The analogy between the individual and international state of nature is imperfect in a decisive sense: the latter condition is not, strictly speaking, a 'status justicia vacuus', that is, 'empty of right' (see 8: 355). Each state is the realization, however imperfect, of the right of its own members, whose claims it at least partially 'executes', that is, gives outward, reciprocally determinate force. The obligation to leave the international state of nature is thus qualified by the prior obligation of states to uphold the rights of their own citizens. States, as Kant puts it in *Perpetual Peace*, have 'outgrown' the status that makes individuals in a state of nature liable to outer compulsion. States are nothing (so far as permitting their members to actualize their rights is concerned) if they are not sovereign. Hence, they cannot be externally forced to submit themselves to a higher sovereign power (*Gewalt*) (8: 356). Kant holds forth a tentative hope that the peoples of the world may one day voluntarily consent to join a world republic (or state of nations) (p. 89).
3. 'What holds in accordance with natural right for human beings in a lawless condition, "they ought to leave this condition, cannot hold for states in accordance with the right of nations (since, as states, they already have a rightful constitution internally and hence have outgrown the constraint of others to bring them under a more extended law-governed constitution in accordance with their concepts of right)' (8: 355–6/327).
4. M. Walzer, *Just and Unjust Wars*, p. 44.
5. Alex J. Bellamy, *Just Wars* (Cambridge: Polity, 2006), p. 2.
6. Alex J. Bellamy, *Just Wars*, p. 2.
7. Alex J. Bellamy, *Just Wars*, p. 2.
8. Alex J. Bellamy, *Just Wars*, p. 5.
9. Georg Cavallar, *The Rights of Strangers: Theories of International Hospitality, the global community and Political Justice since Vitoria* (Aldershot: Ashgate, 2002).
10. *The Rights of Strangers*, pp. 338–9.
11. E. De Vattel, *The Law of Nations or the principles of Natural Law* (New York: Oceana Publications, 1964), p. 237.
12. Cf. Samuel Pufendorf *On the Duty of Man and Citizen* (Cambridge: Cambridge University Press, 1991) p. 168: '1. It is most agreeable to natural law that men should live in peace with each other by doing of their own accord what their duty requires; indeed peace itself is a state peculiar to man, insofar as he is distinct from the beasts. Nevertheless, for man too war is sometimes permitted, and occasionally necessary, namely when by the ill will of another we cannot preserve our property or obtain our right without the use of force. In this situation, however, good sense and humanity counsel us not to resort to arms when more evil than good is likely to overtake us and ours by the prosecution of our wrongs. 2. The just causes of engaging in war come down to the preservation and protection of our lives and property against unjust attack, or the collection of what is due to us from others but has been denied, or the procurement of reparations for wrong inflicted and of assurance for the future. Wars waged for the first of these causes are said to be defensive, for the other causes, offensive.'
13. *The Rights of Strangers*, p. 339.
14. Johann Georg Hamann, *Londoner Schriften* eds. Oswald Beyer and Bernd Weissenborn (Munich: 1993) p. 342. See Cavallar below p. 14.

15. Cavallar, Georg *Die europaeische Union – von der Utopie zur Friedens- und Wertegemeinschaft* (Vienna: LIT Verlag, 2006), p. 14.
16. Cf. Ann L. Loades *Kant and Job's Comforters* (Newcastle upon Tyne: Avero Publications, 1985).
17. *Religion within the Boundaries of Mere Reason*, edited and translated by Allen Wood and George di Giovanni (Cambridge: Cambridge University Press).
18. Consider for instance Vattel's assertion: 'In treating the right to security, we have shown that nature gives man the right to use force when it is needed for the defence and preservation of their rights. This principle is generally recognised; reason asserts it and nature itself has engraved it on the heart of man. Certain fanatics, it is true, taking literally the moderation recommended in the Gospel, have conceived the idea of letting themselves be slaughtered or plundered, rather than resist violence by force. But we need not fear that this error will make any progress. The greater part of mankind will guard against it of their own accord, and it will be well if in doing so they manage to keep within the just limits which nature has set to a right granted only from necessity. To define precisely what those limits are, to moderate, by the rules of justice, equity, and humanity, the exercise of a right inherently severe and too often of necessary application, is the object of this third book'. *The Law of Nations or the principles of Natural Law* third book 'War', p. 235.
19. Hamann was in touch with Kant shortly after his visit to London in 1757. Letter from J.G. Hamann, July 27, 1759 10: pp. 7–16; *Philosophical Correspondence* edited by Arnulf Zweig, Cambridge: Cambridge University Press, 1999, pp. 47–54.
20. Andrew Hurrell, 'Vattel: pluralism and its limits' in Ian Clark & Iver B. Neumann, *Classical Theories of International Relations*' (Houndsmill; Macmillan, 1996), p. 238.
21. Christian Wolff, *Grundsaetze des Natur- und Voelkerrechts* Vorwort Marcel Thomann Hildesheim; New York : Olms, 1980. Reprint of the first edition Halle: Renger, 1754, pp. 796–7.
22. Christian Wolff, *Grundsaetze des Natur- und Voelkerrechts*, p. 857.
23. Christian Wolff, *Grundsaetze des Natur- und Voelkerrechts*, p. 887.
24. *Just and Unjust Wars*, p. 62.
25. 'Kant is neither an "idealist" nor a "realist" in the usual sense. Despite his reputation as a champion of peace and cosmopolitanism, Kant unlike so many idealists, has a robust conception of national sovereignty and of the duty, as well as right, of nations to defend themselves – if necessary, pre-emptively. And unlike so-called realists, who reduce human behaviour to the calculation of advantage, Kant has a lively – and some would say more genuinely realistic – sense of the "irrationalities" that beset human action, especially in politics.' S. Shell 'Kant on Unjust War and "Unjust Enemies"', p. 82.
26. B. Orend, *War and International Justice*, p. 43. Orend continues on the same page: 'the common tendency to read only *Perpetual Peace* (something which Teson and Gallie seem guilty of) is, in particular, a prime source of this confusion' and 'the related tendency to put disproportionate emphasis on *Perpetual Peace*, even when drawing on some other crucial texts (something which both Williams and Geismann seem guilty of), leads to the same

error'. Here I am of course seeking to vindicate my earlier reading of Kant by showing that taken together Kant's texts demonstrate that he does not uphold traditional just war theory.
27. Cavallar, Georg *The Rights of Strangers* Aldershot: Ashgate, 2002, p. 338.

4 The *Metaphysics of Morals* and the Case for Just War Theory

1. Kaufmann, M. 'What is New in the Theory of War in Kant's *Metaphysics of Morals?*' *Annual Review of Law and Ethics* 16, 2008, pp. 147–164.
2. 'What is New in the Theory of War in Kant's *Metaphysics of Morals?*' p. 147.
3. 'What is New in the Theory of War in Kant's *Metaphysics of Morals?*' p. 149.
4. 1769, 1772/23, 1774, 1775, 1777, 1778, 1780, 1782, 1784, 1786, and 1788. See Steve Naragon's excellent website http://www.manchester.edu/kant/notes/notesLaw.htm.
5. Thomas Paine *The Rights of Man* (London: Dent, 1969) pp. 94–5.
6. In his very interesting study *The Invention of Autonomy* (Cambridge: Cambridge University Press, 1998) J.B. Schneewind appears to identify Kant's moral philosophy with the 'collapse of natural law' (p. 141). In Schneewind's view, after Locke and Thomasius 'there were no major natural law thinkers' (p. 11). In terms of a broad historical sweep of the period this may well be correct; however, it appears that Kant does not abandon the perspective of natural law entirely but wants to subsume it within his critical system. This in itself constitutes a very interesting story, which I pursue here although it is not taken up by Schneewind.
7. *Leviathan* ed. Richard Tuck (Cambridge: Cambridge University Press, 1991), p. 91.
8. There is a great deal of discussion in the scholarly literature on Kant's philosophy as to how this relationship between the phenomenal and noumenal is to be understood. Henry Allison has played a prominent role in this discussion suggesting that the relationship should be seen not as one between two worlds but two aspects. See *Kant's Theory of Freedom*, Henry Allison. Cambridge: Cambridge University Press, 1990 and Onora O'Neill's review in *Mind* Vol. 100, July 1992, pp. 373–76.
9. Given Hobbes's doubts about the innate nature of any of our rights it is very intriguing that at the end of his outline of the major natural laws he finds room to praise in such an extravagant way the significance of the laws of nature. Arguably it is from these sections that those who seek to present Hobbes as a normative thinker derive some of the inspiration for their standpoint. On the face of it this is a startling avowal from Hobbes, who has devoted a good deal of space in *Leviathan* up to this point on demonstrating how inadequate natural law theory is. Earlier chapters leave the very clear impression that without the power of sword natural law is impotent. Here suddenly we are confronted by extraordinary confession of faith:
'The Laws of Nature are Immutable and Eternal (*The Laws of Nature are Eternal;*) For Injustice, Ingratitude, Arrogance, Pride, Iniquity, Acceptation of persons, and the rest, can never be made lawful. For

182 Notes

it can never be that War shall preserve life, and Peace destroy it. The Science of these Laws, is the true Moral Philosophy. And the Science of them is the true and only Moral Philosophy. For Moral Philosophy is nothing else but the Science of what is *good*, and *Evil*, in the conversation, and Society of man-kind.' (p. 110). The science of the laws of nature occupies the space of the whole of practical philosophy. It dictates what only is good in society but what also is good in individual conduct.

10. Antonio Cassese in *International Law* (Oxford: Oxford University Press, 2001) describes customs and treaties as 'the two most important sources of international law' which are 'envisaged by two basic "constitutional" rules of the international community'. These are *'consuetudo est servanda*, that is, all international subjects must comply with customary rules, and *pacta sunt servanda*, that is, the parties to international agreements must abide by them'. See p. 149.
11. E. De Vattel, *The Law of Nations or the principles of Natural Law*, p. xvi.
12. E. De Vattel, *The Law of Nations or the principles of Natural Law*, p. xvi.
13. Kant particularly seemed to view republican France in a positive light (7: 85/155) and in the essay 'What is Enlightenment' he speaks with some pride of Fredrick the Great's Prussia (8: 41/21).
14. Szymkowiak, Aaron. "Of Free Federations and World States: Kant's Right and the Limits of International Justice." *International Philosophical Quarterly* 49, no. 2 (2009): pp. 185–206.

5 Bringing the Argument Together

1. Kant appears not to state directly what his purpose in writing and publishing *Perpetual Peace*. I am deducing what cannot have been absent from his intentions from the occasion of the publication. The opening paragraph of *Perpetual Peace* implies that he was seeking the attention of both the public and political leaders since he includes the saving clause to protect himself against any 'malicious interpretation' that 'the practical politician takes the stance of looking down with great self-satisfaction on the theoretical politician as an academic, who with his ineffectual ideas, poses no danger to the state' so the academic's publicly expressed views 'can be allowed to fire off all his skittle balls at once' (8: 343; 317). In the secret article for perpetual peace that Kant added to the second edition of the book, he is more explicit. There he makes clear his view that 'the maxims of philosophers about the conditions under which public peace is possible shall be consulted by states armed for war'. It seems reasonable to suppose, therefore, that Kant saw his own book as part of the process where 'the legislative authority of the state' 'seeks from its subjects (philosophers) instructions about the principles of its conduct toward other states' and so will 'allow them to speak freely and publicly about universal maxims for waging war and establishing peace' (8: 368; 337). Thus Kant sees *Perpetual Peace* as not primarily giving instructions as to how any particular policy should be executed but rather as providing advice as to how policies in general should be shaped. The role of the philosopher who writes *Perpetual Peace* is to 'throw light' on the 'business' of ruling.

2. Gottfried Achenwall & Johann Stephan Puetter, *Anfangsgruende des Naturrechts*, edited and translated from the Latin by Jan Schroeder, Frankfurt am Main, 1995. This is a translation of the 1750 first edition of Achenwall's *Iuris Naturae*. Although Puetter appears as the co-author, in reality his contribution was small.(p. 334). Later editions of the book (by 1781 eight had already appeared) were published under Achenwall's name alone.
3. In the dedication to the *First Principles of Natural Law* Achenwall remarks that 'the Germans are already long used to this new philosophical literature which has sprung up from the academies like a Trojan Horse'. He does not claim that there are 'any new truths in this book'. Indeed he believes it is difficult in 'our century' to say anything new about the subject that is not already known. Their object was to minimize the errors. Gottfried Achenwall & Johann Stephan Puetter, *Anfangsgruende des Naturrechts*, p. 15.
4. Bruno Jahn *Biographische Enzylkopaedie deutscher Philosophen* Munich: Saur, 2001.
5. B. Sharon Byrd & Joachim Hruschka, *Kant's Doctrine of Right: A Commentary* Cambridge: Cambridge University Press, 2010, p. 16.
6. Kant sees Achenwall as making the 'common mistake' 'when the principle of right is under discussion, of substituting the principle of happiness for it in their judgements, and in part that, where there is to be found no instrument of an actual contract submitted to the commonwealth, accepted by its head, and sanctioned by both, they take the idea of an original contract, which is always present in reason as the basis [of the commonwealth], as something that must actually have taken place, and so think they can always save for the people authorization to withdraw from the contract as it sees fit if, though by its own appraisal, the contract has been grossly violated' 8: 301–2/300.
7. Johann Georg Heinrich Feder, *Lehrbuch des praktischen Philosophie* Göttingen, Johann Christian Dietrich, 1776. This is already a fourth edition of the textbook.
8. For a translation of the review which appeared in the *Gottishcen Anzeigen von Gelerhten Sachen* see Bridget Sassen *Kant's Early Critics*, Cambridge: ambridge University Press, 2000.
9. J. G. Feder *Ueber Raum und Causalität, zur Prüfung der kantischen Philosophie*, Göttingen 1787.
10. Feder, *Lehrbuch der praktischen Philosophie*, p. 3.
11. Feder, *Lehrbuch der praktischen Philosophie*, p. 330.
12. Feder, *Lehrbuch der praktischen Philosophie*, p. 334.
13. Feder, *Lehrbuch der praktischen Philosophie*, p. 219.
14. Feder refers to them as *Ansfallskriege* or 'wars of aggression'. Feder, *Lehrbuch der praktischen Philosophie*, p. 221.
15. Feder, *Lehrbuch der praktischen Philosophie*, pp. 339–341.
16. Cf. Mary Gregor, editorial notes to *Kant: Practical Philosophy*, p. 638.
17. Susan Shell's argument in 'Kant on Just War and "Unjust Enemies"' (pp. 99–100) seems to follow this line.
18. Georg Cavallar in *Kant and the theory of International Right* (pp. 94–102) makes a very good case for this view. Particularly notable is his suggestion that 'the line of argument in *Perpetual Peace* is dominated by Kant's newly developed principle of publicity, whereas the *Rechtslehre* focuses on the right to make war and the concept of injury' (p. 95). This is indisputable but does

it not suggest that the *Rechtslehre* though published after *Perpetual Peace* may show Kant's thinking at an earlier stage in his intellectual development?

19. As G. Cavallar shows opinion was divided amongst the 'sorry comforters' themselves as to whether or not it was permissible to go to war against an 'overwhelming or powerful and threatening state'. 'Hugo Grotius, often seen as the founder of modern international law theory, explicitly rejects the right to go to war in order to prevent the growth of a power that might later become dangerous. We are not justified in claiming the mere possibility of suffering from the use of force entitles us to this very use of force.' It is Emer de Vattel who 'first sides with Grotius, claiming that acquiring new territories in itself is no injustice' but then 'absolutely abandons Grotius's position' to argue that 'preventive wars against *potentia tremenda* are legitimate, provided that: 1) The neighbouring country is actually powerful and dangerous; 2) This country has committed an injustice; 3) The imminent evil is considerable; 4) It is more than likely, almost certain that the state in question is planning an aggression. *Kant and the theory of International Right*, pp. 96–7. Vattel stresses the precariousness of relations amongst states: 'The interests of Nations have an importance quite different from the interests of individuals; the sovereign can not be indolent in his guardianship over them; he can not put aside his suspicions out of magnanimity and generosity. A Nation's whole existence is at stake when it has a neighbour that is at once powerful and ambitious.' E. Vattel *The Law of Nations or the principles of natural law* tr. Charles G. Fenwick (New York: Oceana, 1964), p. 249.

20. Gottfried Achenwall & Johan Stephan Puetter, *Anfangsgruende des Naturrechts*, edited and translated from the Latin by Jan Schroeder, Frankfurt am Main, 1995. In the 1750 edition Achenwall sees the right of war in general as arising when a people or nation 'is injured' (p. 317). He connects this point up to his discussion of injury in the first part of the book dealing with in the individual state of nature. There Achenwall maintains 'with every his (Seinen)' – in other words, once property comes into existence – 'the moral capability is given to coerce another. Before an injury this is only a possible capacity after it is an actual one' (p. 149). Thus nations bring war on themselves by acting against what rightfully belongs to another. Whoever is injured 'exercises rightful coercion against the injurer'? (p. 149). Such a nation that has a just cause constitutes for Achenwall a rightful enemy (*hosti iusto*). This rightful enemy who acts according to law is allowed to do everything which can contribute to the creation of complete security. Thus both open and secret coercion are permitted – each act of force is rightful or legitimate. The just or rightful enemy can lay waste (*verwusten*) the territories and population of its attackers and has full rights of occupation once the opponent is defeated. The enemy that acts in accord with law 'has every right against the things of an enemy' (p. 319). Achenwall thus very much favours the rightful or just enemy. Such a combatant is one that is wholly engaged in defending itself and bringing about security. Violence and occupation are legal 'in a just war' insofar as it contributes to the regaining of the condition of full security, however 'when these limits are overstepped' the enemy becomes 'the unjust enemy'. But who is likely to dare enter such a situation – overstep these limits in such a way – where there is such all round confusion (p. 321). Here Achenwall refers us back to his discussion

of individual right where he speaks of the right to war in a state of nature (p. 486).

Achenwall makes the very striking statement that the 'enemy does not cease to be a human being. Thus he is capable of human rights' thus the enemy must hold to contracts which have been made in relation to war. It has to be agreed in advance between the parties that such contracts hold also in war (p. 321).

21. There may be a parallel here with Rawls's notion of the state as a rational actor, which 'as in the traditional account of sovereignty' is accorded 'a right of war in the rational pursuit of a state's national interests' but 'these alone are not a sufficient reason.' For Rawls 'no state has a right to go to war in the pursuit of rational as opposed to its *reasonable* interests. J. Rawls *The Law of Peoples*, p. 90. Rawls seems here to be using the term rational in terms of instrumental/prudential rather than practical or moral reasoning.
22. Carl Schmitt: *The Nomos of the Earth* translated and annotated by G.L. Ulmen (New York: Telos Press, 2003), p. 171: 'If St Augustine says that the idea of war would be still more depressing if filtered through the idea of just war, then the concept of an unjust enemy can increase this depression, because it does not have the act, but rather the perpetrator in view. If it is difficult for people to distinguish between a just enemy and a felon, how can they view an unjust enemy as anything more than a grievous criminal? And in what sense does he remain an antagonist in a war circumscribed by international law? In the final analysis, identification of enemy and criminal also must remove the limits Kant places on the just victor, since he does not allow for the disappearance of a state or for the fact that a people might be robbed of their constituent power. Ultimately, this reinforces the fact that Kant is a philosopher and an ethicist, but not a jurist. On one side, he has the *justus hostis*, and on the other the *unjust enemy* – a concept whose discriminatory power to divide goes even deeper than does that of just war a *justa causa*.
23. Carl Schmitt: *The Nomos of the Earth*, p. 160.
24. S. Shell, 'Kant on just war and "unjust enemies"' p. 102.
25. S. Shell, 'Kant on just war and "unjust enemies"' p. 103. For a critical response to Shell's article see Georg Cavallar 'Commentary on Susan Meld Shell's "Kant on Just War and "Unjust Enemies": Reflections on a "Pleonasm"' *Kantian Review* Volume 11, 2006, pp. 117–124.
26. Balthazar Ayala, *Three Books On the Law of War and the Duties Connected with War and Military Discipline* (New York: Oceana Publications, 1964), p. 59.
27. B. Ayala, *Three Books On the Law of War*, p. 60.
28. Carl Schmitt: *The Nomos of the Earth*, pp. 153/125.
29. Carl Schmitt: *The Nomos of the Earth*, pp. 153/124–5.
30. Carl Schmitt, *The Concept of the Political*, edited and translated by George Schwab (Chicago: Chicago University Press, 1996), p. 33: 'For it is a fact that the entire life of a human being is a struggle and every human being symbolically a combatant... War follows from enmity. War is the existential negation of the enemy.'
31. In his essay 'What is Enlightenment?' Kant even seems to suggest that an enlightened autocracy may present a better form of government to democracy in developing the freedom of a people. 'Only a ruler who is himself

enlightened and has no fear of phantoms, yet who likewise has at hand a well-disciplined and numerous army to guarantee public security, may say what no republic would dare to say: Argue as much as you like and about whatever you like, only obey'. A higher degree of civil freedom seems advantageous to a people's intellectual freedom, yet it also sets up insuperable barriers to it. Conversely, a lesser degree of civil freedom gives intellectual freedom enough room to expand to its fullest extent' 8: 41; *Kant's Political Writings*, edited by H.S. Reiss (Cambridge: Cambridge University Press, 1991), p. 59.
32. *Law of Nations*, p. 237.
33. A.P. D'Entreves (ed.) *Aquinas: Selected Political Writings* (Oxford, Blackwell, 1965), p. 159: 'For war to be just three conditions are necessary. First, the authority of the ruler within whose competence it lies to declare war. A private individual may not declare war; for he can have recourse to the judgement of a superior to safeguard his rights. Nor has he the right to mobilize the people, which is necessary in war.'

Cf. also J. T. Johnson, *Morality and Contemporary Warfare*, p. 46: 'For medieval just war thinkers it reflected the fact that the problem of who actually might authorize resort to force was a major question for the shape of the social order. Indeed, there were two distinct questions. First, at what level in the feudal hierarchy did a person have the right to employ armed force on his own authority? The problem here was the claims of members of the lower nobility, individual knights and men-at-arms, and even on occasion townspeople and peasants to have the right to use arms on their own responsibility as they determined. In practice, this led to a high level of social violence and fragmented – often unjust – rule by local warlords or armed gangs. These claims were opposed by the higher nobility and the Church, leading to efforts by both (such as the Peace of God movement beginning in the South of France in the late tenth century) to impose social order by restricting the right to authorize the use of armed force to the highest level of secular rule in a defined region. The second question was whether authority to employ such force extended to lords of the Church (the Pope, bishops in their dioceses) or only to secular rulers.'
34. *Aquinas: Selected Political Writings*, edited by A. P D'Entreves (Oxford: Blackwell, 1959) p.159.
35. 'Whether the state as a whole or only particular persons are the proper objects of punishment is a harder question...But the implication of the paradigm is clear: if states are members of international society, the subjects of right, they must also be (somehow) the objects of punishment.' *Just and Unjust Wars*, pp. 62–3.
36. *Kant's Practical Philosophy*, p. 638, note 33.

6 Kantian Perspectives on Foreign Intervention

1. See Anthony Coates 'Humanitarian Intervention: a conflict of tradition' in Terry Nardin & Melissa S. Williams (eds.) *Humanitarian Intervention* (New York: New York University Press, 2006): 'Except for terrorism, no issue is

more prominent in contemporary ethical debate about war than humanitarian intervention.... Like terrorism, humanitarian intervention appears to break the existing ethical and legal mold of war' (p. 58).
2. 'This report is about the so-called "right of humanitarian intervention": the question of when, if ever, it is appropriate for states to take coercive – and particular military – action, against another state for the purpose of protecting people at risk in that other state.' *The Responsibility to Protect*, Report of the International Commission on Intervention and State Sovereignty (Ottawa: International Development Research Centre, 2001), p. VII.
3. *The Responsibility to Protect*, Supplementary Volume, (Ottawa: International Development Research Centre, 2001), p. 138.
4. *The Responsibility to Protect*, Supplementary Volume, p. 139.
5. *The Responsibility to Protect*, Report, p. 32.
6. *The Responsibility to Protect*, Supplementary Volume, p. 140.
7. *The Responsibility to Protect*, Report, p. 7.
8. *The Responsibility to Protect*, Report, p. 8.
9. *The Responsibility to Protect*, Report, p. 29.
10. See Terry Nardin & Melissa S. Williams (eds) *Humanitarian Intervention* (New York: New York University Press, 2006) where there are over a dozen entries in the index which compares with one for Hobbes and none for Hegel.
11. Moses, Jeremy Challenging Just war and democratic peace: a critical perspective on Kant and Humanitarian Intervention' *Canberra papers on strategy and defence* (Canberra: 2006) No. 163, pp. 71–83, 71.
12. He has published an excellent brief summary and appreciation of Kant's philosophy *Kant* (Oxford: Oxford University Press, 1982).
13. http://www.opendemocracy.net/articles/ViewPopUpArticle.jsp?id=2&articleId=1749, 2/25/04, 1 For a reply to Scruton see William Mac Bride 'Kant's moral philosophy & the question of pre-emptive war' *Sens Public*, Samedi 5 Mars 2005.
14. It is therefore regrettable that commentators focus on– *Perpetual Peace: a Philosophical Sketch* (1795),the most lucid of Kant's political writings – to the exclusion of the detailed account of republican government contained in and *The Metaphysics of Morals* (1797) elsewhere. http://www.opendemocracy.net/articles/ViewPopUpArticle.jsp?id=2&articleId=1749.
15. Open Democracy, accessed 2/25/04. http://www.opendemocracy.net/articles/ViewPopUpArticle.jsp?id=2&articleId=1749.
16. http://www.opendemocracy.net/articles/ViewPopUpArticle.jsp?id=2&articleId=1749.
17. For an excellent attempt to broaden Kant's international political philosophy to embrace the possibility of humanitarian military intervention see Bernstein, Alyssa R. 'Kant on Rights and Coercion in International Law: Implications for Humanitarian Military Intervention' *Annual Review of Law and Ethics*, 16, 2008, pp. 57–99.
18. Christine Korsgaard expresses this view in her *Creating the Kingdom of Ends* (Cambridge: Cambridge University Press, 1996): 'Peace is important not only because it is the end of violence and injustice. Peace will bring with it the entire achievement of the Kingdom of Ends on earth. It goes hand in hand with the state of affairs where every nation is a republic', p. 33.

19. Fernando Teson, *Humanitarian Intervention: An Inquiry into Law and Morality* (New York: Transnational Publishers, 2005); *A Philosophy of International Law* (Boulder, Colorado: Westview Press, 1998).
20. 'Citizens in a liberal democracy should be free to argue that, in some admittedly rare cases, the only morally acceptable alternative is to intervene to help the victims of serious human rights deprivations' *A Philosophy of International Law*, p. 21.
21. 'Ending Tyranny in Iraq' *Ethics and International Affairs*, 19 (2), pp. 1-20. Teson says of the war against Saddam Hussein's regime in Iraq that 'whatever its value as a defensive reaction against terrorism, the war was indeed justified as humanitarian intervention' (p. 2). Teson sees 'the grand strategy that encompasses the war in Iraq' as 'the natural continuation of an extraordinary idealistic, transformative, liberating impulse of the American Republic, one that ties the current effort in Iraq with Woodrow Wilson's pro-democratic doctrine, Franklin D. Roosevelt's conviction in fighting European fascism, Jimmy Carter's courage in putting human rights at the top of his foreign policy agenda, Ronald Reagan's landmark victory against Communist tyranny, and Bill Clinton's inspired leadership in Kosovo, Haiti, and elsewhere' (p. 19).
22. Jürgen Habermas, 'The Kantian Project and the Divided West' part iv, *The Divided West* (Cambridge: Polity, 2006).
23. 'Bestiality and Humanity: A War on the Border between Legality and Morality', *Constellations* 6, no. 3, 1999, p. 263.
24. 'Bestiality and Humanity', p. 263.
25. 'Bestiality and Humanity', p. 264.
26. 'Bestiality and Humanity', p. 270.
27. 'Bestiality and Humanity', p. 269.
28. Sabine Jaberg, *Kants Friedenschrift und die Idee kollectiver Sicherheit: Eine Rechtfertigungsgrundlage fuer den Kosovo-Krieg der NATO?*, (Hamburg: Institut fuer Friedensforschung und Sicherheitspolitik) Heft 129, 2002.
29. Sabine Jaberg, *Kants Friedenschrift und die Idee kollectiver Sicherheit*, p. 34.
30. 'Habermas does not offer uncritical support for the intervention. He acknowledges reasonable concerns about the conduct of negotiations prior to the intervention, the insufficiently humanitarian conduct of a military campaign based exclusively on air power, the de-stabilizing effects of the campaign on the surrounding regions and, perhaps, most seriously for Habermas the risks attendant in an intervention that lacked the authorization of the UN Security Council and hence the full force and backing of international law.' William Smith 'Anticipating a Cosmopolitan Future: The Case of humanitarian military Intervention', *International Politics* 44, 2007, p. 78.
31. Sabine Jaberg, *Kants Friedenschrift und die Idee kollectiver Sicherheit*, p. 64.
32. Sabine Jaberg, *Kants Friedenschrift und die Idee kollectiver Sicherheit*, p. 64.
33. Sabine Jaberg, *Kants Friedenschrift und die Idee kollectiver Sicherheit*, p. 64.
34. Sabine Jaberg, *Kants Friedenschrift und die Idee kollectiver Sicherheit*, p. 64.
35. 'Bestiality and Humanity', p. 271.
36. 'Bestiality and Humanity', pp. 265-6.
37. Habermas holds that 'UN institutions are on the way to closing the circle between the application of compulsory law and the democratic generation

of law', albeit that 'only peaceful and prosperous OECD-type societies can afford to harmonize their national interests more or less with the demands of the United Nations, which represents a halfway approximation of the *niveau* of global citizenship.' 'Bestiality and Humanity', pp. 270–1.
38. 'Bestiality and Humanity', p. 267.
39. This can also mean 'graves'.
40. 'Bestiality and Humanity', p. 271.
41. 'Interpreting the Fall of a Monument', *Divided West* (Cambridge: Polity, 2007), pp. 28–9.
42. 'The principle that interventions should only be carried out in the event of a serious and substantial humanitarian crime such as ethnic cleansing is clearly being applied in the contrast he draws between Iraq and Kosovo.' William Smith 'Anticipating a Cosmopolitan Future: The Case of humanitarian military Intervention', *International Politics* 44, 2007, p. 81.
43. 'Bestiality and Humanity', p. 267.
44. 'Undoubtedly Kant both believed and hoped that republicanism would become the preferred form of government in all states, but the question remains, how do we get there from here? An aggressive liberalism might see the answer in an ever expanding federation of liberal democracies, but an aggressive liberalism could contribute to resentment and hostility on the part of non-liberal states that are excluded from such a federation. I think it is appropriate to conclude with a teleological question, what is international law for? I think that for Kant, its primary purpose is to protect states from the aggression of other states. If this is true, then international law would be opposed to all forms of jihads, including liberal jihads. International law, of course, is a purposeful endeavour, but it should not be used for the purpose of the advocacy or advancement of any particular ideology. This is consistent, I think, with seeing it as a source of treaty-based agreements among states for the protection of human rights. Just as individual sovereign states can contribute to the growth of human freedom, so, too, can various forms of cooperation among states including ultimately a federation of states. However, it is fundamental from a Kantian perspective that we recognize the limits of the coercive use of the powers of the state or a federation of states. Put bluntly, coercion among states is a denial of the equality which a respect for their moral personality requires.' Burleigh T. Wilkins 'Kant on International Relations', *The Journal of Ethics* (2007) 11/2: pp. 147–159, 158.
45. Mertens, Thomas 'Kant's Cosmopolitan Values and Supreme Emergencies' *Journal of Social Philosophy* Vol. 38, No. 2, Summer 2007, p. 229: 'Humanitarian intervention derives its apparent plausibility from the rather simplistic picture of a brutal criminal regime that violates the basic rights of its innocent citizens who are being rescued by a benevolent outsider, in a situation analogous to the drunkard mentioned earlier who is stopped by neighbours from beating his children. The reality of political communities in trouble, however, is seldom so simple as to allow for such a "domestic analogy." From a pragmatic perspective, the question as to who is to decide when an intervention is justified remains unsolved and, given the unpredictable nature of emergencies, this question seems unsolvable. But if there is no answer as to who decides when humanitarian intervention is justified and appropriate,

the acceptance of a right to humanitarian intervention entails the risk of a sliding scale toward a "right to war," as Kant feared. Humanitarian catastrophes or their likelihood can easily be constructed as a pretext for the use of military force, similar to the situation in which the case for pre-emptive strike leads to an argument for preventive war.'
46. 'Humanitarian Intervention as a Perfect Duty: A Kantian argument' *Nomos*, 47, 2004, p. 5.
47. 'Humanitarian Intervention as a Perfect Duty: A Kantian argument', p. 3.
48. 'Humanitarian Intervention as a Perfect Duty: A Kantian argument', p. 20.
49. 'Humanitarian Intervention as a Perfect Duty: A Kantian argument', p. 2.
50. 'Humanitarian Intervention as a Perfect Duty: A Kantian argument', p. 16.
51. ‚Die bürgerliche Verfassung, obzwar ihre Wirklichkeit subjectiv zufällig ist, ist gleichwohl objectiv, d. i. als Pflicht, nothwendig.' ('A civil constitution, though its realisation is subjectively contingent, is still objectively necessary, that is, necessary as a duty') (6: 264/416).

7 The Hegelian Premises of Contemporary Just War Theory and Their Kantian Critique

1. James Turner Johnson, 'The just war idea: the state of the question', *Social Philosophy and Social Policy* pp. 167–195, 167.
2. Cian O'Driscoll, *Renegotiation of the Just War Tradition and the Right to War in the Twentieth-First Century* New York: Palgrave Macmillan, 2008.
3. As Johnson puts it, 'undertaking to think about war in the idiom of just war discourse opens a window into understanding and appreciating the history that has made us who we are, thus informing and deepening how we think about the moral values relating to political community and the use of armed force in the service of such community.' James Turner Johnson 'Just War as it was and is' *First Things*, January 2005. See http://www.firstthings.com/article/2007/01/just-waras-it-was-and-is-2.
4. For a fuller discussion of Hegel's political philosophy see Howard Williams, *International Relations in Political Theory*, Milton Keynes: Open University Press, 1991, pp. 92–103.
5. References (paragraph number first, page number second) are to G.W. F. Hegel *Elements of the Philosophy of Right* translated by H. B. Nisbet edited by Allen Wood, Cambridge University Press: Cambridge, 1991.
6. *Just and Unjust Wars*, p. xxix.
7. See Gareth Evans et al, *The Responsibility to Protect*, Report of the International Commission on Intervention and State Sovereignty (Ottawa: International Development Research Centre, 2001), VII.
8. There are of course scholars who engage with the literature of just war from a critical perspective such as Robert L. Holmes *On War and Morality* Princeton: Princeton University Press, 1989.
9. *Just and Unjust Wars*, p. xxx.
10. Brian Orend *Michael Walzer on War and Justice* , Cardiff: University of Wales Press, 2000, p. 56.
11. Brian Orend *Michael Walzer on War and Justice*, p. 56.

12. Brian Orend *Michael Walzer on War and Justice*, p. 56.
13. Erskine, Toni 'Qualifying Cosmopolitanism? Solidarity, Criticism and Michael Walzer's "View from the Cave"' *International Politics*, 2007, 44, pp. 125–149), 131.
14. *Just and Unjust Wars*, p. 127.
15. *Just and Unjust Wars*, p. 131.
16. This diffidence is reflected in the views of some contemporary writers on international law. As Antonio Cassese puts it, 'more than any other corpus of legal rules, international law directly and transparently reflects power relations. It only partially restrains States' behaviour. War marks the passage from relatively harmonious relations to armed contention. War is the area in which power politics reach their peak and law relinquishes its control over international dealings. ... Therefore realistically one can simply require international law to mitigate at least some of the most frightful manifestations of the clash of arms. This is precisely what the rules on warfare endeavour to do.' In the previous paragraph Cassese appropriately quotes the distinguished international lawyer Hersch Lauterpacht's dictum that 'if international law is, in some way, at the vanishing point of law, the law of war is perhaps even more conspicuously at the vanishing point of international law.' *International Law* Oxford: Oxford University Press, 2001, p. 325.
17. Jean Bethke Elshtain *Just War Against Terror* New York: Basic Books, 2003, p. 47.
18. Jean Bethke Elshtain *Just War Against Terror*, p. 213.
19. Jean Bethke Elshtain *Just War Against Terror*, p. 214.
20. Jean Bethke Elshtain *Just War Against Terror*, p. 214.
21. James Turner Johnson *Morality and Contemporary Warfare* New Haven: Yale, 1999, p. 41.
22. The moral understanding of the concept of sovereign authority is also what gives states, groups of states, and the Security Council the right to override territorially defined sovereignty when the latter is being abused. When do the rights and protections of sovereignty disappear, on this moral analysis? Under either of two conditions: first, when the governing authorities violate the basic human rights of some or all of their people (since the sovereign's authority to rule follows from service to the common weal, sovereignty is lost, in the moral sense, when state power is used to oppress some or all of the people who live under its rule); and second, in the case of rogue states, states that employ their power to menace others (this, I take it, is the moral meaning of the international-law concept of threats to international peace and security). On this understanding, humanitarian intervention and other uses of force against a state or government that has engaged in massive human rights abuses or that threatens other states or the international order as a whole do not violate the sovereign rights of the state or government that is the object of the intervention, because it has already forfeited those rights by its wrongdoing.' 'The Just War idea: the State of the Question', *Social Philosophy and Policy* 23, no. 1, 2006, pp. 169–95, 187.
23. 'The Just War idea: the State of the Question', *Social Philosophy and Policy* 23, no. 1, 2006, pp. 169–95, 187.
24. 'This conception of war also has as its villains the states who engage in it, so that states, instead of being potential sources of human good, are recast as

the agents of massive evil. The influence of this understanding of war can be easily identified in recent debates over particular uses of force. But as I have noted, the actual face of recent warfare differs markedly from this, as it involves civil wars, uses of force by non-state actors, and massive harm to the innocent not from the use of horrific weapons but because they are made the direct targets of weapons ranging from knives to automatic rifles to suicide bombs. The actual villains here are not states as such but regional warlords, rulers who oppress their people to maintain or expand their power, and individuals and groups who use religious or ethnic difference as a justification for oppression, torture, and genocide. This is, as I suggested earlier, the real "World War III," not a repeated and more horrible update of the London Blitz or the bombings of Dresden and Hiroshima. Those who claim that "modern war" is inherently unjust seem to me to have missed all this.' James Turner Johnson 'Just War as it was and is' *First Things*, January 2005. See http://www.firstthings.com/article/2007/01/just-waras-it-was-and-is-2.
25. *A Theory of Justice* (Oxford: Oxford University Press, 1971), p. 58.
26. *A Theory of Justice*, p. 380.
27. *A Theory of Justice*, p. 380.
28. *A Theory of Justice*, p. 380.
29. *A Theory of Justice*, p. 108.
30. *A Theory of Justice*, p. 110.
31. *Law of Peoples*, p. 86.
32. *Law of Peoples*, p. 86.
33. *Law of Peoples*, p. 92.
34. *Law of Peoples*, p. 92.
35. *A Theory of Justice*, p. 378.
36. *Law of Peoples*, p. 92.
37. *Law of Peoples*, p. 92.
38. *Law of Peoples*, p. 93.
39. *Law of Peoples*, p. 96.
40. *Law of Peoples*, p. 98 Cf. Walzer *Just and Unjust Wars* pp. 251–68.
41. *Law of Peoples*, p. 97.
42. *Law of Peoples*, pp. 97–8.
43. *Law of Peoples*, p. 98.
44. *Law of Peoples*, p. ??.
45. *Law of Peoples*, p. 90.
46. *Law of Peoples*, p. 90.
47. Elshtain places her faith upon just war thinking on such a basis as this. For her it has become the appropriate way to discuss matters of international armed conflict: 'by the beginning of the twenty-first century, the just war tradition had become part of the way in which much of the world spoke of war and peace questions, especially such matters as noncombatant immunity, proportionality, and the treatment of prisoners. International law states that intentional attacks on noncombatants violate not only recognized rules of warfare but universal humanitarian standards', *Just War Against Terror*, p. 53. Cf. also M. Walzer, *Arguing about War* New Haven: Yale University Press, 2004: 'Ongoing disagreements, together with the rapid pace of political change, sometimes require revisions of a theory...faced with the number of recent horrors – with massacre and ethnic cleansing in Bosnia and

Kosovo; in Rwanda, the Sudan, Sierra Leone, the Congo and Liberia, in East Timor... I have slowly become more willing to call for military intervention', pp. xii xiii.
48. M. Walzer, *Arguing about War* New Haven: Yale University Press, 2004: 'Saddam's war is unjust, even though he didn't start the fighting... America's war is unjust. Though disarming Iraq is a legitimate goal, morally and politically, it is a goal that could almost certainly been achieved with measures short of full-scale war.' See p. 160.
49. *Just War Against Terror*, p. 181.
50. Elshtain cites Hannah Arendt's remark that 'politics is not the nursery' in justifying the permissibility of war that is inherent in the just war tradition: 'Practicing a reasonableness based on the calculations of the "humanist" world of infinite negotiations and "logical" explanation is often of little use in helping us to face harsh evidence unfolding before our eyes.' *Just War against Terror*, p. 2.

8 Conclusion: The Kantian Critique of Just War Theory

1. This is how many just war theorists and international lawyers present their position. Cf. A. Cassese 'a realistic assessment of the present condition should not beget despair. Legal rules, however weak and defective do restrict the behaviour of States and introduce a modicum of humanity into utterly inhuman conduct. The absence of normative standards would be even more regrettable: it would leave strong military Powers – or for that matter, any State, even the poor ones, provided they were supported by one of the Great Powers – free of any restraint.' *International Law*, p. 348.
2. This is the defence offered by N. Rengger: 'the tradition is still there – a resource, for those who would understand it and use it aright, that enables us to evaluate and assess the character of our societies' use of force in all of its aspects. It does not think war is a good (only, sometimes a lesser evil); nor does it glamorize or celebrate 'warriors' (as some seem increasingly to wish to do today); rather, it accepts that in the quotidian world in which we all live, there will be circumstances where force is used and even, perhaps, circumstances where it should be used, but most of all, it asserts that in neither case does this absolve us from the requirements of reflection and choice that we should all understand are the necessary partners to our freedom.' 'On the just war tradition in the twenty-first century', *International Affairs*, p. 363.

Bibliography

References (volume and page number) to Kant's *Collected Writings* are made to the *Akademieausgabe* (Berlin: Prussian Academy Edition, 1902 onwards). Unless otherwise stated translations are taken from *Kant's Practical Philosophy* translated and edited by Mary Gregor (Cambridge: Cambridge University Press, 1996).

Other translations of Kant cited:

The Critique of the Power of Judgment translated by Paul Guyer and Eric Matthews (Cambridge University Press, 2000).
The Critique of Judgement translated by James Creed Meredith (Oxford University Press, 1969).
Kant's Political Writings (Cambridge: Cambridge University Press, 1991) translated by H. B. Nisbet edited by H. S. Reiss.
Observations on the Feeling of the Beautiful and Sublime, translated by John T. Goldthwait (Berkeley: University of California Press, 1960).
Philosophical Correspondence edited by Arnulf Zweig (Cambridge: Cambridge University Press, 1999).
Religion within the Boundaries of Mere Reason, translated and edited by Allen Wood and George di Giovanni, Cambridge: Cambridge University Press, 1998.
Toward Perpetual Peace and other Writings on Politics, Peace and History, translated by David L. Colclasure, edited by Pauline Kleingeld (New Haven: Yale, 2006).

Other works

Achenwall, Gottfried *Juris naturalis pars posterior complectens jus faliliae, jus publicum et jus gentium. Editio qvinta emendatior*, Göttingen 1763.
Achenwall, Gottfried & Puetter, Johann Stephan *Anfangsgruende des Naturrechts*, edited and translated from the Latin by Jan Schroeder, (Frankfurt am Main: Insel Verlag, 1995).
Aquinas, Thomas *Aquinas: Selected Political Writings* A.P. D'Entreves (ed.) (Oxford, Blackwell, 1965).
Allison, Henry *Kant's Theory of Freedom*, (Cambridge: Cambridge University Press, 1990).
Ayala, Balthazar *Three Books On the Law of War and the Duties Connected with War and Military Discipline* (New York: Oceana Publications, 1964).
Bagnoli, Carlo 'Humanitarian Intervention as a Perfect Duty: A Kantian argument' *Nomos*, 47, 2004, p. 5.
Bellamy, Alex J. *Just Wars* (Cambridge: Polity, 2006).
Bernstein, Alyssa R. 'Kant on Rights and Coercion in International Law: Implications for Humanitarian Military Intervention' *Annual Review of Law and Ethics*, 16, 2008, pp. 57–99.

Bernstein, Alyssa R. 'Kant, Rawls and Cosmopolitanism': *Towards Perpetual Peace* and *The Law of Peoples*', 17, 2009, pp. 4–52.

Byrd, B. Sharon & Hruschka, Joachim *Kant's Doctrine of Right. A Commentary* (Cambridge: Cambridge University Press, 2010).

Cassese, Antonio *International Law* (Oxford: Oxford University Press, 2001).

Cavallar, Georg *Kant and the theory and practice of International Right* (Cardiff: University of Wales Press, 1999).

Cavallar, Georg *The Rights of Strangers: Theories of International Hospitality, the global community and Political Justice since Vitoria* (Aldershot: Ashgate, 2002).

Cavallar, Georg 'Commentary on Susan Meld Shell's "Kant on Just War and "Unjust Enemies": Reflections on a "Pleonasm"' *Kantian Review* Volume 11, 2006, pp. 117–124.

Cavallar, Georg *Die europaeische Union –von der Utopie zur Friedens- und Wertegemeinschaft* (Vienna: LIT Verlag, 2006).

Coates, Anthony 'Humanitarian Intervention: a conflict of tradition' in Terry Nardin & Melissa S. Williams (eds) *Humanitarian Intervention* (New York: New York University Press, 2006).

Covell, Charles *Kant and the Law of Peace* (London: Macmillan, 1998).

Doyle, Michael 'Kant, Liberal Legacies, and Foreign Affairs, Part 1 & 2, *Philosophy and Public Affairs* 12, 1983.

Easley, Eric *The War over Perpetual Peace* (New York: Palgrave, 2004).

Elshtain, Jean Bethke *Just War Against Terror* (New York: Basic Books, 2003).

Evans, Gareth et al, *The Responsibility to Protect*, Report of the International Commisson on Intervention and State Sovereignty (Ottawa: International Development Research Centre, 2001) VII.

Evans, M. (ed.) *Just War Theory: A Reappraisal* (Edinburgh: Edinburgh University Press, 2005).

Erskine, Toni 'Qualifying Cosmopolitanism? Solidarity, Criticism and Michael Walzer's "View from the Cave"' International Politics, 2007, 44, pp. 125–149.

Feder, Johann Georg Heinrich, *Lehrbuch des praktischen Philosophie* (Goettingen: Johann Christian Dietrich, 1776).

Feder, J. G. H, *Ueber Raum und Causalität, zur Prüfung der kantischen Philosophie*, Goettingen: 1787.

Fukuyama, Francis *The End of History and the Last Man* (London: Penguin, 1992).

Gerhardt, Volker *Immanuel Kants Entwurf 'Zum Ewigen Frieden'* (Darmstadt: Wissenschaftliche Buchgesellschaft, 1995).

Paul Guyer, 'Purpose in Nature: what is living and what is dead in Kant's Teleology', in P. Guyer *Kant's System of Nature and Freedom* (Oxford: Oxford University Press, 2005), pp. 342–72.

Grotius, Hugo *Commentary on the Law of Prize and Booty*, (Indianapolis: Liberty Fund, 2006).

Jaberg, Sabine *Kants Friedenschrift und die Idee kollektiver Sicherheit: Eine Rechtfertigungsgrundlage fuer den Kosovo-Krieg der NATO?*, (Hamburg: Institut fuer Friedensforschung und Sicherheitspolitik, Heft 129, 2002).

Habermas, Juergen *Divided West* (Cambridge: Polity, 2007).

Habermas, Juergen 'Bestiality and Humanity: A War on the Border between Legality and Morality', *Constellations* 6, no. 3, 1999.

Hamann, Johann Georg *Londoner Schriften* eds. Oswald Beyer and Bernd Weissenborn (Munich: 1993).

Hegel, G. W. F. *The Elements of the Philosophy of Right* (Cambridge: Cambridge University Press, 1991).
Hobbes, Thomas *Leviathan* ed. Richard Tuck (Cambridge: Cambridge University Press, 1991).
Hobbes, Thomas *On the Citizen* edited and translated by Richard Tuck and Michael Silverthorne (Cambridge: Cambridge University Press, 1998).
Holmes, Robert L. *On War and Morality* Princeton: Princeton University Press, 1989).
Hurrell, Andrew 'Vattel: pluralism and its limits' in Ian Clark & Iver B. Neumann, *Classical Theories of International Relations'*(Houndsmill: Macmillan, 1996).
Jahn, Bruno *Biographische Enzyklopaedie deutscher Philosophen* (Munich: Saur, 2001).
Johnson, James Turner *Morality and Contemporary Warfare* (New Haven: Yale, 1999).
Johnson, James Turner 'The just war idea: the state of the question', *Social Philosophy and Social Policy*, Volume23, Issue 1, 2006, pp. 167–195.
James Turner Johnson 'Just War as it was and is' *First Things*, January 2005. http://www.firstthings.com/article/2007/01/just-waras-it-was-and-is-2
Kaufman, Matthias 'What is New in the Theory of War in Kant's *Metaphysics of Morals?' Annual Review of Law and Ethics* 16, 2008, pp. 147–164.
Korsgaard, Christine *Creating the Kingdom of Ends* (Cambridge: Cambridge University Press, 1996).
Kersting, Wolgang *Kant ueber Recht* (Padeborn: Mentis, 2004).
Loades, Ann L. *Kant and Job's Comforters* (Newcastle upon Tyne: Avero Publications, 1985).
Mertens, Thomas 'From "Perpetual Peace' to "The Law of Peoples": Kant, Habermas and Rawls on International Relations', *Kantian Review*, Volume 6, 2002, pp. 60–84.
Mertens, Thomas 'Kant's Cosmopolitan Values and Supreme Emergencies' *Journal of Social Philosophy* Vol 38, No. 2, Summer 2007, pp. 222–241.
Moses, Jeremy 'Challenging Just war and democratic peace: a critical perspective on Kant and Humanitarian Intervention' *Canberra papers on strategy and defence* (Canberra: 2006) No. 163.
Mulholland Leslie, *Kant's System of Rights* (New York: Columbia University Press, 1990).
Nardin, Terry & Williams Melissa S. (eds) *Humanitarian Intervention* (New York: New York University Press, 2006).
O'Driscoll, Cian *Renegotiation of the Just War Tradition and the Right to War in the Twentieth-First Century* (New York: Palgrave Macmillan, 2008).
O'Neill, Onora *Constructions of Reason: Explorations of Kant's Practical Philosophy* (Cambridge: Cambridge University Press, 1989).
O'Neill, O. Review of Henry Allison's *Kant's Theory of Freedom* in *Mind* Vol. 100, July 1992, pp. 373–76.
Orend, Brian *War and International Justice: A Kantian perspective* (Waterloo: Wilfrid Laurier University Press, 2000).
Orend, Brian *Michael Walzer on War and Justice* , Cardiff: University of Wales Press, 2000.
Paine, Thomas *The Rights of Man* (London: Dent, 1969).

Pievatolo, Maria Chiara 'The Tribunal of Reason: Kant on the Juridical Nature of Pure Reason', *Ratio Juris*. Vol. 12 No. 3 September 1999, pp. 311–27.
Pufendorf, Samuel *On the Duty of Man and Citizen* edited by James Tully, translated by Michael Silverthorne (Cambridge: Cambridge University Press, 1991).
Rawls, John *A Theory of Justice* (Oxford: Oxford University Press, 1971).
Rawls, John *Lectures on the History of Moral Philosophy* (Cambridge, Massachusetts: Harvard University Press, 2000).
Rengger, Nicholas (2002) 'On the just war tradition in the twenty-first century.' *International Affairs* 78 (2), pp. 353–363.
Russett, Bruce *Grasping the Democratic Peace: Principles for a Post-Cold War Order* (Princeton: Princeton University Press, 1993).
Sassen, Bridget *Kant's Early Critics* (Cambridge: Cambridge University Press, 2000).
Schneewind, J. B. *The Invention of Autonomy* (Cambridge: Cambridge University Press, 1998).
Schmitt, Carl *The Concept of the Political*, edited and translated by George Schwab (Chicago: Chicago University Press, 1996).
Schmitt, Carl *The Nomos of the Earth* translated and annotated by G.L. Ulmen (New York: Telos Press, 2003).
Schwarzenberger, Georg 'The Grotius Factor in International Law and Relations: A Functional Approach', *Hugo Grotius and International Relations* eds. H. Bull, B. Kingsbury & A. Roberts (Oxford: Oxford University Press, 1992).
Scruton, Roger *Kant* (Oxford: Oxford University Press, 1982).
Scruton, Roger 'Immanuel Kant and the Iraq War', *Open Democracy*, online journal, http://www.opendemocracy.net/articles/ViewPopUpArticle.jsp?id=2&articleId=1749.
Shell, Susan 'Kant on Unjust War and "Unjust Enemies" reflections on a pleonasm' *Kantian Review* 10, 2005.
Simari, Andrea *Pace e guerra nel pensiero di Kant : studi su un tema della filosofia critica* Pubblicazioni dell'Istituto di Filosofia del Diritto dell'Università di Roma; Ser. 3,32 (Milan : Giuffrè, 1998).
Smith, William 'Anticipating a Cosmopolitan Future: The Case of humanitarian military Intervention', *International Politics* 44, 2007.
Szymkowiak, Aaron. "Of Free Federations and World States: Kant's Right and the Limits of International Justice." *International Philosophical Quarterly* 49, no. 2 (2009): pp. 185–206.
Teson, Fernando *A Philosophy of International Law* (Boulder: Westview, 1998).
Teson, Fernando *Humanitarian Intervention: An Inquiry into Law and Morality* (New York: Transnational Publishers, 2005).
Teson, Fernando 'Ending Tyranny in Iraq' *Ethics and International Affairs*, 19 (2), 2006, pp. 1–20.
Vattel , Emmerich de *The Law of Nations or the principles of natural law* tr. Charles G. Fenwick (New York: Oceana, 1964).
Vattel, E. *The Law of Nations* eds. B. Kaposy & R. Whatmore (Indianapolis: Liberty Fund, 2008).
Walzer, Michael, *Just and Unjust Wars* (New York: Basic Books, 1992).
Walzer, Michael *Arguing about War* (New Haven: Yale University Press, 2004)
Wilkins, Burleigh T. 'Kant and International Relations' *The Journal of Ethics* (2007) 11/2: pp. 147–159.

Williams, Howard *Kant's Political Philosophy* (Oxford, Blackwell, 1983).
Williams, Howard *International Relations in Political Theory*, Milton Keynes: Open University Press, 1991.
Wolff, Christian *Jus gentium methodo scientifica pertractatum*, Halle, 1750.
Wolff, Christian *Grundsaetze des Natur- und Voelkerrechts* Vorwort Marcel Thomann (Hildesheim; New York : Olms, 1980). Reprint of the first edition (Halle: Renger, 1754).
Wood, Allen *Kant* (Blackwell, Oxford, 2005).
Wood, Allen 'Kant's Compatibilism', in A.Wood (ed.) *Self and Nature in Kant's Philosophy*. (Ithaca: Cornell University Press, 1984).
Yovel, Yirmiahu *Kant and the Philosophy of History* (Princeton: Princeton University Press, 1980).

Index

Achenwall, Gottfried 43–44, 45, 66, 75, 92–94, 102, 166, 175n, 176n, 182n, 183n, 184n
acquired right 77–89; *see also* innate right
aesthetic 174n; judgement 18, 24; power of judgement 23; thinking 40, 173n
aggression 22, 44, 69, 70, 95–96, 148
Anthropology from a Pragmatic Point of View 21–22, 28; *see also* Kant
Aquinas, Thomas 45–46, 67, 110, 113, 176n, 186n; and Augustine 44, 154, 164
Aristotle 11, 28, 46
army 20, 151
autonomy 31, 42, 120, 132
Ayala, Balthazar 105, 185n

Bagnoli, Carla 138–140
Bellamy, Alex J. 59–60, 177n, 179n
Berlinische Monatsschrift 11, 18–19, 37, 53
Blair, Tony 163
Britain 81, 92; *see also* United States of America
Bush, George W. 124, 163
Byrd, Sharon 54–56, 93, 178n, 183n; *see also* Hruschka

Cavallar, Georg 60–62, 70, 172n, 173n, 179n, 180n, 183n, 185n
chivalry 17, 103, 151
Christianity 19, 33, 45–48, 162–163, 186n; *see also* God, religion
citizenship 53, 107–108, 114, 188n
civil war 33, 109, 133, 134; American Civil War 161; *see also* United States of America
Cold War 2, 13–14, 141–142
colonialism 86, 132; *see also* seafaring
communication 26, 38, 78; *see also* language

complacency 32, 170
consent 108, 157; *see also* United Nations
constitution 81, 146
The Contest of the Faculties 21–23; *see also* Kant
contract 70, 79, 86, 102, 127, 158, 183n, 184n–185n; *see also* social contract
cowardice 22, 24
crime 61, 125, 148; *see also* law
Critique of Pure Reason 1, 5, 10–11, 14, 17, 20, 23, 34–37, 39, 40, 65, 94, 167; objective of 34, 35; *see also* Kant
Critique of the Power of Judgment 5, 11, 13, 14, 15, 18, 20, 22, 167; on the value of war 23–26; *see also* Kant
culture 12, 13, 15–16, 22, 121, 149, 151

debate 8, 11, 23, 37, 39, 43, 167–168
defence 49, 67, 69, 81; *see also* self-defence
democracy 115–119, 121, 185; direct 107, 109
democratic peace thesis 1, 2–3, 55; *see also* peace
despotism 15, 117–118
discipline 37, 175n, 185n
'doctrine of right' 28, 65–66, 81, 88–90, 175n; commentary on 54–55, 178n, 183n; Doctrine of Right 5, 6–7, 10, 21, 27, 45, 51–52, 76, 79, 88, 96, 103, 105; and law 82; and war 85; *see also* Kant, *Metaphysics of Morals*
dogmatism 16, 29, 36, 63
duty 15, 27, 31, 89, 132–133, 136–140, 145, 151, 164, 179n; perfect 190n; of political leaders 64; of the sovereign 108; *see also* imperfect duty

Elshtain, Jean Bethke 58–59, 164–165, 191n, 192n, 193n; and Johnson 152–154; and Walzer 169
end(s) 25, 26–27, 39, 47, 74, 78; end of war 23, 89, 117, 149, 151, 169–171; *see also* peace
'The End of all Things' 5, 19–20; *see also* Kant
enemy *see* just enemy, unjust enemy
Enlightenment 1, 3, 79, 93, 129; and natural law 73
equality 53, 57, 78, 79, 104, 119, 120, 130
Erskine, Toni 150, 190n
ethics 130, 132, 138, 143
ethics of war 3, 97, 120, 147
Europe 2, 46, 142, 151–152, 165, 168; European Union 84, 123, 125; history of 87, 146; as a single confederated state 111, 134
evil 20, 22, 27, 32, 42, 87, 106, 143, 153, 191n; greatest of all evils 135; of war 27; *see also* slavery

falsity 22; *see also* God: and Job
Feder, J.G.H. 94–96, 102, 183n
force 42, 50, 58, 83, 114–116; by 87, 98, 99, 116; Kant on 67–68, 119; military 7, 113, 189n; use of 60, 88, 104, 110, 155, 184n; *see also* Kant, military
foreign policy 124–125; *see also* non-ideal theory
free states (federation of) 31, 110–111, 146, 169; *see also* Kant: on politics
freedom 42, 69, 78, 130; concept of 132, 143, 181n; *see also* innate right
French Revolution 21, 27, 76, 121, 132
Fukuyama, Francis 1, 132

Geist 142; *see also* spirit
Germany 133, 153, 162
God 17, 32, 44, 65, 73–74; God's will 46–47; and Job 62–64
good 118, 167, 179n, 181n, 191n

government 109, 112, 117–118, 121–122, 130, 137–140, 185n, 189n
Greece 111; *see also* Roman
Gregor, Mary 55, 172n, 178n, 183n
Grotius, Hugo 45–48, 62, 66, 68–69, 94, 142, 176n–177n, 183n–184n; and Vattel 55, 82; & Vattel and Pufendorf 51, 56, 58, 60, 64, 86

Habermas, Jürgen 7, 124–130, 135, 136, 168, 188n, 195n, 196n
Hamann, Johann Georg 62, 64, 179n, 180n
happiness 27, 38, 74, 131, 137, 171, 183n
Hegel, G.W.F. 1, 8, 141–165
history 10–11, 13–14, 15, 26–29, 31–33, 34–35, 41, 44, 133, 146–147, 174n; of international law 118; philosophy of 28, 167; of political philosophy 142–143; *see also* 'Idea for a Universal History with a Cosmopolitan Purpose'
Hobbes, Thomas 1, 17, 42, 45, 93, 119–120, 122, 129, 172n, 181n, 187n; and the laws of nations 82; and natural right 76–77
honour 24, 26, 152
Hruschka, Joachim 56; *see also* Byrd
human nature 12, 19, 27, 30, 41–42; *see also* Kant
human race 161, 169–170
human rights 7–8, 9, 76, 113, 115, 116, 120–122, 124–125, 130–139, 159, 161, 191n
humanitarian 112, 156, 168; intervention 5, 114, 135, 145, 168, 186n, 187n, 188n, 189n, 190n, 191n; *see also* human rights, intervention, military: military intervention
Hussein, Saddam 116, 119, 121, 188n

'Idea for a Universal History with a Cosmopolitan Purpose' 5, 11, 18, 28, 42, 146; *see also* history, Kant

ideal 160; Kantian 125; of the philosopher 74–75; *see also* non-ideal theory; republican
imperfect duty 137–138; *see also* duty
independence 104, 114, 123, 129, 137, 147–148, 156, 161, 171
innate right 8, 90; *see also* acquired right
instinct 24, 41
international relations 3–4, 10–11, 47, 63, 70, 84, 106–107, 114, 125, 143, 147–149, 162–164, 169–170, 176n, 177n, 189n; *see also* Elshtain, Jaberg, Kant
international theory 1–4, 8, 89, 161, 168
intervention(ism) 130–136; foreign 113–141; *see also* military, Teson
Iraq 2, 4, 7, 116, 117, 124, 129, 134, 141, 155, 163, 165, 188n, 193n

Jaberg, Sabine 126–127, 135, 188n
Jahn, Bruno 93, 183n
Johnson, John Turner 8, 164, 186n, 190n; and Elshstain 152–156; *see also* Elshtain
judgement 167–168; Clash of Judgements 23–27; see also *Critique of the Power of Judgment*
just enemy 96, (justus hostis) 103; *see also* unjust enemy
Just War Theory 40–55; Kantian critique of 166–171; and *Metaphysics of Morals* 72–90, and *Perpetual Peace* 56–71; *see also* Hegel, Rawls, Walzer
justice 81, 95 (*Gerechtigkeit*), 166; cosmopolitan 125; social 150

Kaliningrad 2, (as Königsberg) 11, 64
Kant, Immanuel 1–3, 48, 52, 59, 64, 66, 75, 96–97, 166; critical philosophy of 4, 5, 10, 20, 23, 29–31, 92, 99; on international relations 30, 57, 73, 79, 84, 98; on law of nations 78, 80, 83–84, 91–92, 97–98, 117, 134; on nature 31–32, 43–44, 57, 68, 79, 81, 105, 146; philosophy of 16–23, 30, 40–42, 60, 77, 92–93, 97, 140, 167–168, 175n, 181n, 107n, political philosophy of 3, 28, 31, 37–39, 43, 107, 119, 127, 167, 187n, 198b; political theory of 1, 46, 119, 144; on politics 56–57, 60, 70, 119, 156, 167, 175n, 180n; and his reader(s) 37, 54, 88, 91–92; on war 21, 39–40, 43, 50–54, 67–69, 98–99, 149, 170–171; *see also* Just War Theory
Kaufmann, Matthias 72, 181n
Kosovo 123–130; *see also* Habermas

labour 22, 32
land 32, 87, 139
language 32–33, 59–60, 103, 125, 135, 148, 149
law 36, 75, 78–79, 82, 85, 96, 107–108; internal 38, 45, 138; international 1, 4, 6–8, 19, 21, 26, 46–50, 72–73, 81–84, 88–90, 104–106, 110, 123, 137, 143, 170; of nations 45, 48, 51, 61–62, 66–68, 102, 168, 175n, 177n; and order 109, 140; the rule of 8, 12, 38, 43, 82, 126; system of 8, 74, 125–126; and war 105, 111; *see also* Achenwall, Ayala, Grotius, Hobbes, moral: law, natural law, Rawls, Scruton
Leviathan see Hobbes
liberalism 48, 160, 189
liberty 77, 98, 109, 120–121, 130, 149, 157
Lisbon earthquake 17
Locke, John 1, 45, 73, 176n, 181n

metaphysics 10, 35–38, 49, 74, 144, 164
Metaphysics of Morals 4–6, 10, 45, 50–56, 104–106, 134; and the Case for Just War Doctrine 72–90; and the Just War Doctrine 65–71; and *Perpetual Peace* 52–54, 56–60, 97, 99–101, 111–112, 116, 166–168; *see also* 'doctrine of right', Kant, *Perpetual Peace*, politics

military 59, 145; capacity see *Potentia Tremenda*; military intervention 21, 113–140, 153, 163; *see also* regime change
moral(s) 149, 169; law 27, 136, 154; person 81–82; philosophy 74–75, 144, 149, 164, 181n; *see also* Rawls, Walzer
morality 30–31, 38, 42–43, 55–56, 75, 77, 83; and Hegel 150–151; and nature 94; and war 149; *see also* Walzer

nation (*Volk*) 40, 49, 67, 170, 184n
nation-states 8, 80, 87, 143, 169–170, 178n
NATO 135, 155, 168; *see also* Habermas
natural law 45, 73–77, 80, 92, 119–120; *see also* Achenwall, Enlightenment, Hobbes, law
natural right 21, 78–79, 93–95, 179n
nature 83; international state of 83, 85, 101, 103, 178n, 179n; *see also* Kant, right: rights of state, Shell
Naturrecht 73, 92; *see also* natural law, natural right
Netherlands 59, 92, 177
non-ideal theory 158–164; *see also* Rawls

obedience 119, 122
obligation 102, 136–137, 140, 179n
O'Neill, Onora 175n, 181n
opinion 150, 159
order 76–77, 83–86, 89, 103; cosmopolitan 125; international 115
Orend, Brian 3, 7, 150; and Just War Theory 65, 70; and Susan Shell 50, 54, 56

pacifism 7, 41, 45, 48, 125, 169
patience 95, 135
peace 3, 6–8, 13, 15–26, 27–34, 38, 43, 59, 117, 138, 152, 187n; democratic 115–119; thesis of 1–2, 55; universal 15, 29; *see also* end: end of war, *Perpetual Peace*
Perpetual Peace 2, 5, 6, 10, 89–90; and the case against Just War Theory 56–71; *see also* Kant, *Metaphysics of Morals*, peace, Rechstlehre
philosophy 20–21, 23, 35, 37–39, 59, 74, 92–93, 164; *see also* Enlightenment, Kant, moral: philosophy, science
pleonasm 50, 102–103
political philosophy 45, 49, 58, 73, 92, 142, 150; of Hegel 169, 190n; of Rawls 164; *see also* Kant
political theory 1–4, 46, 115, 150; *see also* Kant
politics 1–10, 30, 38–39, 43, 73, 75, 91, 97, 118, 135, 143, 193n; international 1, 4, 51, 56–58, 60–61, 64, 70, 85–87, 101, 104, 107, 112, 119, 124, 142–150; and law 76, 90, 106
Potentia Tremenda 99–102; *see also* military
power politics 125, 127, 129, 178n, 191n
pre-emptive attack 50–51, 99–100, 116
pride 63–64, 81, 170
progress 30–33, 79, 84, 106, 116, 132–133
property 81, 108–109, 131
prudence 99, 121
psychology 37–38, 41–42; *see also* unsociable sociability
publicity 99, 157, 183n
Pufendorf, Samuel 45, 69, 176n, 179n; and Vattel 49, 61–62; *see also* Grotius, Hobbes
punishment 69, 109–110, 186n

rationality 142–143
Rawls 156–158, 174n, 185n; *see also* non-ideal theory
realism 33, 56, 67, 70, 129, 153–154, 180n
reason 11, 15, 27, 34, 36, 38–39, 41, 43, 49, 73–74, 174n; see also *Critique of Pure Reason*

Rechtslehre 6, 43, 70, 91–92; and Perpetual Peace 96–98, 101; *see also* doctrine of right, Kant
reform 79, 80, 136, 168; -ist 101, 119
regime change 21, 124, 129
religion 28, 32–33, 156, 167–168, 175
Religion within the Boundaries of Pure Reason 18–19, 173n, 175n; *see also* Kant
republican 102, 112; ideal 2, 127
resistance 12, 93, 126
right 85–86, 96–97, 100, 144, 151; condition of 135; right(s) *see* acquired, innate, and human; rights of state 91–98; of war 73–77
Roman(s) 15, 44–46
Rousseau 1, 119

scepticism 29, 37, 102, 129, 169, 176n
Schmitt, Carl 103–106, 185n
Schwarzenberger, Georg 48, 177
science 31, 74, 81, 181n; and anthropology 29; of philosophy 39
Scruton, Roger 116–118, 129, 134–136, 168
seafaring 87; *see also* colonialism
security 15, 64, 83–84, 95–96, 146, 159, 163, 184n; *see also* United Nations
self-defence 84, 90, 96, 98, 159, 162–163, 170
selfishness 24, 26
Shell, Susan 7, 50–51, 56, 69–70, 104, 180n; *see also* Orend
Simari, Andre 17–22, 173n
slavery 86, 170
social contract (theory) 46, 86, 93, 98, 110, 119, 127, 129
sociability 11–12; *see also* unsociable sociability
society 66–68, 126–129, 148; civil 8, 12, 26, 34, 57, 81–82, 135, 146; *see also* Wolff
soldiers 144; *see also* troops
'sorry comforters' 44–45, 48, 51, 55, 58, 60–64, 167–169, 183n; *see also* God: and Job, Grotius, Pufendorf, Vattel
sovereignty 108–110, 114, 121–122, 125–128; absolute 155; national 135, 180n (*see also* nation-states)
spirit (Geist) 142–145; *see also* Hegel
sublime 17, 24, 31, 167; dynamically 23, 25, 40, 174n

teleology 13–14, 18, 20, 22–23, 25, 47
Teson, Fernando 1, 7, 50, 116, 125, 128, 134–136, 168, 180n, 187n, 188n; and hyper-interventionism 119–124
theology 20, 156; *see also* Christianity, religion
transcendent 20, 27, 29, 174n; -al 77, 100
troops 108; *see also* army, soldiers

United Kingdom *see* Britain
United Nations 4, 9, 70, 84, 118, 123, 126, 129, 155, 159, 188n; *see also* security
United States of America 19, 75, 117, 124–125, 129, 154, 161, 163
universalism 2–3, 38, 120–121, 129, 130; *see also* Hobbes, 'Idea for a Universal History with a Cosmopolitan Purpose'
unjust enemy (ungerechtes Feind) 94–96, 102–107, 185n
unsociable sociability 13, 41
utilitarianism 93, 164
utopia 142, 152, 163, 170

Vattel, Emmerich de 45, 48–49; *see also* Grotius
violence 93, 109–110, 115–118, 153
virtue 18–19, 24, 121

Walzer, Michael 44, 59, 69, 110, 133, 160, 164–165, 169, 176n, 179n, 190n, 192n; and the Just War Doctrine 145–152; on morality 144; *see also* Elshtain war 3–8, 12, 34, 61, 66, 85, 91, 95; beneficial consequences of 12–15, 18–20, 23–24, 32, 41; brutality of 20–21, 23, 25, 27, 32, 36, 42, 128, 171; declaring 70, 107–111, 152; dialectic of 10–16, 23; economics and 16; incidence of war in Kant's writings 16–23; and Kantian philosophy 10, 43; legality of 46–50, 59, 129; and politics 153–155; Second World War 19, 123, 147, 153; *see also* Cold War, doctrine of right, evil, Feder, Just War Theory, Kant

welfare 118, 148–149

Weltbegriff (concept of the world) 39, 74–75

will 102, 108, 110, 116–117, 118, 154

Wolff, Christian 45, 66, 73, 176n, 180n

world republic 119, 179n

27682693R00125

Printed in Great Britain
by Amazon